THE PROPHET OF LOVE

THE PROPHET OF LOVE

and Other Tales of Power and Deceit

ELIZABETH KOLBERT

BLOOMSBURY

Published by Bloomsbury, New York and London
Distributed to the trade by Holtzbrinck Publishers

All papers used by Bloomsbury are natural, recyclable
products made from wood grown in well-managed forests.
The manufacturing processes conform to the environmental
regulations of the country of origin.

Library of Congress Cataloging-in-Publication Data

Kolbert, Elizabeth.
The prophet of love: and other tales of power and deceit/Elizabeth
Kolbert.—1st U.S. ed.
p. cm.
Articles originally published in *The New Yorker* and *Mother Jones*.
ISBN 1–58234–463–9 (hc)
1. New York (N.Y.)—Biography—Anecdotes 2. New York (N.Y.)—Politics and govern-
ment—1951—Anecdotes. 3. New York (N.Y.)—Social conditions—Anecdotes. 4. Power
(Social sciences)—New York (State)—New York—Anecdotes. 5. Deception—New York
(State)—New York—Anecdotes. I. Title.
F128.56.K65 2004
974.7'1043'092—dc22
2003024259

First U.S. Edition 2004

1 3 5 7 9 10 8 6 4 2

Typeset by Hewer Text Ltd, Edinburgh
Printed in the United States of America
by R.R. Donnelley & Sons, Harrisonburg, Virginia

CONTENTS

To my boys

Introduction

WHEN AMERICANS are asked whom they trust, politicians routinely fall near the bottom of the list. Just about the only group consistently to score lower are the journalists who cover them. It is tempting to want to contest this ranking—how would the general public even know to mistrust its leaders if it weren't for the hard work of the press?—but the attempt somehow seems misguided. You can't spend your time rehashing the errors of others and then expect to be admired for it.

I began to write about politics not long after graduating from college, when, as a very junior reporter at *The New York Times*, I was assigned to the Albany bureau. I arrived there just as Mario Cuomo reached the peak of his popularity and all over the country was being hailed as the last, best hope of liberalism. In the five years that I spent in the capital, Cuomo didn't run for president twice. The second time, he ended his non-campaign by leaving two chartered planes sitting on the runway of the Albany County airport while the filing deadline for the New Hampshire primary passed him by. (The planes, leased for the flight to Manchester that never took place, set New York's Democratic committee back some thirty thousand dollars.) No doubt my early experiences as a reporter shaped—some would probably say distorted—my view of civic life. If there is any particular theory that informs the pieces assembled in this book it is that the sense of political life is often indistinguishable from nonsense.

All of the stories collected here are about New York and all but one originally appeared in *The New Yorker*, whose staff I joined in 1999. Like most articles written for a weekly, these generally take as their starting point a news event—a campaign, a conflict, a crisis. As a consequence, they record, quite inadvertently, one half turn in the cyclical life of the city. The first piece, "The Charisma of No Charisma," was written shortly after I got to the magazine and discusses the exceptional good fortune of New York's rather unexceptional governor, George Pataki. It was composed at a moment when, in many neighborhoods of the city, becoming a millionaire by age twenty-five seemed no more remarkable than having a bar mitzvah. The following year, the Internet bubble burst, and the year after that the World Trade Center was attacked. On the morning of September 11th, I headed into work early to cover the mayoral primary, which was supposed to take place that day. As I crossed Fifth Avenue, I noticed that everyone was looking south. Several pieces, including "In Charge," about the mayor's handling of the crisis, and "The Chief," a profile of the highest-ranking member of the New York City Fire Department to die in the World Trade Center collapse, were written in the days immediately following the attack. Almost every piece that comes after that is in some way inflected by the tragedy.

Certain people, especially former mayor Rudolph Giuliani, Senator Hillary Clinton, and Mayor Mike Bloomberg, appear and reappear in this book. Others who show up repeatedly, though not elected officials, still would be considered professional politicians; these include, most notably, the Reverend Al Sharpton, who has run for office four times now, albeit never for a post he could actually hope to win. Still others are politicians only in the sense that they are, or were, involved in political struggles. Kathy Boudin, the Weather Underground member who spent more than two decades in prison for her role in the Brink's robbery, falls into this category, as does Wing Lam, a labor organizer who works out of a tiny office in Chinatown. Finally, there is Regis Philbin, who, if asked, probably would say that he's not even particularly interested in politics. He is here because for one brief moment he seemed to me to be the most powerful man in New York, and, at the same time, the source of his power seemed completely mysterious. Perhaps the most entertaining experience I had in the course of reporting these stories was spending a day with a pair of New York City health inspectors, which became the basis for the piece "Everyone Lies." Both of the inspectors were young and quite pleasant, you might even say shy. When they pulled out their badges, though, suddenly invested with authority, they became incredibly intimidating. Men twice their age cowered before them and, of course, immediately set about trying to undermine them. "You know, New York is theatre, street theatre," former mayor Ed Koch once told me, and he meant this not to deprecate the city's political culture, but to celebrate it.

Most journalism, or at least most political journalism, is in some sense a collaboration between the writer and subject. As much as politicians need journalists to reach the public, journalists need politicians to produce copy. A lot of very busy people gave their time to make these pieces possible, and even though they didn't always like the results—indeed, precisely because they didn't always like the results—I am grateful to them.

PART I

Politics

The Charisma of No Charisma

January 1999

I N ALBANY, JANUARY is the season for speechifying. At the beginning
of the month, by law, the governor delivers the State of the State
address, and at the end of the month, by custom, he delivers a budget
address as well. Every four years, there is an Inaugural address, too. This
means that by the time Governor George Pataki began his second term, on
New Year's Day, he had had plenty of practice as a speechmaker. Yet he
never seems to have got the hang of it, or even to have tried.

The theme of this year's Inaugural was "New York Ever Upward." And
so all the usual clichés about "the great march of human progress" and "the
spirit of hope" and "the indomitable force of the human will" were trotted
out, only to plod toward their predictable conclusion like so many cows
being herded into an abattoir. "We stand at the edge of a new century,
which is spread out before us like an undiscovered land of promise," Pataki
told the crowd of state workers and Party stalwarts shivering in the Albany
convention center. "We will keep our state moving forward with policies
that continue to fuel the passion, unleash the power, and tap the vast
reserves of strength, creativity, and determination of New York's greatest
resource—the spirit of our people." Weak public speakers are typically
hampered by embarrassment, anxiety, and paralyzing self-knowledge—
the mortification that accompanies a healthy sense of one's own inade-
quacy. But Pataki, by all appearances, suffers from just the reverse. After
delivering the hoariest of platitudes, he will pause for emphasis and look up
for approval, seeming genuinely pleased with himself and the work of his
speechwriters.

Two months ago, Pataki won reëlection by an enviable margin.

"Historic" was how the Governor described his win at a post-election news conference, where he was vigorously—and to his evident satisfaction—questioned about his national ambitions. In one of the last solidly Democratic states in the nation, he had beaten his Democratic rival, the New York City Council Speaker, Peter Vallone, by more than twenty points. That same day, the State Attorney General, Dennis Vacco, had gone down to defeat, and so had Senator Alfonse D'Amato, leaving Pataki and his lieutenant governor as the only Republicans in statewide elected office.

"I'd love to say it was brilliant politics," Kieran Mahoney, one of the Governor's chief political consultants, said of Pataki's strong showing, "but it seems in retrospect that it was brilliant governing. George Pataki won reëlection before it began, by governing well." Those outside Pataki's inner circle naturally put a different spin on the event: the Governor, cynics maintained, had got credit for an economic recovery he had virtually nothing to do with; had lucked into a surprisingly weak opponent; and, most important of all, had run an almost shamelessly efficient fund-raising operation. For every dollar that Vallone had to spend on the general election, Pataki had ten. "He outspent his opponent by a massive, massive number," Hank Morris, a Democratic political consultant, declared.

Actually listening to Pataki is no way to choose between these rival accounts, but, like a hanging, it does focus the mind. And at the Inaugural reception, as waitresses passed out chocolates stamped with the state seal and champagne in plastic flutes, it was hard not to feel that one was in the midst of something at once bigger and more banal than the victory party of either a disciplined fiscal conservative or an expert fund-raiser. The Governor's State of the State speech on January 6th, which recycled some of the same mangled metaphors he had used New Year's Day, only served to confirm this impression. Although Pataki's win was surely a lot less bizarre than that of, for instance, Jesse (The Body) Ventura, it may say just as much about what voters no longer expect, or even desire, in their leaders. Less isn't more, but for now, at least, it is apparently enough. And, viewed in these terms, Pataki's victory is indeed "historic." New York is, after all, the state that elected Teddy Roosevelt, Al Smith, F.D.R., and Nelson Rockefeller, that is home to Madison Avenue, Mario Cuomo, and MTV, yet in November it voted overwhelmingly for a man who could, by way of inspiration, recount the story of State Trooper Keith Bell. One day, Pataki related in his Inaugural speech, Bell was summoned by an elderly couple whose mailbox had been vandalized: "When his shift ended that day he returned to their home—not as a state trooper but as a New Yorker. He took the mailbox to be fixed, then came back and put it back in the ground. A small moment, but one with big meaning."

When Pataki first ran for governor, in 1994, he stuck to a few easy-to-remember promises: reinstate the death penalty, cut taxes, and end welfare as "a way of life." Running again, this past fall, he could boast that he had come through on all counts. New York has a spanking-new death row, at its prison in Dannemora, and as of this writing two murderers have been sentenced to die by lethal injection, while fifteen other capital cases are wending their way through the courts. The state's top personal-income-tax rate, which was seven and seven-eighths per cent when Pataki took office, has been reduced to six and eight-tenths per cent. New York's welfare rolls have declined by more than six hundred thousand, and state law now calls for recipients to be cut off after five years. In addition, Pataki has overhauled the state's workers'-compensation system, cut corporate-tax rates, and restricted parole for violent felons. He introduced a long-overdue program of discounted fares on the city's subways and buses, secured passage of a one-and-three-quarter-billion-dollar environmental-bond issue, and, most recently, won agreement from the Legislature to create charter schools.

By all objective measures, these achievements are as extensive as those of his predecessor, Mario Cuomo. Yet they have been accomplished with a fraction of the *Sturm und Drang*. Thanks in no small part to Cuomo's habit of starting his day around 5 A.M. and making phone calls to aides, legislators, and groggy reporters not long after, the job of New York's governor had come to seem all-consuming. Albany had grown used to an executive who insisted on making all decisions himself, and on agonizing publicly over most of them.

Pataki has declined to be consumed. Citing concerns about uprooting his children, the Governor still makes the hundred-mile commute to the Capitol from his home, in Garrison. Rather than being a dominating presence in Albany, he seems—and often genuinely is—absent. It is altogether foreign to Pataki's style to dwell on what is hard or morally vexing about his job; his inclination, no doubt dispositional as much as philosophical, is to present the choices that face the state as easy and commonsensical.

The destiny of New York, which just a few years ago seemed too grave a burden for one person, or even eighteen million, to shoulder, now seems no big deal. To quote Howard Stern's blurb on the back cover of "Pataki: An Autobiography," the Governor "took on the massive responsibility of running New York State and made it look simple." Within the pages of "Pataki," which was published last year, presumably in preparation for a national race, the Governor insistently touts his own unassuming efficiency, often using Cuomo's fabled eloquence as a foil. In one of the volume's many vegetative metaphors, drawn from his childhood on a Peekskill truck farm, Pataki charges Cuomo with the gravest of farm-stand sins: putting his best berries on top. "Any respect I may earn," he writes, "will come not from a speech but from a record. . . . We all had it, on the farm: work, not glitz; solutions, not blame; results, not talk. It's what had us putting the big berries in the bottom of the basket."

The neat opposition that Pataki postulates between glitz and solutions allows him to justify—and, in a roundabout way, even celebrate—his own obvious shortcomings. Those who can't speak, as it were, do. But an equally good truck-farm metaphor for Pataki's style might be cherry-picking. His successes over the last four years are real, but virtually every cause that he has taken up is the sort a pollster could happily recommend without so much as bothering to take a poll. No one except the Governor himself knows exactly how much influence his own pollster, the legendarily reclusive Arthur Finkelstein, really exercises, but even Pataki's Republican allies gripe privately that Finkelstein wields something very close to veto power over government policy.

Certainly Pataki, given his ideological commitments, has taken some surprising positions. In the spring of 1997, for example, when the state's rent-control laws came up for renewal, Joseph Bruno, the Republican Senate Majority Leader, insisted that they ought to be scrapped. Of all the examples of wrongheaded liberal social engineering that conservatives love to rail about, rent control has got to rank near the top: it is anathema not just to free-marketeers but to economists of virtually all persuasions, and any politician who, like Pataki, claims to believe in smaller government and unfettered competition surely ought to be against it. Yet for much of the months-long rent-control debate, which infuriated hundreds of thousands of New York City tenants, Pataki said nothing; then, at the last minute, just as the laws were about to expire, he sold Bruno out by agreeing to a deal that preserved the system more or less as it was. Rumor has it that Bruno was so angry when he returned to the Capitol after a Father's Day luncheon with his family and learned the news that he knocked over a chair. Pataki, though he claims Teddy Roosevelt as his hero, never spoke out forcefully on rent control, or used his "bully pulpit" to try to sway public opinion. Had he taken such a political risk, the outcome might have been very different.

"You're not going to make fun of him, are you?" asked the first gubernatorial aide I approached, just after Thanksgiving, about the possibility of getting an interview with Pataki. After nearly a dozen phone calls, I finally got as far the Governor's communications director, Zenia Mucha, but she hardly seemed interested in communicating with me. "You haven't been exactly kind to him," she said, adding by way of further clarification that she had "a ton of other people" requesting interviews. Pataki's relations with the press over the last four years have been civil but decidedly cool. He has never cultivated reporters, nor, one can surmise from the attitude of his aides, has he expected particularly sympathetic coverage. Unlike your run-of-the-mill New York politician, for a whom a day without a press conference is like no day at all, Pataki doesn't seem to live for, or even enjoy, talking into the microphones.

Since the election, however, the Governor has been much in demand, both as a voice of moderate Republicanism who can comment on the mess in Washington and as a possible candidate for national office. My concerns were closer to home. During the campaign, Pataki had left his agenda for a second term indefinite, and this vagueness was clearly strategic. Vallone had never had a chance to press him about it, because Pataki refused to appear on the same stage with him. (At one point, the City Council Speaker was left, literally, to debate an empty chair.) Pataki's excuse for this evasion was that Vallone had debased the race by engaging in personal attacks, a charge that not even the most wide-eyed supporter of the Governor could take seriously.

I finally got in to see Pataki a few days before Christmas. The Capitol was mostly empty again after a brief, hectic sojourn by the State Legislature, which had convened a special session in order to vote itself a pay raise. Pataki has taken the conference room where Cuomo used to hold sometimes two or three press briefings a day and converted it into a private office. It is hung with magnificent paintings of the Hudson River, on loan from various museums, depicting the hills that Pataki climbed as a child, and with a solemn portrait of Teddy Roosevelt. During our interview, Pataki was trying to catch up on his lunch, a turkey sandwich and some fruit salad, and was drinking from a bottle of Diet Snapple, which he kept diluting with bottled water.

In person, Pataki is a lot like the way he is onstage: affable, secure in himself, and utterly uninterested in exploring the dramatic possibilities of being governor. When I asked what we could expect from him over the next four years, he rehearsed the same airy talking points he had relied on in the fall. "What we said in '98 is that the best of New York is yet to come," he told me. "And it is. We're going to have a better state." He noted that, although he couldn't control national trends, "what we can do is build on our successes in improving the economic climate, continue to lead the nation in cutting taxes, continue to work to expand job opportunities and reduce the welfare rolls, continue to change the criminal-justice system to enhance public safety." When he was asked to be a bit more specific, the Governor said, "I can give you dozens of examples in all the areas," but he offered only one new proposal: "We've started a pilot program with the Albany Urban League here where we're taking people who have been trapped on welfare and training them to become painters, carpenters, electricians, plumbers, and in the process you not only give them the skills to be contributing members but you're fixing up old, abandoned buildings and creating housing and economic opportunities. . . . I want to make this a statewide program."

Hoping to elicit something more provocative, I asked the Governor if he had any regrets about his first term. He said he did not. "You know, no one's perfect and you always make mistakes. But if someone had asked me in January of '95 'If you had accomplished what we've accomplished after ten years in office, would you think you had done a lot?' I would have said 'If we had done that in ten years I would have been very proud.' We've done it in four. . . . I don't second-guess myself and say, 'Maybe we should have done something different.' . . . I think we've just been—the state has been enormously successful."

Finally, I asked Pataki about the general perception in the press that he was, well, dull: didn't it bother him? "I'm just a boring guy," he said, and then paused awkwardly, as if waiting for someone to contradict him. "No," he went on. "The press is the press." As I was leaving, the Governor returned to his desk and started to fiddle with his CD player. His favorite CD, I was told, is a soundtrack of birdsongs from species native to the state; Pataki said he was trying to learn to identify the birds by their calls. A bird chirped, and I asked him what it was.

"A grebe," he answered.

Early in Vallone's ill-fated race for the governorship, he commissioned a set of focus groups to gauge his chances of winning. Conducted in Buffalo, on Long Island, and in New York City, with independents and Democrats, the focus groups suggested that Vallone's odds were actually not so bad. "Over all, the discussions were very positive for Peter Vallone," said a memo from his pollsters—a memo that now seems almost poignant.

The pollsters based their optimism on the finding that impressions of Pataki were, in their words, "incredibly thin for a sitting Governor." When pressed by the focus-group leader to say what Pataki had accomplished or how he had changed the state, participants could hardly come up with anything. Only the death penalty and the welfare cuts were mentioned by more than one group. Thus, suggested the pollsters, it should be comparatively easy for Pataki's opponent to cut into his support with a few well-crafted attacks.

But the same report acknowledged that, if focus-group participants were only dimly familiar with Pataki and his accomplishments, they were not inclined to hold him to a particularly high standard. Participants said that they basically liked the Governor. They gave him credit for "trying," for "having exceeded expectations," and for generally "staying out of their lives while times are good." The praise may have been faint, but it wasn't damning.

Like President Clinton, who has been governing by small, mall-tested executive actions, Pataki seems, more than anything else, to appreciate What It Doesn't Take. Clinton, since the debacle of his health-care plan, has consistently avoided setting risky goals or pursuing projects that depend on swaying hearts and minds. Pataki needed no such painful education. As commentators on his State of the State were quick to point out, Pataki has a talent for simply ignoring issues he finds too politically messy to address. Along with the speculation about his Presidential ambitions, there has been a good deal of talk these days about Pataki as a possible Vice-Presidential candidate—much of the talk, it must be admitted, originating from his own aides. To many, either scenario seems laughably unlikely. Why would George W. Bush—or whoever wins the Republican nomination—pick a running mate from a Democratic state like New York, and a hopelessly uncharismatic one at that? Still, Pataki's detractors have always underestimated his appeal; he was reëlected with the largest margin ever achieved by a Republican in the Empire State, though not, as his critics like to point out, with the highest absolute percentage of the vote. He won, it could be argued, not despite his limitations but because those limitations—imaginative as well as rhetorical—are so well suited to the age. We have, it increasingly seems, entered an era of post-inspirational politics. New York's official motto remains "Excelsior," but "Good Enough for Government Work" probably comes closer to the mark.

The Perils of Safety

March 1999

E VERY DAY IN New York City, some nineteen people, on average, file official grievances against the police with the Civilian Complaint Review Board. Their complaints range from charges of verbal abuse to allegations of illegal searches, use of excessive force, and outright physical assault. And every year the city pays out more than twenty million dollars in compensation for this sort of claim. These encounters may be degrading, sometimes even permanently debilitating, but it is rare for one of them to be degrading or debilitating enough to enter the public discourse. As with crime itself, police misconduct has to be abnormal, even outrageous, before it can be tagged as emblematic.

Nineteen months ago, a Haitian immigrant named Abner Louima was picked up after a scuffle outside a Brooklyn night club, taken back to the Seventieth Precinct station, and brutalized so badly that he ended up at Coney Island Hospital in critical condition. As news stories later recounted, Louima had no previous criminal record and had actually been trying to break up a brawl when the police arrived. Even more important to the impact of the story, however, were the grotesque terms of his abuse. Four officers are alleged to have participated at various points, one of them using a wooden stick to sodomize Louima, puncturing his intestines.

When Amadou Diallo was shot, last month, it was again the scale of the violence that turned his death from a private to a civic tragedy. Unarmed and standing alone in the vestibule of his Bronx apartment building, Diallo was shot by four policemen, who fired a total of forty-one bullets, nineteen of which penetrated his body. At the time of the shooting, the officers could not have been standing more than twenty feet away from him.

At the many marches and rallies and protests and press conferences that have been held since Diallo was killed, his case and Louima's have been almost reflexively linked, and for obvious reasons. Both are about police brutality and, more specifically, about the intersection between police brutality and race: the attack on a black man by white cops. Citing concerns about both cases, the United States Commission on Civil Rights announced recently that it would be conducting a broad inquiry this spring into the city's police practices. As a grand jury pursues its investigation of Diallo's death in the Bronx and the trial of the officers accused of beating Louima gets under way in Brooklyn, it seems inevitable that the two will continue to be regarded as symptoms of the same disease.

Linking Louima's beating and Diallo's slaying is rhetorically useful; it makes it that much more difficult for Mayor Rudolph Giuliani or for his police commissioner, Howard Safir, to argue, as the official response to such horrors so often runs, that these are mere "isolated incidents." But, to the extent that the two sensational cases exemplify anything, treating them as the same obscures the meaning of both. Everything we know so far about the attack on Louima suggests that it represents a case of racism in its most familiar—and easily condemned—form. The killing of Diallo, by contrast, seems to be emblematic of something new: a form of racial bias that is statistically driven and officially sanctioned and that, depending on your perspective, may or may not be racism at all.

Over the last several years, as crime in New York City has dropped, the most impressive, and also the most reliable, figure has been the city's falling murder rate, and the most important component of that figure has been the decline in the number of people killed with guns. According to Police Department records, gun murders in the city were the highest they had ever been in 1991—one thousand six hundred and five. Last year, that figure was down to three hundred and seventy-five, a decline of almost seventy-seven per cent. Over that same period, the number of murders committed by other means also fell, but less rapidly, from five hundred and forty-four to two hundred and fifty-four, or, roughly, fifty-three per cent.

Getting guns off the street has been one of the N.Y.P.D.'s top priorities ever since Mayor Giuliani took office and hired his first police commissioner, William Bratton. Yet almost as soon as the department began to search more aggressively for handguns, the number of gun arrests actually began to go down. This development clearly complicated the department's claims of success, and there are some people who point to it as evidence that the city's falling crime rate—and, indeed, the entire country's—has had relatively little to do with police tactics. Nevertheless, the N.Y.P.D. wisely took credit for it, arguing that it was proof that the owners of illegal guns, increasingly fearful of arrest, were now leaving them at home. An unlicensed handgun left in a drawer is, to be sure, still an unlicensed handgun, but one that is that much less likely to be used to commit a crime.

The department's tactics were never particularly subtle, or even, many would argue, very new. Quite simply, the police increased the number of people they stopped and frisked for weapons, often using minor violations such as fare-beating, public beer-drinking, and loud radio-playing as pretexts for a pat-down. In 1995, the department proudly told the *Times* that the number of frisks in one precinct, the Thirtieth, in northwest Harlem, had increased by a hundred and fifty per cent in just one year.

The campaign against illegal hand-guns was in keeping with the new emphasis that Giuliani and Bratton placed on preventing, rather than just reacting to, crime. But it put the cops in an ambiguous relationship with the people they were supposed to be protecting: virtually everyone became a potential suspect. Bratton, who has been widely quoted since Diallo's death as advocating a reassessment of some of the very policies he pioneered, told me recently that the department always "clearly understood" that the focus on seizing illegal guns was going to increase the number of "negative encounters" between cops and civilians. "We weren't born yesterday," he added.

Spotting an illegal weapon, as opposed to just taking one off a fare beater, is a skill, and one that, according to those practiced in it, is so subtle that it requires something very close to innate ability. Where the inexperienced eye would see nothing at all amiss, those who have the skill can guess from someone's gait (slightly off balance) or his gestures (perhaps he unconsciously pats his pocket as he jogs across the street) or the hang of his clothes (is one side of his jacket ever so slightly lower than the other?) that he is carrying a gun. There are even plenty of cops who are otherwise perfectly competent but will never be able to detect a concealed gun; they simply do not, in police parlance, "have the eyes."

In the N.Y.P.D.'s battle against illegal handguns, one section of the department has played a starring role, and that is the élite Street Crimes Unit. In the mid-nineties, Street Crimes members constituted roughly half a per cent of the force but purportedly made twenty per cent of all gun arrests. A few years ago, the Street Crimes Unit was expanded greatly, against the recommendation of its then commander, Richard Savage. Too much growth, Savage argued, would threaten the group's cohesiveness and its selectivity. After expressing his concern, Savage was promoted out of his post. Currently, the unit's members constitute about one per cent of the police force and, according to the department, make forty per cent of all gun arrests. Although the N.Y.P.D. has declined to reveal the racial makeup of the special unit, it is almost certainly even less diverse than the department as a whole, which remains almost seventy per cent white.

The members of Street Crimes are not assigned to any particular precinct. Instead, they are dispatched to those neighborhoods where, according to the very latest statistics, crime is running highest. The four cops who approached Diallo on the night of February 4th were all members of Street Crimes. Diallo, a street peddler who sold an assortment of CDs and videotapes, had come home from work at about midnight and, his roommates later told reporters, was heading out again to get something to eat when the police arrived. At this point, it is impossible to know what provoked them to start firing: the officers have said nothing publicly about the incident, and have not yet spoken to the grand jury. On that night, they were searching for a serial rapist responsible for some forty-five attacks since 1993, and Diallo, according to another cop who had looked for this rapist, could be described as a "rough match" with a police sketch. A lawyer for the police union, who is representing one of the cops, has said that the four thought that Diallo had a gun.

The Street Crimes Unit, understandably, has come under a great deal of scrutiny since the slaying, and its motto, "We own the night," which is supposed to celebrate its part in making the city's streets safe to walk on after dark, has been interpreted by critics as a bald declaration of aggression. In defense of Street Crimes, officials of the N.Y.P.D. have pointed to its impressive record of seizing illegal guns. They have also released for the first time figures indicating the extent of the unit's efforts. In 1997 and 1998, its members performed forty-five thousand and eighty-four frisks.

In the abstract, there is nothing racially biased about the Street Crimes mission, or about the fact that its members have patted down so many people—or, indeed, about the department-wide emphasis on performing frisks at the slightest provocation. In reality, however, both critics and defenders of the force agree, these practices have resulted in thousands upon thousands of young black and Latino men getting searched for weapons— or, as the cops would say, "tossed." As Savage, who has now retired, pointed out to me recently, "In the precincts that we worked in, it would be difficult to *find* a white guy."

Diallo died where he was shot, in front of 1157 Wheeler Avenue, a brick row house in the Soundview section of the Bronx. When I visited the building recently, the front door, which is painted red, was propped open, as it must have been on the night of the killing, and several bullet holes were clearly visible in its side. In the vestibule, there were gashes in the walls, where bullets had apparently torn into the plaster, and through the diamond-shaped window of a second door I could make out still more holes in the walls of the hallway.

Since Diallo's death, the building has become a shrine, with buckets of wilted flowers sitting out front and messages of anger and condolence lining the entryway. A poem addressed to the cops and attached by duct tape to the brick façade read, in part:

> When you look at me what do you see
> Am I innocent until proven guilty
> Am I your enemy
> Or were you sent here to protect me

Hanging next to the poem, a Teddy bear wrapped in plastic clutched a box of Valentine's candy. In the thirty minutes or so that I stood in front of the building, taking notes, I spoke with half a dozen people who told me that they had come expressly to contemplate the spot where Diallo had been killed. "I wanted to come and see for myself what it looked like," one of them said. An elegantly dressed woman wearing a fur hat stopped by and silently added a fresh bouquet to a bucket.

I made my visit in the company of Francisco Gonzalez, the district manager for the local community board, who over the last few weeks has become a de-facto spokesman for the surrounding neighborhoods. A short, stocky man who was once an Army chaplain's assistant, Gonzalez grew up in the nineteen-sixties in the South Bronx, or, as he refers to it, Fort Apache. He sees nothing inherently wrong with the N.Y.P.D.'s current approach. On Elder Avenue, just a block away from Diallo's apartment, Gonzalez pointed out to me a stack of blue N.Y.P.D. trestles. They had been used, he said, to close off the street as part of a campaign to drive out drug dealers, a campaign that he felt had been largely successful.

"I got to tell you, Giuliani has the right idea in terms of how to address crime," he told me. He said he thought his views were generally shared by his neighbors. "If you speak to the average Joe, he'll say, 'I'm really happy. At 9 P.M., I can go to the bodega and buy some milk.'"

At the same time, Gonzalez said, he had heard a lot of complaints in the last few years about overaggressive policing. Just among the local officials that he dealt with, he knew of several instances of people stopped and questioned for no apparent reason other than the way they looked. In one case, it was a community-board member visiting his son-in-law. "He happens to be white," Gonzalez said. "They assumed he was doing drugs."

Even the local State Assemblyman, Ruben Diaz, Jr., has a story of being stopped. Shortly after his election in 1996, Diaz, then just twenty-four, was driving through his district with a couple of his friends when he was pulled over. Diaz's pockets were patted, and a friend was frisked. It was clear that the officers suspected that his car, a 1994 Toyota Camry, which had Assembly plates, had been stolen. "I hate to be racial," Diaz said, with the restraint of a much older politician, "but I don't think a white twenty-four-year-old would have been asked to get out of that car."

*   *   *

In order to "toss" someone, a police officer must reasonably suspect that the person is armed and presents a danger, and he is expected to be able to articulate why he felt that way. This "reasonable suspicion" standard has evolved from a landmark 1968 Supreme Court decision, Terry v. Ohio, and it is significantly lower than the "probable cause" standard that the cops must meet to make an arrest or to obtain a search warrant. Just how much lower has been the subject of much debate and considerable litigation. The courts have consistently held that simply being of a certain race or fitting a certain type or hanging out in a high-crime area does not constitute sufficient grounds for frisking. Making a furtive gesture or having a bulge in your pocket, on the other hand, does.

Even though stops based on race are illegal, the practice of "racial profiling" by law-enforcement agencies clearly goes on. That it happens on some of the nation's highways, for instance, has been established with something approaching statistical certainty. When researchers studied traffic data for I-95 north of Baltimore, as part of the settlement of a 1993 class-action lawsuit, they found little disparity in the rate at which blacks and whites violated the traffic laws but huge disparities in the rate at which they were pulled over. (Police often use traffic stops as a pretext for gun or narcotics searches.) An expert witness in the case described the odds of this disparity's occurring by chance as "less than one in one quintillion." Similarly, statistics produced in a 1994–95 case of minority drivers arrested for drug or weapons possession on the New Jersey Turnpike showed that on the southern section of the turnpike cars with black occupants represented only fifteen per cent of those violating the speed limit, yet they accounted for forty-six per cent of the drivers pulled over.

The N.Y.P.D. has consistently maintained that it regards racial profiling as anathema. Department officials have said, and ordinary cops confirmed to me, that at the Police Academy new officers are drilled insistently on what does and does not constitute reasonable grounds for a frisk. Members of Street Crimes also receive a copy of the department's training manual, "Street Encounters," which expressly stipulates that if an officer's reason for approaching someone "is a personal prejudice or bias, such as the person's race or hair length, the encounter is unlawful."

Critics of the department argue, though, that what matters is not what the cops are taught, but what actually happens on the street. Just last week, the National Congress for Puerto Rican Rights filed a class-action lawsuit against the Street Crimes Unit, accusing it of engaging in racially motivated searches. But measuring bias on the streets of New York is a lot harder than measuring it on a stretch of highway. As the city's corporation counsel, Michael D. Hess, pointed out in response to the announcement of the suit, it would "not be surprising" if a high proportion of those frisked by the Street Crimes Unit were black and Latino, given the neighborhoods the unit has been sent to protect. To fight violent crime most effectively, "you wouldn't send the majority of your people to do stop-and-frisks at Seventy-second Street and Park Avenue," Hess told me. The city's murder statistics "don't lie and cannot be fudged," he has said, which is why, he might have added, some of the questions raised by Diallo's death are so difficult to answer.

If you are a black resident of New York City, your chances of being murdered are at least five times as high as they are if you are white, and the odds that you've been arrested for murder are more than ten times as high. This disparity means that the police will see more behavior by blacks that they will legitimately identify as suspicious. At the same time, it means that they will, almost inevitably, come to see criminal behavior as a black phenomenon, which is not only profoundly unfair but also unlawful. The more aggressive policing becomes—the more the cops try to anticipate crimes before they occur—the more such structural biases are brought out into the open.

Of course, the segregation of crime, by income, by neighborhood, and, especially, by race, is what makes such a strategy politically practical in the first place. Crucial constituencies have little directly to lose from it. The cost of aggressive policing may be a collective erosion of civil rights, but only some groups feel the immediate impact. "Most people are prepared to pay those costs," observed Tracey Maclin, a Boston University law professor who has written extensively about race and the Fourth Amendment, "because, frankly, it is not them." Just three months after the assault on Abner Louima, Mayor Giuliani was resoundingly reëlected—largely, it seemed, because of his record on crime.

Six weeks after Diallo's shooting, it seems much less likely that this latest crisis will dissipate so quickly. Recent polls show that the Mayor's popularity is down roughly thirty points from its high of seventy-four per cent, in February, 1998—a decline that is most pronounced among blacks but that cuts across all racial groups. In the city there is a feeling, which is harder to quantify than mayoral popularity, that the very meaning of New York's drop in crime has shifted.

The difference may be in part that Diallo died. Or it may be that he was shot at so many times, which seems to suggest not only panic and confusion but also terrible fear and hostility. Or it may be that Diallo and Louima together are just more potent, that the repetition has forced New Yorkers to acknowledge a connection that they would have preferred to ignore.

But it may also be that people sense, if only intuitively, the fundamental difference between the two cases. Allegedly, as the cops beat Louima in their squad car on the way to the station and then tortured him inside it, they taunted him with racial epithets. The very explicitness of their racism was something to condemn, but also to take some comfort in: What those cops did to Louima, you could tell yourself, clearly had nothing to do with doing their job. It is much harder to say that about Diallo.

Postscript: Because of the protests and publicity surrounding the case, the trial of the four officers accused of killing Amadou Diallo was moved to Albany. On February 25, 2000, all four officers were acquitted. The Diallo family brought a lawsuit against the city, which was settled, for $3 million, on January 6, 2004.

Running on Empathy

February 2000

I N ANY CAMPAIGN, there are big lies and there are little ones. The difference is not so much moral as practical, just as it is in everyday life. What might at first have been fascinating about the Clintons but is, by now, mostly just maddening is the deliberate muddle they have made of this distinction.

Last month, the First Couple completed their long-awaited move— "move" here being understood in the loosest possible sense. If not yet the most photographed five-bedroom home in America, 15 Old House Lane is well on its way, and the elegant lines of its gambrel roofs are probably by now familiar to most New Yorkers. Naturally, the Clintons were concerned about the symbolism of the event, and they decided, at the last minute, that the President would have to arrive with his wife, even though that meant putting off their entrance until after dark. The next morning, in what is known in the trade as a carefully orchestrated appearance, Bill strode outside, put his arm around Hillary, and spoke about how happy he was to be in Chappaqua.

"We're seeing some things we haven't seen since we moved to the White House, and some things we haven't seen in seventeen years," the President told reporters, striking a theme that Mrs. Clinton returned to, even more emotionally, a few days later, at a news conference in White Plains. "You know," she said, "it's hard to describe, but when we began pulling things out of storage, which I'm still doing, I mean, we have wedding presents we've never gotten a chance to use, and so I'm putting them up in cabinets and unpacking boxes with mementos people gave us or things that I have from my grandmother that I haven't seen for a long time." Then she added, in all apparent earnestness, "It's a very, you know, great personal experience for both of us."

The first year of Mrs. Clinton's New York experience is just ending, and on Sunday she is scheduled to announce officially her candidacy for the United States Senate. Things are not, on the whole, going well. Her halting and always implausible campaign has, so far, consisted mostly of gaffes, wasted opportunities, and prurient questions from the press. Just two weeks after she and her husband unpacked their things, the First Lady was ambushed by reporters in Buffalo and forced to declare publicly that, no, she did not intend to get a divorce, nor had she ever had sex with Vince Foster. Meanwhile, literally hundreds of journalists show up whenever she does anything the slightest bit noteworthy, and when she is in control of the agenda she uses the occasion to say at some length almost nothing. After visiting forty counties in the state—an accomplishment she recently boasted about to David Letterman—she keeps coming back to the same tautology: she cares deeply about those issues about which New Yorkers deeply care.

When Mrs. Clinton first decided to take the race on, it was a bold act that seemed to demand an even bolder follow-through. How does someone mount a Senate campaign from a state where she has never lived if she has no record of accomplishment to point to and is, on top of all that, widely distrusted? The answer that is emerging is, like the First Lady's sentimental musings on her tchotchkes, at once stranger and more ordinary than could have been expected: she is planning, it seems, to base her candidacy on the quality of her concern, the heartfeltness of her convictions, and the depth of her feeling—to run, in other words, on her sincerity.

Mrs. Clinton likes to talk about the issues, or, perhaps more accurately, to talk about talking about the issues. Her favorites are education and health care, which polls show to be precisely the same ones New York voters put at the top of their lists. Often, when the discussion seems to be headed in a direction she doesn't care for, Mrs. Clinton invokes "the issues" to reorient it. What she means by the term, however, is a bit slippery.

"What's important to me are the issues," she said at a recent press conference at the Westchester County Democratic Committee headquarters, in White Plains. "I mean, who, at the end of the day, is going to improve education for the children of New York? Who's going to improve health care for the people of New York? Who's going to bring people together? And that's what I'm going to be talking about."

Later, she observed, along the same lines, "I think that the real issue ought to be who cares about the children of New York City, and who will work day in and day out to advance the interests of the education system."

In principle, at least, questions of public policy are not equivalent to questions of disposition. But Mrs. Clinton insistently conflates the two. A few weeks ago, I went to hear her address an interfaith breakfast at Riverside Church, in upper Manhattan. Like most of her appearances so far, this one was before an audience predisposed in her favor; in addition to clergy members and social activists, there were several prominent Democrats in the crowd, including former mayor David Dinkins. Twenty tables had been set up in the church's large vaulted assembly hall, each with eight seats. Mrs. Clinton arrived at the event half an hour late, dressed, as she almost always is these days, in a dark pants suit with a long flared jacket. She proceeded to make her way around all the tables until she had shaken hands with every guest. Then she moved on to the kitchen staff.

Mrs. Clinton alludes often to the "challenges before us," and also to "commitment" and "hard work" and the importance of "bringing people together" or, alternatively, "to the table." She is emphatically in favor of doing more to "support" people. "Parents are a child's first teachers, and we have to do a better job of supporting families in that most important function," she said at one point at Riverside Church. "All children can learn, if they are given the support," she added a little bit later on. "I want to work very hard to make sure that the Congress supports school districts that are supporting schools that are making the changes that will really help students learn," she said just a few moments after that.

In putting together her campaign staff, Mrs. Clinton has rehabilitated several former White House aides who had fallen out of favor; most of them share a pronounced liberal bent. Harold Ickes, a senior adviser to the campaign, for example, is a onetime aide to Jesse Jackson who left the Clinton Administration after being passed over for White House chief of staff. Mandy Grunwald, another top campaign adviser, was one of the aides the President blamed, quite probably unfairly, for the Democrats' loss of Congress in 1994. The First Lady's inner circle, as the Giuliani camp likes to point out, now bears a strong resemblance to the President's in the days before he took up triangulation. It is thus tempting to read her freehanded promises of "support" and her frequent protestations of "concern" as evidence of an ideological program in code. But that would be almost too generous.

As unsympathetic as reporters may be to the First Lady, they have, in a desperate search for news from her campaign, obscured the extent to which her remarks routinely drift off into a haze of good intentions. Mrs. Clinton brings to her public appearances a great deal of poise and seriousness of purpose, which, more than anything she actually says, is what the events tend to be about. This was the singular insight of the First Lady's unprecedented "listening tour," during which she tried to elevate nodding into a kind of political philosophy: so long as the "issue" is attitude, a politician doesn't have to say much of anything to make a point.

"I think it's appropriate to take a few minutes to reflect on some of the issues that people of faith have in common, and from my perspective, as I have travelled extensively now through New York and been in the company of so many different New Yorkers from so many different walks of life, I agree that the challenges before us, as individuals, as members and leaders of the community of faith, as those who already hold positions of public responsibility and those who seek them, that we do all share and should be committed to an understanding of how we make progress, but we define that progress broadly, deeply, and profoundly," Mrs. Clinton told the crowd at Riverside Church, giving special emphasis to the words "deeply" and "profoundly."

In New York, there is no right answer to the question "Are you going to march in the St. Patrick's Day parade?"—just degrees of wrongness. Though the parade may seem, to outsiders, mostly to be an excuse for public drunkenness, it is also a forum for the long-running battle over the rights of religious organizations to exclude homosexuals. Mrs. Clinton apparently did not realize this when, back in early December, she blithely declared, "I would hope so!"

A lot of the First Lady's blunders so far have been those of an outsider: first, the donning of the Yankees cap; then the reminiscences about a childhood pit stop in Elmira; then the revelation of a Jewish stepgrand-father—all were efforts to find a connection, no matter how piddling, to her adoptive state. But even taking into account the inevitable hazards of carpetbagging, Mrs. Clinton has proved maladroit at it. Sometime after the contretemps over clemency for members of a Puerto Rican terrorist organization (she first supported it, then opposed it) but before the contretemps over embracing Suha Arafat (she said she did not realize Mrs. Arafat was accusing the Israelis of poisoning Palestinian children), a lot of Democratic politicians in New York began to lose heart.

In public, the tone of their pronouncements about the race has grown increasingly wan, abstracted, and noncommittal. In private, they mostly just complain. "I don't think she has the instincts for it," one Democratic elected official from the city told me. Of Mrs. Clinton and her advisers, "They seem to have a tin ear for New York politics," a longtime party activist from upstate said. "She's got nobody who understands the grit of it all," another influential New York City Democrat griped to me. Indeed, Mrs. Clinton's campaign was, until quite recently, essentially a Washington-based operation; not until December, when she hired a campaign manager, Bill de Blasio, a former aide to Housing Secretary Andrew Cuomo, did anyone of real authority in the organization even live inside the state.

What, exactly, Mrs. Clinton is doing in New York is the dead cat in the eaves of her campaign. It affects everything, and it is the one thing that no one wants to deal with. Right before the Clintons' move, one of her advisers told me, in all apparent seriousness, that after the novelty of her living in Chappaqua wore off people would forget that where she came from had ever been an issue. The First Lady declined to be interviewed for this article, or, for that matter, for more than a hundred others, but at one of her recent press conferences I did manage to shout out a question about whether the fact that she was not a New Yorker was relevant to the race. In response, Mrs. Clinton said she didn't want to presume too much: "I would not prejudge how that decision will be made by any individual New Yorker." Then she steered the discussion back to the depth of her feeling.

"I think it's fair that people say to themselves, 'Well, I want to be sure that she's committed to New York, that she cares about New York, and that she's going to fight for New York,'" she said. "And I think I will be able to demonstrate all three of those attributes during this campaign."

When pollsters ask voters what they most dislike about Mrs. Clinton, her not being from the state is at the top of the list. Last winter, before she had started shopping for real estate and when the race was still largely hypothetical, the First Lady was leading the Mayor in the polls by more than ten points; now they have reversed positions. Particularly disturbing to Party leaders is the reception she is getting from other suburbanites: among voters in this group she is more than fifteen points behind Giuliani. More ominous still is the response of other women. When blacks, who overwhelmingly favor the First Lady, are taken out of the sample, she trails Giuliani among female voters by several points.

Whatever this gap is about, it is clearly not about the issues, at least as conventionally defined. To the extent that Mrs. Clinton's campaign has a strategy, it is to press her inherent advantage on abortion rights, the environment, and gun control, as well as on health care and education. Without offering anything very substantive on these topics—Mrs. Clinton will not even say, for example, whether or not she still believes in the basic precepts of the health-care plan she proposed seven years ago—she can nevertheless count on a majority of New York voters assuming they agree with her. In recent weeks, she has taken up what will doubtless become a major theme of her campaign: the vulnerability of Roe v. Wade and the makeup of the next Supreme Court. To eke out a victory, Mrs. Clinton hopes to inspire a heavy minority turnout in the city, to convince suburbanites that the Mayor does not, in the end, share their values, and to appeal to job-hungry districts upstate with a message of economic hope. All of which is to say that she is aiming to win as a fairly ordinary Democratic candidate, in spite of her extraordinary history and the resentments it has inspired.

The Mayor's pollster, Frank Luntz, told me that a few months ago he conducted his own "listening tour" of New York to assess the First Lady's strengths and weaknesses. He said that he was struck by how much bad feeling there was out there toward her that defied reasoned analysis.

Women in particular expressed their distaste in strong but inchoate terms. "The theme was 'I don't like her,' " he said. "Why? 'I just don't!' " Luntz, of course, is a biased listener, but two prominent Democratic officials told me, independently, that they had noticed much the same pattern in talking to female friends and constituents. They used the same word to sum up their findings: the feeling, they said, was "visceral."

For weeks, Mrs. Clinton declined David Letterman's invitation, but when she finally appeared on his show, smiling, kidding, and exchanging flattery with the "Big Guy," it was hard to see why. Their conversation was the closest that Mrs. Clinton has come for more than six months to providing an extended sitdown interview, and as a media event it could hardly have gone more smoothly. New Yorkers got a chance to see the First Lady face the tough questions in what turned out to be the safest possible context: Letterman broached the delicate issue of her not being from New York but did not press the matter, and before giving her a "pop quiz" on state trivia—state bird, state tree, and so on—he warned her about it in advance. Mrs. Clinton was smart enough to laugh at herself and self-possessed enough to do so in a way that, for all the event's evident staginess, seemed genuine.

It is a disarming fact about Mrs. Clinton that, in spite of all she has been through, she retains an implicit faith in herself and in her ability to appeal to voters on a personal, even intimate, level. If the calculated emptiness of her rhetoric often makes her seem detached, under the right circumstances she can still manage to project a sense of warmth and engagement and, finally, sincerity. This is a considerable strength in a politician, and it explains what may seem, on the face of it, to be her self-defeating electoral strategy. More than one Democratic official suggested to me that the key to the campaign would be how many New Yorkers the First Lady could get out and meet face to face, and while in practical terms this is a dubious notion—just five per cent of the New York electorate is five hundred thousand handshakes—it does get at something important about the race.

Recently, I met up with Mrs. Clinton on the two-day swing through western New York during which she was harried by questions about divorce and adultery. By the time she got to her final stop, at a senior center in Cheektowaga, a suburb of Buffalo, members of her press entourage were happier than they had been for weeks. The First Lady's press secretary, Howard Wolfson, meanwhile, looked as if he were about to be sick.

Whatever Mrs. Clinton might have been feeling, she didn't show it. A crowd of more than two hundred had gathered to meet her in a huge room decorated with foil snowflakes. Over and over again, elderly women told the First Lady that she looked prettier or skinnier than she does on TV, and she thanked each with the effusive surprise of someone hearing such a compliment for the first time. One woman was so choked up to meet Mrs. Clinton that she could barely speak. Another launched into a lengthy, and, to me, largely incomprehensible account of how her mother's house had been foreclosed, and how some sort of law ought to be enacted to prevent such things from happening. The First Lady listened intently, and then, when it was all over, said in a tone of deep appreciation, "Thanks so much for bringing that to my attention."

Mrs. Clinton lacks many of her husband's political skills—among them his flexibility, his sense of nuance, and his gift for improvisation. But she shares with him a genius for gestures of empathy. Unlike most people, and even most politicians, she stares unflinchingly into the eyes of those she is meeting, and in the midst of a noisy crowd still seems entirely focussed on whatever they are saying. After she had passed by, I asked several people what their impression of the First Lady had been, and the same words kept cropping up: "honest," "open," "nice," "sincere."

"While you're talking, she's actually listening to what you're saying," Helen Anzalone, a retired teacher, told me. "She doesn't just want to get away."

The first time I met Mrs. Clinton was in August of 1992, at the height of the Presidential campaign and six months after her famous appearance with her husband on "60 Minutes." The Clintons were in the midst of one of their bus tours, winding somewhere through the scrub of east Texas, and I bumped into Mrs. Clinton as I was making my way to the back of the candidate's bus to interview him. She put out her hand, and I remember being struck by the intensity of her gaze, but even more by what she said: "Hi, I'm Hillary Clinton." This seemed to me a pretty good joke on celebrity, and I recall being about to smile but then catching myself. She wasn't, I saw, poking fun at the situation but, rather, insisting on a sort of sublime humility: since she didn't know my name, perhaps I didn't know hers.

There is no inherent contradiction between enormous personal ambition and a genuine commitment to helping others. Indeed, there are probably few public figures who have had a lasting impact in whom these two motives have not both been at work. But the Clintons have never wanted to suggest this about themselves. Instead, they have made the most of the neediness of the electorate, or, if one prefers, its narcissism. From "Putting People First" to the listening tour, the message has always been one of elaborate deference and solicitude. What they saw early on, and with exceptional clarity, is that voters would forgive an awful lot in a politician who could manage to say convincingly that he really cared.

But extending this pretense—that the campaign is all about the voters rather than the candidate—to Mrs. Clinton's current quest pushes its logic to the breaking point. It is a little like robbing Peter to pay Peter, or, as Fabian in "Twelfth Night" observes, "This is to give a dog and in recompense desire my dog again." To run for the Senate after the carnage of the last eight years is nothing if not an extraordinary assertion of self. It makes sense only if the First Lady has an exceptionally strong motive, be it personal or political. Yet this is precisely what she cannot—or will not—provide.

Personal and Political

May 2000

L AST THURSDAY, RUDY Giuliani held a press conference in the Blue
Room at City Hall to announce that he had prostate cancer. The day
before, the Mayor had been spotted leaving Mount Sinai Medical Center,
and so, even before his announcement, there had been rumors about his
health. He told reporters that he had decided to discuss his condition
publicly to bring this speculation to an end. The cancer, he said, had been
diagnosed early and was a "treatable form."

Throughout the press conference, Giuliani seemed relaxed and cheerful,
even, as one television reporter subsequently put it, "serene." Asked several
times and in several different ways whether the diagnosis would affect his
Senate candidacy, the Mayor said he did not yet know; he hoped to remain
in the race, but he would base that decision on the course of therapy his
doctors recommended. When, at the end of the press conference, he was
asked whether his illness would make him any nicer, the Mayor was more
definitive. "No way!" he responded. The very next day, speaking at a
Republican dinner in Saratoga Springs, he proved the point by trashing the
President and describing as "Clintonian" words that "don't mean what
they say."

A life-threatening illness has a way of softening most, if not all, hearts,
and Giuliani was inundated with expressions of concern, including one
from the First Lady. He had become a figure of sympathy, something
that—as the question about his temperament and his answer, however
joking, suggest—would have seemed almost inconceivable just a few
hours earlier.

For as long as Giuliani has been Mayor, his reputation has oscillated between toughness, which is a political virtue, and meanness, which is not. After the shooting of Patrick Dorismond by an undercover cop seven weeks ago, it seemed to have rocked once too far in the wrong direction. So many New Yorkers were disturbed by his response to the shooting that the polls, which had shown him leading Hillary Clinton for almost a year, suddenly reversed. Attention that had been focussed on the First Lady's peculiar compulsion to represent a state where she has never lived shifted, almost overnight, to the Mayor's equally peculiar, but darker, compulsion to offend. On a more comic note, even his wife, Donna Hanover, appeared to have lost patience with him; after years of stable half-estrangement, which entailed her not being seen with him but also not embarrassing him, she suddenly joined the cast of "The Vagina Monologues." A cartoon in the New York *Post* showed the Mayor reading the news and fainting dead away, little clouds of steam rising from his temples.

The fact that Giuliani has cancer has obviously overshadowed his wife's provocative behavior, and, to a certain extent, his own, and it is impossible to predict what the Senate race will look like in a few weeks, or even if he will still be in it. But Giuliani's illness also points up what was most unfortunate about the Dorismond episode: the Mayor's refusal to identify with those in pain or to take the subsequent criticism of his actions at all seriously. At any given moment, this refusal may have reflected a simple lapse in judgment or a temporary loss of control, but, taken together, the events of those weeks, and, indeed, of his entire campaign so far, suggested something different. The Mayor, it seemed, was not so much trying— unsuccessfully—to hide his contempt for others as attempting something much more ambitious, which was to run on it.

The New York Senate race could be said to have officially begun back in February, when Mrs. Clinton formally announced her candidacy in a lengthy ceremony that included an eighteen-minute biographical film, several introductory speeches, and a twenty-seven-minute address by the candidate herself. There were plenty of things to disagree with in all the remarks by and about the First Lady, but the Mayor decided to take issue with "Captain Jack."

Someone, almost certainly not Mrs. Clinton, had mixed "Captain Jack" into the soundtrack that played before the ceremony began. The song, written by Billy Joel, tells the story of a lonely young man who spends Saturday night listening to music and getting stoned, and it conveys a rather gloomy message about drug use. Nevertheless, at a news conference the day after the First Lady's announcement, Giuliani read a line of the lyrics out loud—"Captain Jack will get you high tonight, and take you to your special island"—and declared its import to be "Let's say yes to drugs, let's glorify drugs, let's glorify pot." The next day, speaking on a Rochester radio station, he broadened his criticism, saying that the song also encouraged masturbation.

In the months following, the fuss over "Captain Jack" proved to be central to the emotional logic of Giuliani's election effort. Almost every day, the First Lady would attend a gathering of concerned citizens in some obscure town like West Henrietta, or issue a position paper pushing some esoteric government program like the Broadband Deployment Grant Initiative. The Mayor, meanwhile, made fun of Arkansas.

Not long ago, I caught up with Giuliani during one of his infrequent upstate trips. The Mayor clearly doesn't like to travel north of Van Cortlandt Park, and there are many who have posited that he wouldn't have entered the Senate race if, under the city's term-limits law, he weren't soon to be out of a job. Last week, when he revealed his diagnosis, many people speculated that he would welcome the opportunity to withdraw from the race, but by the following night the Mayor seemed to be trying to tamp down the speculation. "I'm very hopeful it's all going to work out, in all respects," he told a roomful of cheering Republicans.

On the evening I was following him, the Mayor had travelled two hundred and fifty miles, to Syracuse, for just one public event, a speech at a dinner hosted by the local Chamber of Commerce. The theme of the dinner was "The Grass Is Greener Here," a choice that, given the city's decades-long decline, seemed ironic in ways that the chamber probably did not intend, and on each table there was a centerpiece made out of a little plot of turf. Giuliani likes to start his speeches with a mob reference—often, nowadays, to "The Sopranos." This time, however, he chose another of his stock openings, an imitation from "The Godfather": "Thank youse for invitin' me heah tonight." He then moved on to his accomplishments in lowering crime ("Seventy per cent fewer murders"), reducing the welfare rolls ("More people moving from welfare to work than any place in America"), and improving the economy ("What we did is give you your money back so you decide how you want to spend it"). Of all his achievements, Giuliani said, he was proudest of having converted New York City welfare offices into "job offices," a change that was brought about, as he put it, "because we care about people in a responsible, adult, mature, loving fashion, not out of some kind of sense of our own guilt." As for why he should be elected to the Senate, the Mayor implied that he would do for the rest of the state what he has done for the city, but what he had in mind in terms of federal legislation, or financing, or even advocacy, he never specified.

Afterward, the Mayor spoke to a group of local reporters outside the banquet hall. Someone had given him an orange Syracuse basketball jersey, which he was wearing over his shirt and tie. There was time for only about half a dozen questions before he was due back at the airport, and Giuliani took almost every one as an opportunity to twit his opponent. Asked about "soft money," he said, "I think the Clintons have to learn the following: New Yorkers are not dumb. We are not suckers." Asked about Mrs. Clinton's criticism of his education record, he replied, in mock amazement, "The Clintons are raising the trust issue? You've got to be kidding me."

At the heart of the Dorismond episode is a tragedy that the Mayor had nothing directly to do with. On March 16th, Patrick Dorismond, an off-duty security guard, was standing outside a bar in midtown Manhattan when he was approached by an undercover narcotics officer, who reportedly asked if he knew where to buy drugs. He is believed to have told him to move on, and, for reasons that are still unclear, a scuffle ensued, during which another officer fired a single, fatal shot. Dorismond, who was twenty-six, was unarmed.

The shooting occurred at a time when racial sensitivities in the city were particularly raw; just three weeks earlier, a jury had acquitted the four police officers who killed another unarmed black man, Amadou Diallo. The day after Dorismond's death, the Mayor, in the name of balance, authorized the release of his juvenile-arrest records. Generally, such a move requires a court order, but Giuliani proceeded without one, under the novel theory that, since Dorismond was dead, his privacy rights had, albeit without his consent, been waived. With the exception of the city's corporation counsel, just about every lawyer familiar with the statute took issue with this theory, and at a hearing on the matter convened by the State Legislature one witness after another testified that the Mayor's actions had violated the law's intent. Even many Republicans complained that Giuliani had crossed the line, and wondered what possible purpose his conduct could be serving.

Despite the near-unanimity of opinion, the Mayor remained steadfast. He continued to intimate that the dead man had been responsible for his own shooting, and declined to attend Dorismond's funeral. At one point, Giuliani declared that Dorismond had been no "altar boy"; later, upon being advised by a reporter that Dorismond had, in fact, been an altar boy, he refused to comment, calling the question "argumentative."

A few weeks ago, I went to see the Mayor at City Hall. He spoke to me in his office, which is decorated in shades of burgundy and gold and contains a large portrait of Fiorello LaGuardia, along with busts of Abraham Lincoln and Ronald Reagan. It was one of the first extended interviews that he had granted since the shooting, and I asked whether he had had any second thoughts about releasing Dorismond's records.

"I read the law myself," he said. "The law contains no prohibition against releasing the records if someone is dead. It doesn't speak to the subject, and therefore it leaves, even granting the other side as much leeway as possible, an ambiguity. The purpose of sealing is to protect the ability of someone who got in trouble to get a job, to not be discriminated in housing, et cetera, et cetera. All these things have to do with life. If the State Legislature wanted to create a protection beyond death, they should have written it into the law. So legally I don't have any reconsideration."

I tried again. Even if his action had been legal, given the anguish it had provoked, did he have any regrets? "The ultimate result is that it's helped the city, even if it isn't understood at the time," he said.

But wouldn't it have made sense to offer some expression of remorse, simply for the sake of peace in the city? "I can only do the things that I believe," the Mayor said. "I don't believe this was the wrong thing to do. If I did, I would say it immediately. I know it would help me politically. And I don't have a resistance to doing that if I believe it. But I think we have to talk to each other honestly. We can't allow the domineering impact of political correctness to have us lie to each other."

Later in the interview, I asked the Mayor about some of Mrs. Clinton's criticisms of him. How would he respond to her charge that she is running on issues, while he is avoiding them? "I can't figure out the issues," he said. "I hear the slogans, but I haven't figured out the issues she's running on. I would say she's running on slogans. I think I'm running on issues. There isn't a single thing that I'm running on that I haven't done already, in great detail."

How about the criticism that he is uncaring? "What I would ask people to do is think a little bit deeper about the difference between substance and perception," he said. "For the Clintons, this has largely become a slogan that works, because it's sort of Pavlovian, but it doesn't go any deeper than that."

Giuliani is the only politician I have ever interviewed who gives the impression of being more cautious and deliberate in private than in public. This, of course, in large measure reflects his public excesses. (Even among all the elected officials making overheated comments about Elián González last week, Giuliani managed to stand out by referring to the federal agents as "storm troopers.") Still, the contrast raises interesting questions about how the Mayor has chosen to present himself. He routinely declines to speak to reporters in the more considered setting of a one-on-one interview, offering the explanation that press conferences provide more "direct" communication with the electorate.

On one of the few beautiful afternoons of this wet, raw spring, the Mayor decided to hold his daily "press availability" in the town of Bedford, on the grounds of the local Shell station, where the price of gas was two dollars and twenty-three cents a gallon. The ostensible reason for choosing Bedford, about an hour's drive north of Manhattan, in Westchester County, was the high price at the pump. The real reason, though, was obvious: Bedford is right next to Chappaqua. "You should have some familiarity with Bedford, New York," the Mayor said, addressing himself to the absent Clintons. "It's kind of close to another part of New York that you claim to be part of."

Giuliani kicked off the event with some remarks on the President's energy policy, which he called "bankrupt," and his foreign policy, which he labelled "feckless." "This Administration is napping, hibernating, asleep, unfocussed—whatever you want to call it—with regard to what's going on with gasoline," he said. "That's spelled n-a-p-p-i-n-g." Then he opened the press conference to questions on other topics. A reporter asked him about efforts by the City Comptroller, Alan Hevesi, to block several "welfare to work" contracts approved by the Giuliani administration.

"I think this is an attempt by Alan Hevesi to bring us back to where we used to be," the Mayor declared. "These are the people who created the philosophy of dependency, and they are apparently annoyed that we have five hundred and fifty thousand fewer people on welfare, and that we're down to the lowest number of people on welfare since 1967. After all, they created and supported and did nothing about over one million people on welfare when they had a chance to run city government."

Hevesi, a Democrat, has argued not that the contracts are a bad idea but, rather, that they were awarded using improper bidding procedures. Giuliani, however, does not have much patience for such procedural debates. His world view allows for just two types of people: those who are for him and those who are either misguided, blind, or simply corrupt. He is widely feared for his tendency to exact retribution from those he considers to be in the latter camp; New York City's Public Advocate, Mark Green, describes him as "the embodiment of the Machiavellian ethic 'Better to be feared than loved.'" A few weeks ago, when a state court sided with Hevesi, the Mayor responded as follows: "Democratic judge. Democratic decision. Jerky decision."

Not infrequently, the Mayor's press availabilities devolve into public scoldings, during which he castigates reporters for various forms of psychological and moral degeneracy. In response to a recent question about whether it was appropriate for him to send his children to private school, for example, Giuliani accused a reporter of "voyeurism." In response to another recent question, about Mrs. Clinton's economic proposals, he responded, "You guys, you're unbelievable; you're, like, knee-jerk, knee-jerk, knee-jerk," and he suggested that the reporters go "join the Democratic National Committee."

Giuliani's reluctance both to travel and to grant interviews means that much of his Senate campaign has been conducted through his availabilities, a decision that may seem perverse, except that a lot of his rhetoric requires the presence—real or imagined—of a disbelieving enemy. In this sense, the press is not so much an actual antagonist as a stand-in for a whole class, perhaps a whole stateful, of people who, Pharisee-like, continue to resist his message. At the Bedford Shell station, the Mayor several times complained that reporters were not paying enough attention to higher fuel prices, even as more than two dozen of us jostled for space around the gas pumps, desperate to record every word. "Things like this would be major issues if there were a Republican President," he said at one point. "So maybe you should examine the way in which you look at the world."

The press conference Giuliani gave last Thursday was impressive for a lot of reasons, not the least of which was that it was so straightforward, and, as much as anything could, it seemed to vindicate the Mayor's faith in the format. Giuliani outlined what he knew about his condition, which was that his cancer appeared to be confined to the prostate, and how he had come to know it, which was through a blood test and then a biopsy. He expressed confidence that he would be cured, but he noted that prostate cancer had killed his father. He did not seem to be trying to wring emotion from the occasion, nor did he have much to say when reporters pressed him for a big thought.

"Absolutely," he said, on being asked whether the diagnosis had made him reconsider his values. "Just the contemplation of it for the last two weeks makes you think about what's important in life, what are the most important things. But, you know, you should be thinking about that anyway. But do I have an answer yet? No, I don't have an answer yet."

These days, it is pretty much obligatory to lament the consumerist, poll-driven, finger-in-the-wind style of American politics and to speak nostalgically of an age, perhaps mythic, when elected officials sought guidance in something more lasting than focus groups. Giuliani, it is safe to assume, follows the polls as carefully as the next guy, and a lot of his positions reflect the very pragmatic calculations of a Republican running in a Democratic state, as does his decision not to spend a lot of time talking about these positions.

But the Mayor appreciates, in a way that most other politicians apparently do not, the paradoxical effect of paying too much heed to public opinion. His best impulses, which were on display last Thursday, when he spoke so unaffectedly and without self-pity, reflect this, and so, too, do his worst. Giuliani's irascibility, his insensitivity, and his towering self-righteousness are clearly not the product of any considered study, and his Senate campaign has been based on the premise that these qualities can, with a certain amount of squinting, be taken for assets: the more unattractive and obviously damaging his conduct, the more authentic it must be. Bruce Teitelbaum, Giuliani's campaign manager, summarized the Mayor's appeal as follows: "Even if we disagree with the guy, we respect him for standing up for what he believes in."

Nothing is more authentic than mortality, and on a human level, as much as on a political level, the Mayor's announcement last week was so powerful precisely because it was so real. In the end, reconciling the calm and the grace with which he is facing his illness with the many less appealing features of his recent campaign is not that difficult if one simply accepts what has been the Mayor's account of himself all along: when he says he really doesn't care what anybody else thinks, he really means it.

The Prophet of Love

June 2000

G OOD-LOOKING IN a placid, boyish sort of way, Rick Lazio is the kind of politician who, at forty-two, still talks a lot about his mom. He lists as his outside interests guitar playing and numismatics, and when he says he has no skeletons in his closet one is inclined to believe him. This week, the Long Island congressman is to receive the nomination for United States Senate at the New York Republican Convention, in Buffalo—a development that his fellow party members must regard with a mixture of heartsickness and relief.

Lazio had always made it clear that he wanted to run for the Senate; still, his campaign has taken shape at an astonishing speed. Just twenty-two hours after Rudy Giuliani's withdrawal from the race, Lazio held a kickoff rally, in the gym of the West Islip High School, where campaign T-shirts with the slogan "Made in New York" were already on hand. The next day, after making the rounds of the Sunday-morning talk shows, he embarked on a two-day fly-around that included appearances in nine cities. When I caught up with him last week, at his final stop, in White Plains, his wife and his press secretary looked as if they were about to keel over. Lazio himself was exuberant.

"I put my Mets hat on when I was six years old," he told a cheering crowd on the small lawn of the Westchester County Republican headquarters, the very same line he had trotted out to similar cheers in West Islip, and presumably also in Buffalo and Elmira and Utica and Albany. "I have never needed an exploratory committee to figure out where I wanted to live. New York is my home once and for always. I am one of you."

It is perhaps peevish to complain about Lazio's lack of subtlety. One of the unwritten rights of a political nonentity is to define himself however he wants to, or, at least, however he can get away with. And there is, all things considered, something disarmingly modest about the case the Congressman is making. He may be the first politician to mount a native-son campaign for statewide office. "I've fished and clammed in our waters," he likes to say.

What's unnerving about watching Lazio has to do, rather, with the bizarre history of the race he is stepping into. Before Giuliani withdrew, he, too, loved nothing more than to taunt Hillary Rodham Clinton about her carpetbaggery, and, to the extent that he ever really mounted a campaign against her, the confected nature of her identity was at the heart of it. The Mayor not only anticipated Lazio's strategy, however, he also blew it to smithereens. For months, he ragged the First Lady about her Yankees cap, her Chappaqua home, her centrist posturing—her pretense, in short, of being something that she was not—only to discover at the very last minute that it was he who was living a lie.

Reporters who arrived at the City Council hearing room on the afternoon of May 19th came expecting to hear a dispirited Mayor drop out of the race. They were met by a prophet of love. "The reason I'm such a fortunate man is that I have people that love me and I love them, and they care for me and I care for them, and that's the greatest support that you can have in life," Giuliani said to the crowd. "I'm also very, very fortunate because not only do I have very good friends and people that I love and love me but I have a job as the Mayor of New York City, being the Mayor of the city that I love very much, people that I've always had a great deal of connection to and love for."

The next day, Giuliani gave a follow-up interview to Tim Russert, of NBC News, expanding on what his recent diagnosis of prostate cancer had taught him. "I tend to think now that love is more important than I thought it was," he said. "I think about all the love that I've received and it's amazing. . . . I've gotten thousands of letters giving me support, giving me love. And I think about the people that have to face this alone, without this incredibly large system of support and encouragement, and it has to be terrible."

The overriding message of all this—that love will make him a better mayor—would hardly be remarkable as a narrative of loss and recovery were it not for the fact that it contradicts just about everything Giuliani has ever said about himself, the city, and the nature of leadership. His philosophy, which some might say was always an elaborate rationalization for a reflexive bellicosity, took as its first principle the idea that sentiment has no place in the formation of public policy.

Only a few months ago, I watched the Mayor meet with some of the city's poorest and most desperate citizens. Most of them were welfare recipients, and they were begging him to sign a bill that would have made adjustments in the city's workfare program. As he sat in stony silence, they offered up tearful accounts of mistreatment, sexual harassment, and physical danger. Giuliani made not even a perfunctory show of sympathy. "I would be less than candid if I didn't say I'm inclined to veto," he said when the testimony was over, and that is exactly what he did.

The Mayor has often asserted that what liberals call compassion is really just a twisted form of guilt. Most of the programs of his predecessors, he likes to say, were inspired by such thinking, and, as he told a campaign gathering in April, amount to little more than giving "people some silly irresponsible slogan in their head that just makes things worse." At his most ambitious moments, Giuliani was willing to trace just about all the problems of the inner city to one form or another of bogus, and ultimately self-serving, sentimentality.

The timing of the Mayor's withdrawal left Republicans exactly ten days to agree upon a replacement. It was, he reported, surprisingly difficult to resolve on a course of cancer treatment. "I didn't understand the impact of this," he said. "I thought of it as a budget—I know this sounds silly—but I thought of it like a budget decision or a legal decision." Giuliani's discovery was a moving one, but it came dangerously close to confirming the suspicions of his critics. Even at this most vulnerable moment, he seemed to be implying that making decisions that affect millions of other people was, for him, emotionally uncomplicated.

If the Mayor's epic farewell-to-the-Senate news conference set a new standard for weirdness in New York politics, it was only by beating out his farewell-to-Donna news conference, nine days earlier. On that occasion, he announced that he would be relying even more on his "very good friend," Judith Nathan, and was seeking a separation. One of the reporters present had the good sense to ask the Mayor how his wife of sixteen years felt about this development:

REPORTER: Is this a mutual place that you've come to—you talked about formalizing an agreement?

MAYOR: I don't know. I'm speaking—no, we haven't done that. I believe that that's what we should do, that that would be the best thing to do to protect our children, to protect ourselves, to protect everyone, and to maybe deal with it more honestly and directly.

Most sex scandals occur because of private indiscretions that become public. In Giuliani's case, it seemed to be the reverse: everything that was most damaging occurred in front of a bank of cameras. According to news accounts, Donna Hanover learned about her husband's decision only when she was called by friends who had been watching him on television. A few hours later, she summoned reporters to Gracie Mansion and, in a tone more of sorrow than of revenge, announced that he had wrecked their marriage with a pair of affairs, including one with his former press secretary. The Mayor refused to respond to these allegations, on the ground that his marriage, which he had finished off on live TV, was now a private matter. "Don't you realize that you embarrass yourselves by doing this in the eyes of everybody?" he growled at reporters one afternoon. The very next evening, he went out for dinner on the Upper East Side and cheerfully posed for pictures with his new "friend."

For his entire mayoralty, Giuliani has been the scourge of illicit pleasures, closing down the sex shops, banishing the hot-dog venders, even trying to enforce the laws against jaywalking. All along, his faith in his own moral compass has never wavered. Much like Angelo in "Measure for Measure," who sets out to impose the death penalty for fornication (and then propositions a woman training to become a nun), the Mayor often seemed to derive a certain icy satisfaction from pointing up the frailties of others. New York Republicans, confronted with his infidelities, struggled to explain away the hypocrisy. One county chairman I spoke with gamely argued that the Mayor's conduct wasn't really duplicitous because, as everybody knew, his marriage had been a sham all along.

For his part, the Mayor never even acknowledged the contradiction. Usually quick to assign blame, he has, on the subject of his own marital difficulties, been magnanimous to a fault. "The fact that we've grown independent, we've grown more separate over the years—who knows why those things happen?" he mused. In dropping out of the Senate race, he rejected the suggestion that sex or scandal had anything to do with it. "This decision is a health decision," he said categorically.

If the Mayor's withdrawal speech had the tone and structure of a confession, it was, of course, to a different lapse entirely, and this substitution was the truly inspired element of his performance. At this point, it doesn't really matter whether reporters were convinced by his conversion narrative, or by his promise to be more inclusive. Instead of being asked about how and when and why he cheated on his wife, Giuliani is now being confronted with much less awkward questions, about his spiritual awakening.

"There is luck, good luck and the luck of the Clintons," William Goldschlag observed the other day in the *Daily News*. Not long ago, the consensus in New York politics was that the First Lady is a deeply flawed candidate who is running a mediocre race. Now the consensus is that she's a deeply flawed candidate who is running a mediocre race and is likely to win the election.

Last week, Mrs. Clinton continued to campaign much as she always has, speaking at a Boys and Girls Club in Mount Kisco, a union convention in Albany, and a senior citizens' center in Mount Vernon, but the jagged terror that characterized her operation for so long was gone. Lazio may well turn out to be a formidable opponent—polls already show him narrowing the gap with the First Lady—but the race has clearly lost its sense of high drama. In Mount Vernon, one of Mrs. Clinton's aides was asked whom she was rooting for in the N.B.A. playoffs, and he was relaxed enough to joke that although she was a longtime Bulls fan, she had, of course, also always had a soft spot for the Knicks.

At the senior center, the First Lady seemed cheerful and self-assured. She voiced her support for helping children and old people; people who take care of children and old people; and, finally, people who have no one to take care of them at all. Afterward, she called some bingo numbers and then walked over to speak to members of the press, who were roped off in the back. One reporter asked her about Lazio's recent criticisms. She furrowed her brow and pursed her lips. "I'm going to continue to do what I've done, and that is to run a positive campaign about the issues that I've been talking to people here at the center about," she said. "I've been a little disappointed. I thought it was unfortunate that he seems to be running a campaign of insults."

While Mrs. Clinton was working the room, I spoke with about a dozen of the bingo players, and with each one I tried out Lazio's nativist argument. Responses ranged from "If you can come in and do the job, that's what counts" to "Americans are transient people" to "It takes guts to move to a new state." One youthful-looking retiree went so far as to suggest that it might actually be better for New York to have a senator unburdened by an overintimate knowledge of local affairs. "I've always been one who thinks you can see things much better from a distance," she said.

Last winter, when I asked advisers to the First Lady how they planned to deal with the problem of her carpetbagging, they said they wouldn't really need to, since after a few sightings of her buying groceries in Chappaqua it would simply cease to be an issue. At the time, I found this notion laughable, but, like so many of the most cynical political predictions, if the senior center is any guide, it has turned out to be true. In this sense, Lazio's current strategy may be not just ham-handed but quite possibly also self-defeating. One can claim to be the real thing for only so long before it starts to seem just another posture.

Even at the darkest hour of the Mayor's indecision, all the Republicans I spoke to said they preferred the sick and wounded Giuliani to the bushy-tailed Lazio. Obviously, this was a reflection of the Mayor's name recognition, his record of achievement, and his huge war chest, but it was also a reflection of his innate talents. Too headstrong and self-destructive to be considered a master politician in conventional terms—it's unclear at this point whether he has left himself any future in politics at all—Giuliani, at least before he discovered love, knew how to swing a tire iron. When he took a swipe at Mrs. Clinton, it was in the spirit of spoof rather than of self-affirmation, and he never confused the absurdity of her position with a justification for his own. We will miss him.

The Inside Game

October 2000

N OT LONG AGO, a dozen former members of the all-black 503rd
Field Artillery Battalion were having drinks and canapés in a small
function room in the basement of the Rayburn House Office Building.
They had come to Washington, some from as far away as Texas and
California, to commemorate the outbreak of the Korean War, fifty years
before, and that afternoon they had taken a bus to Arlington to lay a wreath
at the Tomb of the Unknown Soldier. The next morning, they were due to
leave for Seoul from Andrews Air Force Base, wheels up at 8 A.M. Most of
the men were in their seventies, and it had been a long day, so after a few
drinks they gravitated toward some folding chairs set up along the walls.

Congressman Charles Rangel, the party's host, arrived late. He had
served with the 503rd in Korea, first as a corporal and then as a sergeant. In
November of 1950, when the Chinese crossed the Yalu River and surprised
the Americans with a devastating counterattack, Rangel was wounded near
Kunu-ri. Nevertheless, he led a group of several dozen men through the
frozen hills to safety, and for his valor in that disastrous campaign he was
awarded a Purple Heart and a Bronze Star. After making a few remarks to
the group, Rangel introduced a Cabinet official from the Office of Veterans
Affairs, who presented everyone with a special lapel pin, and then he joined
the other men telling war stories at the edge of the room.

It was hard for an outsider to follow much of the conversation, which
turned on events that had occurred half a century and half a world away.
Still, it seemed pretty clear what kind of history the group in general, and
Rangel in particular, was constructing. " 'You can walk along with that
clipboard, but you're going to get your ass shot off,' " Rangel said at one

point, mimicking the words of a commander of his. At another point, I heard him say, to much hilarity, "I crossed the same goddam river three times. People thought I knew what I was doing."

By the conventions of American politics, Rangel's life has been an exemplary one. Not just the decorated service in Korea but the poor childhood on Lenox Avenue, the struggle to get through college, the succession of odd jobs during law school—all would fit effortlessly into a story about grit and hope that is also, perforce, a story about a nation of opportunity. Yet something prevents Rangel from telling it that way.

When he and the other members of the 503rd returned from their trip, I tried, mostly unsuccessfully, to extract from him a clearer account of his contribution to the war effort. "This crew that I went to Korea with reminded me that they never really knew what my job was," he told me, giving a deep, raspy laugh. "'How the hell did *he* make corporal? All he does is walk around with a clipboard!'" As for his heroism, Rangel dismissed it as a case of the blind leading the blind; he had struck out, for no particular reason, in one direction, and forty-three soldiers had fallen in behind him.

Rangel, who is seventy, is a heavy man with a large, almost rectangular face, a small mustache, and eyebrows of operatic proportions. His voice, when he is telling stories, is gravelly almost to the point of parody. Rangel has represented Harlem for three decades, and during that time he has suffered his fair share of defeats, but he describes his career as virtually free of disappointment. "I swear I've never had a bad day," he told me. "Never had a setback that I couldn't deal with, in saying, 'You lucky son of a bitch.'"

Next month, if the Democrats regain control of the House, Rangel will become the chairman of the Ways and Means Committee. If that happens, he will be the highest-ranking African-American in congressional history. The chairmanship could be seen as one last spectacularly lucky break for Rangel—the perfect ending to his picaresque tale. Or it could be seen as proof of just how far, even in politics, a gift for the picaresque can take you.

*   *   *

On the morning of the second day of the Democratic National Convention, in Los Angeles, I found myself wandering with Rangel through a men's-clothing store in Santa Monica. That evening, he was to give a three-minute speech on the floor, just inside prime time. A rehearsal of his remarks, which had been scheduled for the previous night, had never taken place, even though Rangel had waited around the Convention Center nearly forty-five minutes for it, and now he was on his way downtown to try again. When he spotted a mall, he announced that he wanted to treat himself to a new shirt.

Rangel is a snappy dresser—the only time I ever heard him criticize Al Gore was when the Vice-President showed up at an environmental event in rumpled clothes—and on this particular day he had on a dark-blue suit, a sky-blue shirt, and a maroon-striped tie with a matching handkerchief, as well as two large rings and a heavy gold-link chain bracelet. The first thing Rangel did when he got into the store was ask what was on sale. "If the price is right, I'll wear the label on prime time," he announced. He picked out a dress shirt with a white-on-white herringbone pattern and a gold tie-and-handkerchief set. Something that one of the clerks said to him about sleeve length prompted him to tell a long joke that involved hunching his shoulders and limping around the store, the punch line of which was "Yeah, but that suit sure fits great!" Upon being told that the shirt was sixty-nine dollars—knocked down, especially for him, from eighty-nine—and the tie set forty-nine, he put back the tie set.

After Rangel had paid for his purchase—in cash—he went to look around the atrium of the mall. Several shoppers recognized him and came over to wish him well. He greeted each one with an expression of surprised pleasure. "He's the reason I'm a Democrat," one man told me. "He's always speaking up for a good cause." Rangel noticed a stand that sold smoothies, and decided that he wanted one. I said I would treat, and he told me that he thought I should get a drink for his driver as well, a gesture that from many other politicians would have seemed almost too solicitous.

At roughly the time that Rangel was pricing shirts in Santa Monica, several hundred black delegates were meeting a few miles away with Senator Joseph Lieberman at the Westin Bonaventure Hotel. Two days earlier, Congresswoman Maxine Waters, of Los Angeles, had declared that because of Lieberman's stand on affirmative action she might not be able to back the Democratic ticket, and the day after that a meeting of the black caucus of the Democratic National Committee had been suspended when it seemed about to be overtaken by the issue. The controversy was getting a lot of news coverage, including a front-page story in the special Convention issue of the Washington *Post*.

When it suits him, Rangel is as apt to make trouble as the next guy, but in Los Angeles this clearly wasn't what he had in mind. Several times I heard reporters try to prod him into saying something controversial, only to be met with a definitive, Rangelian brushoff: "Your question is far too sophisticated for me" or "That's above my pay grade." Rangel obviously knew about the meeting with Lieberman—I had heard him mention it in the car—and just as obviously had decided to be somewhere else when it happened. As soon as he arrived at the Convention Center, reporters tried to get him to take a position on what they clearly hoped was a widening racial conflict; in a tone of regret, he told them he couldn't help them, since he hadn't been at the meeting.

Later, after Rangel had run through his speech and repaired to a sky box high above the Convention floor, I asked him about the issue, hoping that in a quiet moment I might have more luck. He responded with a comic parable. During a national Party Convention once, he and a number of other African-American delegates had had some by now forgotten grievance, and they had threatened the Party chairman that they were going to walk out over it. "No, you won't," the chairman had told him. "Because we're going to provide you with *bicycles*."

"I would think Lieberman's going to have bigger problems with me than I'll have with him," Rangel said by way of conclusion. Then he lay down on a couch and took a nap.

Under the United States Constitution, "all Bills for raising Revenue shall originate in the House of Representatives," and before the House can vote on them they have to go through Ways and Means. The committee's jurisdiction extends from the tax code through trade policy to Social Security and Medicare. Its work is thus at once technically demanding, tortuously dull, and extremely consequential.

One day this spring, I sat in on a Ways and Means markup of a Medicare prescription-drug bill, H.R. 4680. The markup took place in the committee's Longworth Building meeting room, which is very large and very formal, with a round recess in the ceiling and a fierce-looking eagle perched in each corner. Virtually everything that was to occur during the session could have been predicted in advance, having been orchestrated by the Democratic and Republican House leaders to inflict maximum damage on one another. Nevertheless, the room, which can easily hold several hundred people, was full. Most of the first hour was taken up with a read-through of the proposed bill: "Section 307 on page thirty-three would phase in a new risk adjustment method based on data from all settings gradually in ten years in one-tenth increments starting in 2004." Rangel left in the midst of this exercise to attend to other business, and I followed him, but some six hours later I was told that the meeting was still, excruciatingly, grinding on.

When Rangel was named to Ways and Means, in 1975, he was the first black person ever to serve on the committee. He pushed hard for the assignment, and he finally got it, he intimated to me, by supporting the 1974 New York gubernatorial candidacy of Congressman Hugh Carey, a Ways and Means committee member. Given the concerns of Harlem, one might have expected Rangel to seek a seat on the budget or the appropriations committee, where he would have been in a position to funnel aid directly to his district. But Rangel is keenly sensitive to the power that comes from having something that someone else wants.

"When you represent a poor community, and you're looking in the long range, you have to be in a bargaining position with those who have an entirely different agenda," he told me once. "There's not a tax bill that poor and working people don't come out ahead on because of my efforts. It's not because I'm that good—it's just because other people want so many other things that I can say, 'Hey, hold it. Stop the parade!'"

Rangel is the kind of politician who earns ratings of a hundred per cent from the A.F.L.-C.I.O. and zero per cent from the American Conservative Union. He favors expanding federal aid for education, and training, and housing, and drug treatment, and he vigorously opposed the welfare-reform act of 1996. Most of his major legislative accomplishments involve using the tax laws to encourage the rich to help the poor, and his minor ones generally involve using the tax laws to help New York City. "Charlie has used his position consistently to tweak every piece of legislation that went by him," Kathryn Wylde, the president of the New York City Investment Fund, told me. "He has used it shamelessly parochially, and for that we are very grateful."

Not surprisingly, the prospect of someone with Rangel's politics heading the committee that writes the nation's tax code has given a lot of people pause. First of all, there is the direct power that comes with the post, which previous Ways and Means chairmen like Wilbur Mills and Dan Rostenkowski leveraged into virtual veto authority over major legislation. Then there is the indirect benefit of the job's fund-raising capacity—with so many tax breaks to hand out, it is nearly limitless— which nowadays is almost as important.

Rangel seems to take a certain pleasure in all the discomfiture. He likes to tell stories about nervous executives who have gradually lost their sense of color the closer he has come to the chairmanship, and he has openly exploited his proximity to the post to raise millions of dollars for the congressional Democrats. At the same time, he seems to be taking some pains to try to ease the anxiety. Many in the business community interpreted his vote this past spring to normalize trade relations with China as one such gesture; the vote ran counter to the position advocated by most of Rangel's traditional allies in organized labor, and infuriated many of them.

"I'm the C.E.O.s' new best friend," Rangel told me, chuckling. "Some of them say, 'Have I ever told you about the great job you're doing?' And I say, 'No, I don't think you have.'"

The southern border of Rangel's congressional district starts at the Hudson at 127th Street, follows a sawtooth pattern around the top of Central Park, and ends at the East River, at 96th Street. The district's original lines were drawn by a reluctant New York State Legislature in the early nineteen-forties as part of one of the nation's first efforts to create a black seat. It has since had only two occupants, Rangel and, before him, Adam Clayton Powell, Jr.

Rangel lives roughly in the center of the district, at 135th Street and Lenox Avenue, directly across from Harlem Hospital. One morning this summer, I visited him at his apartment, which is spacious and bright and eclectically decorated with vases and mirrors and various knickknacks from the Congressman's assorted travels. Rangel has been married for thirty-six years, and has two children, Alicia, who is an advertising executive in New York, and Steven, who is a lawyer in Washington. Shortly after I arrived, Rangel's wife, Alma, whom he frequently describes as long-suffering, brought us a tray with coffee, croissants, and melon. She urged me to let her husband talk so that I could eat, and her tone suggested that she did not think he would need much encouragement.

Rangel's talk about himself is so much more irreverent than that of most successful politicians that it is easily mistaken for candor. Rangel, who never really knew his own father, grew up with his mother and grand-father, Charles Wharton, in a brownstone at 132nd Street and Lenox Avenue; at one point during our conversation, he took me over to the balcony to point out the building. By his own account, he was an unpleasant child, adored by his mother but scorned by his grandfather. "I was just a mean little son of a bitch," he told me. "I am so nice to kids now. Even bastard kids I'm nice to, because I see myself."

On Saturdays, Rangel and his younger sister used to go downtown with their grandfather to the criminal courthouse, where Wharton worked as an elevator operator. Rangel now believes that the trips with his grandfather are what drew him to the law, but for a long time, he says, he refused to admit this to himself.

"Because of seniority, my grandfather became the head elevator operator, which meant he took up only the assistant district attorneys, the district attorney, and the judges," he said. "And, oh, he would bow and scrape! And they would say, 'Hey, Charlie, how're you doing?,' and he was 'Oh, O.K., Mr. O'Dwyer, have you met my grandchildren?' And I'd never seen my grandfather bow and scrape. He was a tough little man—tough on me, tough on the people in the block. He wore this damn uniform of his in the block, he wore this little badge, and he was respected, because he was no ordinary elevator operator."

Before Rangel went off to Korea, he had dropped out of high school, and when he came back he held down a series of lousy jobs, culminating in one that involved hauling lace through the garment district. One rainy afternoon, he had an epiphany, or at least half of one, on Thirty-sixth Street. The hand truck that he was pushing got away from him, the boxes fell into the street, and cops began cursing him for holding up traffic. Then and there, he resolved to make something of himself, though he was not at all sure what, and he walked away, leaving the hand truck and the boxes in the gutter. "My grandfather, when I told him that I was going to go to college—he laughed himself to death," Rangel said. "He didn't know anybody that went to college. *I* didn't know anybody who went to college."

With help from the G.I. bill, Rangel graduated from New York University in 1957, and then received a full scholarship to attend St. John's University Law School. While at St. John's, he interned at the Manhattan District Attorney's office with some of the same lawyers his grandfather was still taking up in his elevator. "They gave me a going-away party there, and I invited my grandfather," he recalled. "He was so pissed off, because all the people that had called him Charlie were calling me Mr. Rangel."

Rangel explains his entrance into politics with yet another story about his grandfather. Wharton was nearing retirement age, and was afraid that he would be forced out of his job at the courthouse. To keep that from happening, Rangel joined the local Democratic club. After a few years of trying to work his way up in the club, he left it and joined a group of self-styled young "reformers," led by Percy Sutton. When Sutton became the Manhattan borough president, he installed Rangel in his old seat in the State Assembly. To this day, the two are the closest of friends and political allies. "Incidentally," Rangel informed me, apparently not wanting to leave any mistaken impressions, "Percy never was a real reformer."

Frank Guarini, a former Democratic congressman from New Jersey, served with Rangel for fourteen years on Ways and Means, and also for a time on the Select Committee for Narcotics Abuse and Control. He recalls travelling with Rangel to Burma and meeting the country's dictator, General Ne Win, to discuss drug trafficking in the region. Toward the end of the meeting, Win asked the delegation members if there was anything more he could do for them. Rangel said yes. The General was dressed in his military uniform, and Rangel particularly admired one of his insignias. Could he take it home? Flattered, the dictator handed it over. "Charlie could charm the Devil," Guarini said.

Like most politicians, Rangel is immensely gregarious. He is also, at least in his private dealings, a reflexive optimist, who sees possibilities where others see only barriers or limits. That warmth helps explain what is otherwise a rather puzzling fact about him. For years now, Rangel, as a public figure, has been known as one of the most outspoken, most partisan, and most caustic members of Congress, which is why he is so much in demand on the political talk-show circuit. Rangel, a Catholic, once lashed out at John Cardinal O'Connor, saying, "If the Church paid nearly as much attention to life after birth instead of life before birth, it would make a greater contribution." Five years ago, in a fight over eliminating a tax break for broadcast properties sold to minority-owned businesses, he likened the current Ways and Means Committee chairman, Representative Bill Archer, of Texas, to Hitler.

And yet Rangel has a network of friends which extends in virtually all directions. Former Representative Guy Vander Jagt, a conservative Republican from Michigan, describes Rangel as his "polar opposite" politically but also as one of his best friends. "Charlie is a tremendous consensus builder," he told me. "He's going to find a way to make things work." Once, I watched Rangel spar on MSNBC with Representative David Dreier, of Los Angeles, another Republican and ideological opponent. Afterward, when the cameras were off, Dreier pleaded with Rangel to set a lunch date with him. (Rangel promised to check his schedule and get back to him.)

Representative Gregory Meeks, a black Democrat from Queens, considers Rangel his mentor. He told me that it was Rangel who taught him "how to get things done," and he described the Congressman's teachings as follows: "First, you establish a personal relationship with someone—try to understand why they do what they do. Sooner or later, they'll need a favor. Then they'll come back and deliver for you."

In representing the interests of New York City on the Ways and Means Committee, Rangel frequently depends on the favors of others. The city's many idiosyncrasies—its high cost of living, for example, and its high rate of poverty—mean that it is almost always seeking federal formulas or income criteria that are different from those sought by the rest of the country. Typically, Rangel measures his success by a number buried deep inside some bill, which has been recalculated to reflect the difficulties of life in New York, and to which a lot of other lawmakers, with other agendas, had to agree.

Politics of this nature is not just an inside game; it is inside the inside, and also almost entirely white. Rangel helped found the Congressional Black Caucus, but at the same time he has always been close to congressional Democratic leaders, starting with Thomas P. (Tip) O'Neill, who was the majority whip when Rangel arrived in Washington, in 1971, and continuing today with Richard Gephardt, the House minority leader. In 1984, when Jesse Jackson ran against Walter Mondale for the Democratic Presidential nomination, Rangel, unlike practically every other black politician in the country, supported Mondale, who had served in the Senate. "It was a very, very political decision," Rangel told me when I asked him about this. "A very practical political decision." (The decision did not, however, prevent him from becoming friends with Jackson. When the two ran into each other in Los Angeles, they embraced, and I heard Rangel joke to Jackson, "I vote for you all the time.")

Rangel was, perhaps most significantly, also a good friend of Rostenkowski's when Rostenkowski ruled Ways and Means. The former chairman told me that he had always been able to count on Rangel's support when he needed it. "I used to get a kick out of it," Rostenkowski said. "He would say, 'Dan, what did I decide to do here?'" Frank Guarini, who himself did not always get along with Rostenkowski, told me that Rangel had been able to "charm" Rostenkowski, "and so he got what he wanted."

In Harlem, Rangel measures his success by his involvement—typically protective, and often self-protective—in the life of his district, and as he has risen through the ranks in Washington he has never lost interest in the details (some would say the minutiae) of neighborhood affairs. Rangel is the only congressman in New York who remains a Democratic district leader, which means that if he wanted to he could vote at the kind of meetings where local judicial nominations are decided.

Rangel won his seat by running against Adam Clayton Powell, Jr., in a race that was made possible—and, according to Rangel, necessary—only by Powell's growing indifference to the district. A legendary figure in black New York, and for a time the most powerful African-American politician in the country, Powell was, by the late nineteen-sixties, sick, under investigation, and living in virtual exile in Bimini. Rangel was afraid that if he didn't run against Powell someone else would, and run him—Rangel—out of politics as well. "Adam had lost the confidence of the people in Harlem," he told me.

For a long time after the 1970 election, Rangel and Percy Sutton, along with a few other friends, including David Dinkins, who served as the city clerk and then as the Manhattan borough president before becoming mayor, effectively controlled Harlem politics. This was a wonderful irony, given that Sutton's rise had been predicated on the notion that he was fighting the machine. The "reformers" more or less set up their own machine, and Rangel's career reflects the strengths and also the weaknesses of this way of operating.

By valuing friendship and loyalty as much as he does, Rangel often seems to give short shrift to other qualities, like talent or technical know-how. For more than two decades, for example, he was the patron of a group called the Harlem Urban Development Corporation, a state-government agency that was created in 1971 to foster economic growth in the neighborhood and was dissolved in 1995. Even the most benign account of what the group did with the tens of millions of dollars in public funds it received would have to acknowledge that a considerable amount of it was spent ineffectively; many critics, however, have gone much further, and accused H.U.D.C. of basically being a high-priced patronage operation. When New York began turning over city-owned housing to private developers for rehabilitation, H.U.D.C., in its efforts to protect its own turf, largely prevented this from happening in Harlem, with the result, as one housing expert put it to me, that the neighborhood is now "a decade behind the rest of the city."

"Charlie, to his credit, won't let anyone push him around, and he insists that if it's in Harlem he's going to have control," this person told me. "No one has ever thought he lined his own pockets, but he trusted others who have not served him well."

During the recent investigation by the state attorney general's office into allegations of mismanagement at the Apollo Theatre, Rangel's style was publicly, and painfully, put on display. For many years, Rangel was the chairman of the board of the nonprofit group that ran the theatre, while a company owned by Percy Sutton produced a weekly television program there, "It's Showtime at the Apollo." A lawsuit by the attorney general, which named both men as defendants, accused Rangel's board of failing to collect millions of dollars it was owed by Sutton's enterprise. Both men were eventually cleared of criminal wrongdoing, but after months of newspaper coverage most New Yorkers had probably already concluded that the former borough president had received favorable treatment from his friend the congressman. Perhaps even more damaging, the scandal drew attention to the fact that during the years Rangel had control of the board the theatre itself had only sunk further into disrepair.

Over the last three decades, Rangel has obviously steered a great deal of government largesse toward Harlem, which is one of the primary reasons he wields so much influence in the district. Along with another ideological opponent, former Congressman Jack Kemp, Rangel was a moving force behind the creation of federal empowerment zones—specially designated areas that receive favorable tax treatment and certain forms of aid—and, not surprisingly, one is situated in his district. The Upper Manhattan Empowerment Zone has succeeded, among other things, in attracting a new mall, Harlem U.S.A., to 125th Street, the completion of which has led to much hopeful talk about a commercial revival in the neighborhood, and even, somewhat hyperbolically, of a second Harlem Renaissance. Several knowledgeable people made the case to me that, while Rangel deserved enormous credit for the zone's creation, its success owes much to the fact that he subsequently lost control over its day-to-day operations.

Not long ago, when Congress was in recess, I spent a day with Rangel in his district. His first stop that morning was the auditorium of Harlem Hospital, for the dedication of a new emergency facility, which was being named in memory of a local community activist, Marshall England. According to a bio prepared by the hospital under the title "A Saint for Our Times," England, who died in January, was a tireless organizer, and always carried with him several bags filled with petitions. For the ceremony, a ribbon made of kente cloth had been stretched from one side of the stage to the other.

When Rangel arrived at the auditorium, the program listed eight speakers before him; nevertheless, he was immediately ushered onto the stage. "I've ofttimes said that when Judgment Day comes for me, and St. Peter tries to give me a hard time, I'm going to tell him that all of my public life I've represented Harlem Hospital, and I'm entitled to a break," he told the crowd. Rangel spoke in praise of England as a man of "integrity," as someone who "never stopped caring for his community," and as "an irritant to those people who really just wanted to accept the status quo." At one point, he broadened his remarks so that England's struggles became a metaphor for the struggles of Harlem, saying, "We've had our fights with every mayor, and yet we never allowed anyone from outside of our community to come in and criticize our hospital."

In many ways, Rangel is an anomalous figure in Harlem, where protesters and grassroots organizers like England are more the mainstream. As Rangel's own remarks indicate, his community is extremely suspicious of established political power, and he, too, would probably have been suspect if he ever seemed to want to claim that his success validated the system, or even one man's hard work and determination. But Rangel's rise, at least by his own account, has been a result of very different qualities— shrewdness, opportunism, and luck. "After that bitter ambush that I got caught with in Korea, I have never, ever, ever had a bad day," he once told me. "I can't complain about the cold, because so many of my friends froze to death. I can't complain about hard times, because I came from absolutely nothing to become a member of the United States Congress. And sometimes, in teasing people who are bitching and complaining, I say I wish I could do that, but if I did I'd hear this booming voice saying, 'Rangel! Didn't you just thank Me this morning?'"

After Rangel spoke at Harlem Hospital, he went on to a street naming, at 143rd Street and Convent Avenue, where he once again praised the honoree as a man who had struggled on behalf of unpopular causes, and then to his district office, which is in the Adam Clayton Powell, Jr., State Office Building, on 125th Street. The waiting room of the office was filled with people who wanted help in fighting Con Edison or their landlords or, in many cases, the Immigration and Naturalization Service. Rangel had a meeting with one of his staff members about some projects in East Harlem, and made it clear that I was not invited to attend, so I went to sit in a conference room.

The room was lined with dozens of pictures of Rangel: with Nelson Rockefeller, with Tip O'Neill, with Walter Mondale, with Jimmy Carter, with Mario Cuomo, with Nelson Mandela, with Dr. Ruth. There were also several pictures of Rangel with J. Raymond Jones, who was the first black Democratic leader of Manhattan, and was known as the Harlem Fox. Rangel worked against Jones for a time, and then later with him. Jones died nearly a decade ago, at the age of ninety-one, and in one corner of the room I found a framed piece on him that had once run in the *News*. In it, Jones offered some advice to aspiring black politicians: "When they think you are going to hit them from the inside, you do it from the outside. Then when they think you are coming from the outside, you hit them from the inside."

Postscript: The Republicans narrowly retained control of the House in the November 2000 election and picked up seats in November 2002. As of this publication, Congressman Rangel remains the ranking member on the Ways and Means Committee.

In Charge

September 2001

S HORTLY BEFORE NINE o'clock on Tuesday morning last week, Mayor Rudolph Giuliani was on Fifth Avenue, at Fiftieth Street, on his way to City Hall, when he got word that a plane had crashed into the north tower of the World Trade Center. He sped downtown and got there in time to witness what he subsequently described as "the most horrific scene I've ever seen in my whole life." The Mayor spoke to some of the fire commanders at the scene, including the chief of the department, Peter Ganci, who was killed moments later. In a gruesome irony, the city's new emergency command center was situated directly inside the World Trade Center—not in one of the two towers that were hit but in a third building, which also lay in ruins by the end of the day. Since that location was obviously unsafe, Giuliani went to a suite of city offices a block away, at 75 Barclay Street, where he and his aides intended to set up an alternative command post. When the first World Trade Center tower collapsed, debris started to rain down from the ceiling of 75 Barclay, and they had to evacuate that building as well. They had just finished an impromptu news conference at Chambers Street and West Broadway, and had begun walking north, when the second tower collapsed. It was at that point that the Mayor of the city of New York, along with everybody else in lower Manhattan, found himself running for his life.

Mayors always rush to the scene of disasters; this is as much a part of the job as submitting budgets and making sure the garbage gets picked up on time. No mayor, however, has ever had to react to a disaster of the magnitude of last week's, and few could have done so with more forcefulness, or steadiness of purpose, than Giuliani. On the day of the attack, the Mayor spoke publicly at least half a dozen times, the last around midnight, and then he went back to the scene to speak to the rescue teams working through the night. Each time he spoke, he managed to convey at once grief and resolve, and his presence offered the kind of reassurance so disconcertingly absent in Washington, where the President was, for much of the day, missing.

"New York is still here," the Mayor said at one point. "We've undergone tremendous losses, and we're going to grieve for them horribly, but New York is going to be here tomorrow morning, and it's going to be here forever." He described speaking to Ganci, who had been a member of the Fire Department for thirty-three years, just before he died, and telling him, "God bless you." And he urged the people of the city to try to resume their normal lives without bitterness.

"Hatred, prejudice, and anger are what caused this terrible tragedy, and the people of the city of New York should act differently," he said. "We should act bravely. We should act in a tolerant way. We should go about our business, and we should show these people that they can't stop us." By all accounts, the command center the Mayor eventually did establish, at a location that reporters were asked not to divulge, functioned effectively. "It was magnificent, really," Representative Jerrold Nadler, a frequent critic of the Mayor, said after attending a meeting there.

Andrew Kirtzman, a political reporter for NY1, the city's cable news channel, was running alongside Giuliani on the morning of the tragedy. Kirtzman described the Mayor as entirely composed, even though, for nearly an hour, no one seemed to know where he should go. At one point, Kirtzman recalled, the Mayor bumped into a young black police officer: she said something to him, and, like a father, he touched her on the cheek. Eventually, he found a temporary office in a fire station, but since all the crews at the station had already left for the World Trade Center, someone had to jimmy the lock in order to let him in.

One of the mysteries of Giuliani's tenure has always been why, in moments of civic calm, he creates such havoc, and then, in genuine crises, behaves so calmly. This mystery will never entirely be solved; the attack occurred on the very day that the city's mayoral primary was to have taken place—it was postponed until September 25th—and there are now fewer than four months left in his term. But the role that the Mayor played last week was one that he, at least, had apparently foreseen for himself. Giuliani had pushed for the construction of the new emergency command center, widely derided at the time as his "bunker," and, even though he made a dreadful miscalculation in putting it inside the World Trade Center, his concerns about New York's vulnerability, and the need for sure leadership in case the worst occurred, were more than borne out. Too much of the past year had been given over to the Mayor's usual battles—with his estranged wife, with the city comptroller, with museums that he accused of offending decency. Now, in the context of last week's terrible events, something of Giuliani has been restored to him and, by extension, to the city.

The Chief

October 2001

T HE FIRST AND second alarms, which were transmitted together,
sounded at 8:47 A.M., the third at 8:50. At 8:55, a 10-60 went out,
signalling a major emergency, and four minutes later a fifth alarm sounded.
The New York City Fire Department has no formal designation for a blaze
that requires more than five alarms, but on September 11th there were five
for the north tower and another five for the south tower, and still the alarms
continued to ring, first in firehouses in Chelsea and Chinatown, and then in
Brooklyn Heights and Williamsburg, and then all across the city, so that in
less than thirty minutes more than a hundred companies had been called
out. Ladder 24 was called from midtown, and Engine 214 from Bedford-
Stuyvesant, and so was Squad 288 from Maspeth, Queens, and Ladder 105
from downtown Brooklyn. Even after the two towers collapsed and tens of
thousands of people came streaming out of lower Manhattan covered with
ash, the firemen kept coming.

That afternoon, Liz Feehan and her sister Tara waited for news together
at Tara's house, in Belle Harbor, Queens. Three of the men in their family
were firefighters, and all three were at the World Trade Center that day:
Liz and Tara's father, William, the department's first deputy commissioner; their younger brother John; and Tara's husband, Brian Davan.
When the phone rang, Tara picked it up and started yelling. Liz
immediately concluded that the call was about one of the two younger
men. Their father, the second-ranking official in the F.D.N.Y., was, she
assumed, too far up the hierarchy to die in the line of duty.

William Michael Feehan had joined the F.D.N.Y. in 1959, and during
the next forty-two years held every possible rank in a department that was

thick with them, from "proby" to lieutenant to battalion chief to commissioner—something only two or three other people have done in the department's history. Feehan helped fight some of the worst fires in New York, including the Brooklyn Navy Yard fire, in 1960, which killed fifty people, and the Madison Square blaze, in 1966, which killed twelve. For his long, distinguished career, he was venerated by his fellow-firefighters, and also sometimes teased by them. "Billy," his friends used to say, "when you joined the department what were they feeding the horses?" At the time of his death, Feehan was seventy-one years old, six years past the mandatory retirement age for firefighters in the city, and for nearly a decade he had held what is technically a civilian post. Still, he kept handy a helmet and a rubberized suit—known as "turnout gear"—and was fit, and willing, enough to help lay hose.

Before Feehan died, few outside the department or the insular world of city government had heard of him. He did not court publicity, and he rarely attended the functions that high-ranking city officials are invited to. (A favorite excuse of his was that he had tried to stop by but couldn't find a parking space.) As first deputy commissioner, Feehan served under three different commissioners and two different mayors, a tenure that testified at once to his ability and to his equanimity. "He would quietly suggest to you to do something differently, and you always knew that it was good advice, and you always took it," the current commissioner, Thomas Von Essen, told me. Even after Feehan became deputy commissioner, his men continued to address him as "Chief," a lower but, to them, more honorable title.

Feehan began his career with Ladder 3, on East Thirteenth Street in Greenwich Village. One week after the disaster, I went down to the firehouse, a squat brick building constructed under Mayor Jimmy Walker, in 1929. The men in the company refer to it as Ladder 3 Recon, for "reconnaissance," and they like to say that when rescue units get into trouble they call Ladder 3 Recon to get them out of it. The house sits next to a photo shop and across the street from a New York University dormitory. A construction-paper sign posted in one of the dorm's windows read "NYU ♥ FDNY." Normally, the men would have been upstairs, in the firehouse kitchen, cooking dinner and watching TV, but this night they were out on the street receiving condolences, as were firemen all over the city.

On September 11th, Ladder 3 was called on the third alarm. The day shift was just arriving, and the night shift going off duty, which meant that there were two full crews in the house. The company lost twelve men out of a total force of twenty-five. It is still not known where, or how, they died. Someone had pasted pictures of the missing on a piece of poster board, and around this poster, which was propped on an easel, the sidewalk had been transformed into a makeshift shrine. There were dozens of bouquets with notes pinned to them, and candles flickering in pools of wax, and silver balloons, clearly designed for less grave occasions, printed with the message "Thank you." It was six in the evening, the time when New Yorkers start to arrive home from work. People kept coming by to drop off doughnuts and cakes and homemade cookies. An elderly man brought over a plate of apples and honey, in honor of Rosh Hashanah; a woman with red and blue tinsel stars in her hair stopped in to offer the men Shiatsu massages. A woman in her forties brought a mixed bouquet. She seemed unwilling to just add it to the general pile, so she waited for one of the firemen to notice her, and handed it to him. "You guys are the best and the bravest," she said. Then she started to cry.

The attack on the World Trade Center left thousands of people mourning fathers and mothers, colleagues, close friends, and children. It left thousands of others, in the city and beyond, who hadn't lost anyone, searching for a focus for their grief. In this context, it was natural for people to gravitate to their local firehouses. One former Manhattanite I know drove in from Westchester to visit the firehouse in his old neighborhood. He had brought a check for the relief fund—the company had lost nine members—and when the fireman he gave it to thanked him he had to turn away, he told me, because he found himself weeping uncontrollably. Not a single firehouse in the city was untouched by the disaster. Among the three hundred and forty-three firefighters who are either dead or missing are members of at least sixty companies.

The only men left in Ladder 3 are those who were not on duty on the morning of the eleventh. I asked one of them, a lieutenant, whether he felt fortunate to have been off that day. He told me the opposite was true. "I wish it was me instead of them," he said, and he felt sure, he told me, that had the situation been reversed his colleagues—his "brothers"—would have felt the same way. "The camaraderie that you have with your brothers—you'd do anything for them," he said.

William Feehan was born in Queens on September 29, 1929, and grew up in Jackson Heights. His father was a firefighter with Engine 21, and one of his uncles was a priest. In the tradition of old Irish New York, these were the career choices presented to Feehan, and although his parents tried to steer him toward the church he eventually chose the F.D.N.Y. From an early age, Feehan loved fires—he used to run down to Northern Boulevard to watch the engines go by—and in 1956, after graduating from St. John's University and serving in Korea, he joined the New York Fire Patrol, a private force financed by the insurance industry, which is still in operation.

At about the same time, a new F.D.N.Y. commissioner, Edward Cavanagh, instituted a mandatory-retirement policy, and Feehan's father, who was sixty-seven, immediately became overage. In 1992, the year he became first deputy commissioner, Feehan spoke about his father's disappointment in an interview with his oldest son, William, Jr., a human-resources executive, and a friend of his, Harvey Wang, a photographer. "My father lived till he was in his early eighties, and to the day he died I think he felt that Edward Cavanagh passed that bill just to hurt him," Feehan recalled. "I don't think a day went by when he didn't have something unkind to say about Edward Cavanagh for cutting his career short, in the prime of his life, and he carried that bitterness to the grave with him."

From the beginning, Feehan's solidity impressed those he worked with. James Manahan, a firefighter who trained with him, told me, "Billy really made his own reputation. In firefighting, it's crucial how you're perceived by the people you're working with, because when you go above a fire you've got to have trust in the guy that's beneath you. No one would think twice about going above Billy."

In 1956, Feehan married Betty Keegan, whom he had met, also in the tradition of Irish New York, in the Rockaways. Over the next decade, the couple had four children. They moved to a single-family house in Flushing, and, because it wasn't easy to support the family on a fireman's salary, Feehan moonlighted—first as a substitute teacher and later as a security guard for the Helmsley hotels. (Whenever the kids made cracks about Leona or Harry, Feehan asked them if they wanted to take out another college loan.) He also studied hard for the department exams that determine promotions. In 1964, after just five years in the department, Feehan made lieutenant. In 1972, he became a captain, and in 1979 the chief of a battalion.

A week and a half after Feehan died, I went out to the house, on Twenty-eighth Avenue in Flushing. It is, by today's standards, modest, and following Betty's death, in 1996, Feehan continued to live there alone. The day I visited, Liz Feehan, a slim, lively woman who works as a court clerk in Manhattan, was at the house, and so were her brother John and his wife, Debbie, who is a nurse. We sat in the dining room, at a table covered with a lace cloth, surrounded by the bags of Mass cards that had been left at Feehan's wake.

According to his children, Feehan was a man of great faith, and also of great optimism. When they were young, everything they presented to him was "the most special—fill in the blank—in the world," and, when they got older, every house or apartment they moved into was a "gem" or a "home run." "He was your biggest fan," Liz said. "Nothing could not be overcome. He'd say, 'We'll move on and get through this.'"

John looks a lot like the photographs of his father—the same square face and wide-set eyes. He told me that his father hadn't pushed him to become a fireman but had been relieved when he did: "He didn't know what the hell I was going to do, so he was happy that I had a job." Everyone in the department knew him as "Feehan's kid," John said. "It sounds way too pretentious, and I don't mean to be, but it was kind of like I was a prince," he told me. Often, on Saturdays, the two men would have breakfast at the North Shore Diner, in Bayside, and "talk fire." On their days off, they also liked to "buff" fires together—watch their colleagues handle a blaze and later, like a pair of critics, review it.

All of Feehan's children had felt a certain trepidation about the upcoming mayoral election and the inevitable arrival of a new administration. Their father had told them that, no matter who became mayor, he didn't think it likely that he would be asked to stay on. Liz described how their mother, long before Feehan's retirement was even on the horizon, had worried about it: "She used to say, 'I hope your father goes in a fire.' We'd say, 'Speak for yourself.' But she meant that's how he would have wanted to go."

Feehan liked to tell stories. In the interview that he did with his son and Harvey Wang, he told one about how he almost didn't make it into the Fire Department, because of his bad eyesight, and another about the time he was a captain in Harlem and the commissioner, who had come for a visit, ended up posing for photographs with a bookie. He also spoke about Charlie, a fire buff who lived for a while at Ladder 6, in Chinatown, and, having been convinced by the men that Feehan's wife was Chinese, was always plying him with fortune cookies.

Feehan was a member of Ladder 6 when, in 1970, the company was called to a fire at One New York Plaza, a fifty-story office building at the corner of Water and Broad Streets. The blaze killed two people, and helped bring about the passage of Local Law 5, which requires that all high-rises have sprinkler systems and fire alarms on each floor.

"When we were dispatched to the fire," Feehan recalled, "we left the firehouse heading down East Broadway, and an air line broke. We came to a dead halt and the chauffeur"—the driver of the fire truck—"jumped out and said we were out of service. I was a fairly young lieutenant and this was going to be my first high-rise fire, and there was no way that I was going to miss this fire. There was a hardware store right on the corner, so I sent a guy in, and I said, 'Get some tape,' and we taped this thing up. They called us, and said, 'Ladder 6, what's your location?' We lied and said that we were three blocks from them.

"I remember the chief of the department then was John O'Hagan. I remember him telling us to go to the floor above the fire, and see whether or not there was an access from one floor to the next. We went up the stairway and the floor was just so hot that we couldn't crawl in. My chauffeur, who was very senior, and a very experienced guy, said, 'It's just too hot, we've got to get out of here.' We did, and we went back down and reported to Chief O'Hagan, and told him we couldn't get in on the floor, and he said, 'If you can't make it, you can't make it.' It was like a knife in your heart.

"A short time later, there was a report that there were some people on the upper floors, and we jumped up, because we were kind of depressed from not doing the other job. A guy from the building said, 'I have an elevator that will take you directly up to the top floor.' We went down to the lobby to get this elevator, and he said, 'I'm pretty sure this elevator—' We said, 'Hold it. Pretty sure is not good enough. If we're going to get on this elevator, we have to be sure it is not going to let us off on the fire floor.' Well, to make a long story short, he couldn't guarantee that. The only way to get there was to walk. We walked from the thirty-second floor to the roof and opened the roof, and of course the people reported being trapped weren't there, and now we had to get back down.

"I remember walking down. We had to stop on every floor, because we were totally exhausted. And I remember one of the senior guys—we were sweating profusely now, we were dirty and grimy, it must have been about eleven o'clock at night—and I remember him sitting on the stairs and looking over, and he said, 'You and your frickin' tape.'"

The F.D.N.Y. has its headquarters in a building in the Metrotech complex, in downtown Brooklyn, and the deputy commissioner's office is on the eighth floor, next door to the commissioner's. A week after the attack, a new first deputy, Mike Regan, was already in place, and when I went to visit I could see that someone had dropped off a half-inch-thick departmental memo entitled "Missing as of September 17, 2001, 1400 hours." Otherwise, things in the office appeared to be pretty much as Feehan had left them. Arranged on the desk were half a dozen pictures of his grandchildren and a stack of his business cards, which he kept in a holder shaped like a fire hydrant. A collection of toy fire engines was displayed on the windowsills, and on the walls were fire-prevention posters drawn by New York City schoolchildren. Feehan's red appointment book was still lying near the phone.

In every municipal department, the commissioners are political appointees, while the people who work for them are civil servants. This distinction is keenly felt, and nowhere more so than among the members of the F.D.N.Y. At the headquarters, I picked up a copy of *Fire Works*, the department's internal newsletter. The issue, which had been published in July, included a Q. & A. with the commissioner. In answer to a question about mandatory training days, Von Essen had written, "When you look up hypocrisy in the dictionary, it should have UFA/UFOA written next to it." The U.F.A. is the firemen's union; the U.F.O.A. is the officers' union.

Feehan's accomplishment, almost unheard of at the Fire Department, was to be equally popular with labor and management. "Very few people are loved by City Hall and the firefighters," Vincent Dunn, a retired F.D.N.Y. senior deputy chief, told me. "Bill Feehan was to the fire commissioner what Colin Powell and Dick Cheney are to the President. He always made the top command look stable." This was not, by all accounts, because Feehan had an accommodating nature; as one of his friends put it, "He was a tough fucking guy." Feehan didn't care for whiners, and he was especially hard on shirkers. In firefighting, it is usually left to the junior man to carry the extinguisher, or "can." One of Feehan's favorite expressions was "If you're the can man, be the can man," and it meant "Just do your job."

Once, Feehan was sitting in a restaurant when he overheard a firefighter at another table boasting that he was fit enough to return to work but planned to squeeze a few extra days out of his medical leave. The next day, the man found himself, with no explanation, assigned to a desk just outside the commissioner's office. Only after he had spent a few days wondering anxiously what had happened did Feehan call him into his office to, as another Fire Department official put it to me, "read him the riot act." More recently, Feehan was involved in a minor traffic accident while driving to the funeral of a firefighter in Staten Island. When he arrived at the office the next day, he saw his name on the list of people who were on medical leave. "More than one person got chewed out for that," John Feehan told me.

Feehan served briefly as the fire commissioner in the last days of David Dinkins's mayoralty. When Rudolph Giuliani was elected, he appointed Howard Safir to head the department, and asked Feehan to stay on as Safir's deputy. A few years later, Safir moved on to become the police commissioner. Feehan thought that he might be reappointed fire commissioner, and when Giuliani passed him over he confided his disappointment to Von Essen, the man who got the job. But, in keeping with his "be the can man" work ethic, Feehan put that disappointment aside and, Von Essen told me, "worked tirelessly to teach me and to mentor me."

During the more than four decades that Feehan served in the F.D.N.Y., the city's composition changed fundamentally, but the department's did not. The *Times* recently published two pages of pictures of the missing firefighters; there were barely a dozen African-American faces and not a single woman's. In the 1992 interview, Feehan acknowledged that critics were right to fault the department for its lack of diversity. "We have failed in that," he said. But he went on to say that he was pained by the way the critics had broadened their attack. "When they talk about a firehouse culture, they talk about it negatively, and this disturbs me, because there is maybe not a firehouse culture but a department culture," he said. "If you destroy the culture this department has, that tradition this department has, you destroy a very basic part of this department, and we just become another city agency. I don't think that when you have a department whose men and women are expected to be ready at any moment to put their life on the line to go to the aid of a stranger, I don't think you can pay people to do that job. There has to be something beyond money that makes them do that, and I think it's the culture of the department."

"High-rise firefighting is a whole art in itself," Feehan once said. "I spent very little time in a high-rise area, and there are chiefs who know more about high-rise firefighting than I'll ever know. When you have your first high-rise fire, the thing that strikes you most is just how long it takes you to get the thing done. It is twenty or twenty-five minutes after you arrive at the scene before you are getting water out of the nozzle on the fire floor."

On the morning of September 11th, Feehan was in his office, where he typically arrived by seven-fifteen. He was at his desk when his son John called with a question about the bibliography for the upcoming lieutenant's exam. Feehan told him that it would be available soon—it was just awaiting the commissioner's approval. A few minutes later, the first plane struck.

There was no precedent for the World Trade Center fire, and no way to fight it except as if there were. Feehan rushed from his office directly to the fire's command post, which, following standard protocol for a high-rise fire, had been set up in the lobby of the burning north tower. Every fire of any significance has such a post, which is basically nothing more than a metal folding table and a set of magnetic tabs labelled with the numbers of the F.D.N.Y. companies. Whoever is in command draws a rough sketch of the site directly onto the table with a felt-tip pen and then uses the magnetic markers to keep track of where the companies have been assigned. Also following standard protocol, the first companies to arrive at the World Trade Center were ordered to get hoses up to the blaze and to try to keep the stairwells open.

When a plane hit the south tower, the command post moved to West Street. Feehan's executive officer, Henry McDonald, was at home monitoring radio traffic. "The last thing I heard over the radio was that they were moving the post 'by orders of Chief Feehan,' " he told me.

Partly shielded by the north tower, the command post on West Street survived the collapse of the south tower, at 9:59 A.M., at which point Feehan and the chief of the department, Peter Ganci, decided to move the post farther north. But before they could do so, the north tower fell. (Von Essen had been called away to brief Mayor Giuliani, and this is why he survived.) Liz Feehan told me she was sure that her father would not have regarded his death as heroic. "We don't know exactly what happened to Dad," she said. "But he would have said, 'I'm not a hero—a wall fell on me. How does that make me a hero?' That's exactly what he would have said."

Feehan's body was one of the first to be pulled from the ruins; it was found that afternoon, while his son John and his son-in-law Brian Davan were nearby, assisting with the rescue operations. The funeral was held the following Saturday at St. Mel's, in Flushing. Among the mourners were Mayor Giuliani, Commissioner Von Essen, and the Speaker of the City Council, Peter Vallone. Ganci was buried on the same day, as was the Fire Department's chaplain, Mychal Judge.

William, Jr., delivered his father's eulogy. He spoke of Feehan's love for his family, his sense of humor, his profound optimism, and, above all, his pride in his work. He told about how, on the night after the attack, he had gone down to the site of the fire to see where his father had died and had found a certain comfort there—a comfort perhaps incomprehensible to someone who is not part of a fire family. Standing amid the wreckage, which at that point was still smoldering, he realized, he said, that "there was no place on earth my father enjoyed more than a fire scene."

The Long Campaign

October 2001

A FEW MINUTES before Mark Green came down to address the crowd in the Imperial Ballroom of the Sheraton New York hotel last Thursday, campaign workers began handing out placards with the slogan "Unite to Rebuild." The slogan referred, of course, to the events of September 11th, but Green, the city's public advocate, took it up in another, more immediately relevant sense. "Freddy Ferrer called me an hour ago to congratulate me and concede," he said. "I told him no—I wanted to first say to him congratulations because of his extraordinarily passionate and skillful and effective campaign. He turned out to be an extraordinary leader of idealism, and vision, and eloquence." Then, as if addressing Fernando Ferrer, the Bronx borough president, directly, Green continued, "Your contributions to the city have only just begun. We need you, we need your ideas, and I can't wait till you and your supporters unite with us to win in November.

"I stand before you, awed, honored, and humble, to be the Democratic nominee for mayor," Green went on, turning his attention back to the crowd. He thanked his supporters, took some shots at his Republican opponent, the billionaire Michael Bloomberg—"Now more than ever, New York needs the experience that money can't buy"—and, finally, returned to the theme of unity. "If you want a united New York, which will focus on our common ground and our shared dreams, where everyone has a voice and a seat at City Hall, join our campaign."

Between the fawning and the gloating, the self-promotion and the perfunctory humility, victory celebrations are rarely tasteful affairs. Even so, Green's party last Thursday posed an unusual challenge. The runoff between Green and Ferrer had fallen on the one-month anniversary of the World Trade Center attack and also on the same day that the F.B.I. issued a new terrorism alert. On top of all that, the celebration was only in the narrowest technical sense really about a victory.

Green had entered the runoff with nearly every possible advantage over Ferrer. He had all along been the favorite in the race, and, when the World Trade Center was destroyed, it was assumed, at least by members of the city's white political establishment, that the disaster would trump all other concerns. Green, accordingly, reoriented his entire appeal, adopting the "Unite to Rebuild" slogan and issuing paper after paper on what the city would need to do to recover. Ferrer hardly reacted, and, when he did, what he said often seemed beside the point. He refused to renounce, or even really modify, any of the promises he had made earlier in the campaign, when, seeking to become the city's first Latino mayor, he had run on an appeal to "the other New York." And yet it was the tragedy or, to be more exact, the bathos that followed it that almost cost Green the election. At the party, Green's supporters were swapping stories about how badly he had fared in different office pools, while his own aides joked openly about all the free time they had expected to have after the election. Elizabeth Holtzman, the former city comptroller, addressed the issue perhaps a little too directly when she told the crowd in the ballroom, "It wasn't very long ago that people were writing off Mark Green."

New York's mayoral primary was supposed to have taken place on the very day of the attack, and was cancelled at 10:40 A.M., eleven minutes after the second tower collapsed. By that point, the polls had been open for nearly five hours, enough time for one "wave" of exit polls. The results of that wave, which were never officially released, showed Green comfortably ahead, leading the four-man Democratic field and just two points shy of the forty per cent that he would need to avoid a runoff. By the time the primary, rescheduled for September 25th, had been completed, it was Ferrer who came in first, with thirty-six per cent of the vote, and Green's troubles were just beginning.

The next day, a few hours before the beginning of Yom Kippur, Mayor Rudolph Giuliani summoned all the mayoral candidates to his command

post on the West Side, to issue his so-called "ultimatum." The choice that
the Mayor offered the candidates—either they let him stay on for an extra
three months or he would run for a third term—was empty of real
significance. The candidates had no power to grant his wish, and he had no
power to make good on the threat. But this only heightened the purity of
the symbolism. Bloomberg, who had just won the Republican nomination,
had, all along, been trying to link himself to the Mayor. He leaped at the
offer; Giuliani's idea was such a good one, he declared, that the inaugura-
tion should be pushed back permanently, from January to April.

Green, too, immediately acquiesced to an extension, ostensibly in the
interest of a smooth transition, but clearly also out of fear. Just a day earlier,
someone on the Mayor's staff had—ominously—told the *Times* that the
public advocate "had not attended enough planning meetings" since the
World Trade Center attack, and that he had "fiddled with his Palm Pilot"
during one of them. ("Mark doesn't even have a Palm Pilot," one of his
aides complained to me. "He has a BlackBerry.") The Mayor himself,
meanwhile, when he was asked if the candidates had been "helpful" in the
crisis, said darkly, "Some have and some have not."

Ferrer took a day to respond to the Mayor's proposal. Then he rejected it,
equating Giuliani's actions with extortion, or—more provocatively—
terrorism. "There are pressures that come on you as a candidate, as a public
official, or as mayor," he said. "Someone might hold a figurative gun to
your head. But, if you can't deal with the pressure at any moment in time,
how do you persuade people that you are ready, and that you are up for the
challenges of being mayor of the toughest city in America?" After a while,
Giuliani publicly dropped the idea of running for a third term, but Ferrer
didn't. He kept returning to the theme of courage under fire, at one point,
nearly a week after the ultimatum, delivering an entire speech on what it
felt like to be tested and found worthy. "None of us knows how we will
react under pressure until our moment arrives at its chosen time," Ferrer
told his audience—mostly reporters—at the City University Graduate
Center. "My time came last Wednesday, in a room with Mayor Giuliani."

Over the years, Green has been accused of many things—stubbornness,
arrogance, self-absorption, and runaway liberalism—but shrinking from a
fight was not one of them. During his tenure as public advocate, Green

spent so much time wrangling with Giuliani that there were many who wondered if he had the time—or the inclination—to do anything else. Ferrer, for his part, enjoyed just the opposite reputation. A product of the Bronx Democratic machine, he belonged, by training and also, apparently, by temperament, to a group given more to dealmaking than to idealism. Just four years ago, when he thought his chances for winning the Democratic mayoral nomination lay in running to the right, Ferrer switched his position on the death penalty and also grumbled about abortion. "Every time a mother hiccups, that's no reason to abort a child," he said.

All this history, however, was immediately forgotten. Green had chosen, for once, not to fight with the Mayor, and this turned out to be the one fight that anyone cared about. Taunted by Ferrer—and watching his African-American support slip away—Green lost heart. (He later told me that the reaction to his decision had broken down almost entirely along racial lines.) He cycled through one self-defeating rationalization after another, until he finally hit bottom. In an interview on WLIB-AM, Green announced, "I actually believe that if, God forbid, I had been mayor during such a calamity, I would have been as able or better than Mayor Giuliani." The line alienated just about everyone, especially those who had sympathized with his original decision.

Junior's, on Flatbush Avenue in downtown Brooklyn, is an anachronism, a Jewish deli that continues to thrive in a neighborhood that is now almost entirely black. On the Saturday before the October 11th runoff, former Mayor Ed Koch was scheduled to attend a campaign event at the restaurant, and when I got there I found him sitting on a banquette, facing a group of reporters over a table set with bowls of pickles and beets and coleslaw. He was wearing a green windbreaker, a green shirt, and a pair of rumpled chinos.

In the primary, Koch had backed the City Council speaker, Peter Vallone, the most conservative of the four Democratic candidates, whose election effort was based on an unapologetic appeal to white voters in the outer boroughs. Before the primary, Vallone had accused Ferrer of conducting a racially divisive campaign, but the day after it, in one of those moves that make sense only if you give up the notion that they're supposed to, he endorsed him. (Vallone, it was rumored, had been irritated by a call from Green on primary night pressing him, a little too early, to concede.) A few days later, Koch, too, switched over to Ferrer. When I sat down at the table, the former mayor was explaining that he had done this "because Freddy stood up to Giuliani when Mark caved." I asked him whether, beyond that one issue, he agreed with Ferrer's positions. He replied that, in fact, he and Ferrer shared the same political philosophy. "Freddy is a guy who has middle-class values," he said. I tried to pursue this point, noting that Ferrer's campaign was ostensibly based on a different premise entirely.

"But he *is* middle class," Koch replied. "Freddy lives in Riverdale. He has a wonderful view of the Hudson River from his apartment." Finally, somebody asked Koch whether he could point to a fundamental difference between Green and Ferrer. "Mark Green is obnoxious, and Freddy is not," he said cheerfully. "That's a fundamental difference."

After about a quarter of an hour, Koch was joined by his old nemesis the Reverend Al Sharpton. Sharpton, who entered the restaurant talking intently into his cell phone, had on a three-piece suit, black with electric-blue pinstripes. The outfit showed off his new, prison-trimmed physique—he had recently served ninety days for trespassing on United States military property while protesting bombing exercises in Vieques— and Koch greeted him by asking how he was managing to keep off the pounds. "One meal a day and no fried food," Sharpton responded. "I don't want to have to go back to jail to lose it again."

Sharpton had also waited until late in the campaign to endorse Ferrer. It is theoretically possible that the delay reflected real indecision, but just barely. Everyone, including Bloomberg, courted Sharpton while he carried out his deliberations; Green even took the Reverend and his wife to see "Judgment at Nuremberg," which was playing on Broadway last spring. Sharpton's endorsement, at the end of August, was crucial to Ferrer, it finally elevated him to what he had claimed to be all along—the leader of a black-Latino coalition. At the same time, the endorsement represented an obvious opportunity for Green. In the days leading up to the runoff, reporters practically begged him to denounce the Reverend, but Green didn't quite have the will—or the nerve—to do so. The furthest he would go was to insist that he had never sought Sharpton's support, a claim that hardly seemed strong enough to satisfy Sharpton-haters, and that only invited mockery. "I learned one thing from Mark," Sharpton said at Junior's. "From now on, when someone wants my support I'm going to tell him to write it, notarize it, and send it to my lawyer, because I misunderstood. Maybe I had the wrong impression. Maybe I was gullible. But I thought that when he was explaining to me what he would do for the city it was because he wanted my support."

Finally, Ferrer arrived. The group moved out onto the sidewalk in front of the restaurant, Ferrer not quite leading the way. A reporter asked the borough president about his shifting stand on the death penalty, an issue that had been raised by Green that morning. Ferrer's expression grew sorrowful. "Well, you know, I'm sort of troubled by a long memory," he said with a sigh. "Primary night, Mark Green said, 'We're not going to engage in negative campaigning, we will be talking about the future of this city.' And every day he has launched yet another barrage of negative attacks. Now, I thought he was a man of principle. Apparently, he is uncomfortable with the decision he made accepting the Mayor's deal for ninety days and he feels he has to launch these attacks. I think that's sad." Ferrer answered most of the other questions posed to him in a similarly aggrieved tone. "I know that Mark has been, since the election, since he saw that I was ahead of him by about five points in the first round of the primary, concerned about that," he said in response to a question about "the other New York." "He has to launch these negative attacks. I think it's absolutely wrong. I was hoping Mark wouldn't do this."

When the press conference was over, Ferrer and Koch and Sharpton headed down Fulton Street, side by side. The street was crowded with weekend shoppers, and people began to trail after the trio, mostly, it seemed, in order to meet Sharpton. Someone began to chant, "Freddy is ready," and the crowd took up the call. I happened to be standing next to Ferrer at that moment. He turned to me with a faint smile and shrugged. "Who would have thunk it?" he said.

On Columbus Day, with only two days to go before the runoff, and polls showing the race in a dead heat, Green aired what was labelled, accurately,

the first negative ad of the mayoral campaign. Aimed at middle-class—
mostly white—voters, it questioned Ferrer's competence to run the city in
the aftermath of September 11th. The ad lifted, not entirely in context, a
phrase from a *Times* editorial, calling Ferrer "borderline irresponsible." Its
tag line was "Can we afford to take a chance?"

It is impossible, at this point, to know what the full cost of the World
Trade Center attack will be. Recently, the city's comptroller, Alan Hevesi,
who himself ran for the Democratic nomination and came in last, issued a
report estimating that the total—including everything from the loss of
lives, or "human capital," to the bill for Police and Fire Department
overtime—would run between ninety billion and a hundred and five
billion dollars. Felix Rohatyn, the investment banker who helped save
New York from bankruptcy twenty-five years ago, declared last Tuesday
that "the city is in greater economic jeopardy today than it was in the fiscal
crisis of 1975." That same day, Mayor Giuliani signed an executive order
freezing a billion dollars in city spending.

Either Ferrer genuinely didn't appreciate the gravity of the situation—
or he simply didn't want to deal with it. His first response was to compare
the destruction downtown with the general urban decay he had confronted
as borough president; later, he likened the disaster to a long list of others,
including the draft riots of 1863, the Triangle Shirtwaist Factory fire, in
1911, and the Happy Land Social Club blaze, in 1990. Not until a week
after the primary did he address, in any concrete way, the problem of
rebuilding, and when he did so there was little more to his plan than a
proposal to appoint a "blue-ribbon panel" to consider the matter. And, in
spite of the enormous new costs imposed by the attack, Ferrer insisted that
he would not back away from commitments he had made earlier in the
campaign to spend more on, among other things, teachers' salaries, after-
school programs, affordable housing, and parks. Partly as a result of this, he
won the endorsement of the city's largest municipal unions, District
Council 37, which had previously backed Vallone, and the teacher's
union, which had backed Hevesi.

"While it's critical to rebuild our financial center, it's equally critical to
rebuild our schools," Ferrer declared. "While it's essential to house the
businesses and residents displaced by the events of the past few weeks, it's

equally important to house the working families of New York struggling to find an adequate and affordable place to live. The towers of the World Trade Center have crumbled, but our priorities have not." Whenever Green tried to press him on his response to the crisis—or lack thereof— Ferrer fell back on his more-in-sorrow routine. During the second debate of the runoff, the two engaged in an exemplary exchange.

"Well, you know, I'm disappointed," Ferrer said. "I had hoped this would be a different kind of campaign, where we'd discuss ideas, and, as Mark put it, be relentlessly focussed on the future of this city. Let's do it in that way. Now, to compare our ideas is fine. To denigrate ideas and say, 'Mine's a big idea' and 'Yours is a little idea,' is not only beside the point, it's frankly apart from what there should be in this debate, Mark."

"It's not beside the point," an obviously frustrated Green shot back. "It *is* the point!"

Last Tuesday, I met up with Green at the entrance to the Utica Avenue subway station, in Crown Heights. It was six o'clock in the evening, and every few minutes a new crowd surged up the stairs. Just about everyone on the street was African-American, except for an occasional band of young Orthodox Jews, on their way to synagogue to celebrate Simchas Torah. Green was, for all his missteps and misfortunes, upbeat. He told me he was convinced that "the tide had turned," and that voters were, finally, attending to the "closing issue," by which he clearly meant the challenges ahead. I asked him why this had taken so long, and he blamed Giuliani.

"After the primary, people were still extremely distracted because of the catastrophe and because of Mayor Giuliani's—um—efforts to either overturn term limits or stay on ninety days longer," he said. "It was only when his efforts stopped, and the public started focussing on which of two Democrats would be the mayor for four or eight years, that the final questions started being asked."

Green stood at the subway station for about forty-five minutes, and during that time he must have greeted four or five hundred people. He had taken off his jacket, and although he described himself as "bone tired," he appeared to have tapped into some reservoir of giddy energy. A middle-aged woman told Green, who is Jewish, that Jesus loved him, and that He was coming soon. A few minutes later, a young man walked by shouting, "Fuck the Jews, fuck the Jews." Neither Green nor anyone else responded. "I need your help on Thursday," Green kept saying as he stuck out his hand. "I need your help on Thursday." One woman asked him about housing, another about education, and a third about whether he could prevent her sons from being deported, but apart from that the only questions people put to him had to do with his response to the Mayor. "I got to tell you something, I was really disappointed that you actually agreed to extend Giuliani's term for ninety days," a man in a business suit told him. I asked Green whether, if he had it to do over again, he would make the same decision. He said yes, but I wasn't sure I believed him.

Strictly speaking, there is probably no way that the election could have lived up to the events of September 11th. The problem was too big, and not just for this set of candidates. As has often been observed, the very circumstances that made the race so important—it may well turn out to be one of the most consequential in the city's history—also tended, inevitably, to obscure it. The final debate of the runoff was held less than an hour before the United States began bombing Afghanistan. And, on the evening of the contest, televisions all over the city were tuned to the President's prime-time news conference.

Still, it would be wrong to say that the campaign settled nothing, or even, as Green put it, that it got sidetracked. For all its speciousness, triviality, and embarrassing antics—at one point, the Green campaign actually hired an acrobat to do flips as a metaphor for Ferrer's ideological inconstancy—this race turned on the same questions that New York City elections almost always do. The campaign's theatrics came just close enough to the real issues to be accepted as proxies for them; ultimately, it was a contest about race, about how to divvy up limited public resources, and about attitudes toward authority. In the end, Green beat Ferrer fifty-two per cent to forty-eight; he won only because whites are still the largest group in the city electorate and they supported him by a margin of five to one. As the talk about rebuilding gives way to the costly business of doing so, the divisions that have—once again—been exposed seem likely only to widen.

The Mogul Mayor

April 2002

MICHAEL BLOOMBERG IS impatient with words but likes numbers. His public appearances, while notable for their brevity, nearly always feature some figure or factlet that he finds salient—the size of the city's police force, say (forty thousand officers), or the year the World Trade Center was conceived (1960), or the proportion of New Yorkers who are African-American (one in four). Among the first pledges that he made upon taking office was that every month he would post on the Internet an exact head count of his staff. Current total: four hundred and ninety-seven.

Bloomberg himself is New York's hundred-and-eighth mayor, a job he acquired by spending more money on his campaign than anyone in the history of the country (seventy-four million dollars). He recently turned sixty, and, based on his stake in Bloomberg L.P., the privately held financial-data empire that he founded, he is, according to *Forbes*, the seventy-second-richest person in the world, up ten places from last year. Bloomberg's driver's license puts his height at five feet ten, which means that he is either taller than he looks or shorter than he says. His girlfriend, Diana Taylor, is five feet nine and a half, and when they stand next to each other, as the *News* recently pointed out, she towers over him.

Every new mayor recasts the job in his own image; Bloomberg, perhaps not surprisingly, has already pushed this further than most. He has, for example, declined to move into Gracie Mansion. (The city-owned residence, completed in 1804, has not, Bloomberg explained, "had a face-lift for some time.") Instead, he has opted to remain in his five-story town house, on East Seventy-ninth Street, which features a foyer done in Egyptian porphyry, French Empire sideboards, and a library whose hue

Bloomberg's decorator once compared to "a bottle of cognac held up to the light, all glowing cognac colors." Shortly after his victory in November, Bloomberg held an intimate get-acquainted dinner for the five borough presidents at his town house. He served Château Haut-Brion, which retails for at least a hundred and fifty dollars a bottle, and sent each guest home with a giant cookie decorated in icing with the seal of his or her borough. The fifty-one members of the City Council he invited over for cocktails. Afterward, some of them wondered about their host's decision to serve caviar at a time when the city seems headed toward the worst fiscal crisis since perhaps the Depression, but in the end the consensus was that it had been the right thing to do. The Mayor has four other homes, in Westchester, Vail, London, and Bermuda. When he takes the weekend off, he refuses, on principle, to say where he's headed.

Bloomberg is the first to point out that, according to the numbers, New York is in deep trouble. In February, when he presented the outline of his spending plan, he dispensed with the usual preliminaries and instead of lowballing the problem, as is City Hall custom, forecast a budget gap bigger than anyone had predicted. Bloomberg put the size of the gap at $4.8 billion, which is, by coincidence, roughly the size of his own personal fortune. To meet a shortfall of this magnitude, he pointed out, sacrifice would be required from everyone. "The two hundred and fifty thousand people who work for New York City do a pretty good job," he said. "So you can't just rush in and say, 'Let's just do things better.'" (Later, the Mayor qualified this, saying that a more accurate number to use for the city workforce might be three hundred and six thousand or, alternatively, three hundred and sixty-three thousand.)

Depending once again on how you count, the mayoralty is either Bloomberg's third or fourth career. In the previous ones, he was so enormously successful that he was often asked to share his secret for getting ahead. Bloomberg is fond of aphorisms, and the advice he used to dispense consisted of lines like "Always be building," "Do what you love," and "Bring a gun to a knife fight." Just by virtue of winning the election, he has already exceeded what was expected of him politically, and his first hundred days in office have mostly gone smoothly. As mayor, he has made strong appointments, reorganized City Hall, calmed the bond-rating agencies, and reached out to many groups in New York that are not normally considered the constituencies of a Republican billionaire. How he will manage the graver challenges that lie ahead is obviously the central question of the next four years, but it is not one that Bloomberg himself seems in any way troubled by. "He doesn't have self-doubts," Morris Offit, who runs a capital-management firm and is an old friend of the Mayor's, told me. "There's no hand-wringing. It goes back to the trader's mentality: you take a shot, and if you're wrong you go on to the next one."

On an average day, Bloomberg appears at three or four events around the city. One morning not long ago, his first stop was a topping-out ceremony for the huge new AOL Time Warner headquarters, which is rising above Columbus Circle. The project, conceived in a happier, more expansive moment for New York, is also to include condominiums, a Mandarin Oriental hotel, and a new home for Jazz at Lincoln Center. Hundreds of people were milling around the sixth floor of the unfinished building, which, lacking walls, provided a spectacular view of Central Park.

As soon as the Mayor arrived, wearing a gray suit and tasselled loafers, he was ushered to a makeshift stage. He offered his factlet, declaring, not altogether accurately, "Seventy-five years ago next month, there was an American flag raised as part of the topping-out ceremony on the Empire State Building," and added a few upbeat words of praise: "We've really got a wonderful thing for our children, and thank you." Eventually, an American flag went up over the building, while Wynton Marsalis played "Buddy Bolden's Blues," but by that point Bloomberg was already long gone.

His next stop was a news conference at One Liberty Plaza, a block north of the World Trade Center site, to announce construction of a temporary pedestrain bridge over West Street. Since September 11th, large sections of lower Manhattan have been effectively isolated, first by the wreckage and now by the cleanup effort. Governor George Pataki was also at the news conference, and so was the State Assembly speaker, Sheldon Silver, whose district happens to include the Trade Center site. While the other two men tried to grapple, not altogether successfully, with the gravity of the occasion, Bloomberg was evidently bored. He rocked back and forth on his heels, and twice had to stifle a yawn. Bloomberg spoke after Pataki, who is six feet five, and when he got to the lectern the microphone was pointing at the middle of his forehead. "Well, I see that this podium was set for the governor's height," he observed dryly.

The day's third event was a celebration of Chinese New Year, out at the public library in Flushing, Queens. Thanks to his policy of not using his police siren, Bloomberg arrived at the library a full hour late, but he received a standing ovation nevertheless. He was introduced by the local city councilman, John Liu, who greeted the crowd in Chinese. Bloomberg began by reading aloud from a proclamation that he had issued on the occasion of the lunar new year, but then broke away.

"Let me just digress for a second and point out to you that in New York City roughly eleven per cent of the population is of Asian extraction," he said. "And John Liu is the first Asian-American to be elected either at a state or a city level." Finally, Bloomberg joked, as he often does, about his own ethnic background. "Happy New Year," he said. "I would love to tell you in Chinese, but John stole my thunder and my accent's not as good. If you want me to do it in Yiddish, I could probably do better."

Bloomberg campaigned for mayor as Rudy Giuliani's successor—one of his slogans was "New York's Next Step"—and in the last days of the campaign he poured millions of dollars into airing and re-airing a sixty-second ad in which Giuliani all but anointed him. When you're actually following Bloomberg around, however, it's hard to see much connection between the two men. Giuliani loved the theatre of the mayoralty—the rushing to emergencies, the issuing of edicts, the public wrangling and denunciations. Just about any event he appeared at he dominated, partly by virtue of his rhetorical skills but mostly as a result of his monumental certainty in his own moral rectitude.

Bloomberg, by contrast, is the kind of guy who once opened a business meeting with a joke about a nurse who liked to masturbate her patients. Another time, at a sales conference, he is alleged to have announced, "I would like nothing more in life than to have Sharon Stone sit on my face." As mayor, he has forgone this approach, but still he resists all forms of pomp, or Giulianiesque sententiousness. Even as he is speaking, the implicit message seems to be that the real work of his mayoralty is taking place somewhere else. Bloomberg is casual to the point of offhandedness—often he is referred to as Mayor Mike, or simply Mike—and he seems altogether uninterested in the dramatic possibilities of office. Not long ago, I heard him address a group of New York City police officers at a charity dinner. "You do something that the rest of us don't have to do," he told them. "And there's no easy way to say thank you other than 'thank you.'"

Bloomberg's last appearance of the day was back in Manhattan, at the Plaza Hotel, at an awards dinner sponsored by the Jewish Community Relations Council of New York. He arrived at the hotel at around eight-fifteen and was up onstage by eight-twenty-five. The award for community service was going to one of his deputy mayors, Dennis Walcott. "Just as I think the best is yet to come for New York City, I think we're going to get the best out of Dennis in the future," the Mayor said. He congratulated Walcott, and then departed. When the dinner's m.c., Neil Cavuto, of Fox News, got back to the podium, he made a show of searching for Bloomberg in the crowd.

"Did the Mayor leave already?" he asked. "I guess he's on the way to Bermuda."

Bloomberg was born in 1942 on, as he likes to point out, Valentine's Day. Growing up in Medford, Massachusetts, a mostly blue-collar suburb of Boston, he appears to have enjoyed an all-American childhood, as inflected by a kosher home. Bloomberg's father, William, was an accountant for a dairy, and his mother, Charlotte, was a housewife. (Charlotte, who is ninety-three, still lives in the house that the family bought in 1946.) While preparing for his bar mitzvah at the local Conservative synagogue, Bloomberg sold Christmas wreaths door to door to finance summers at Boy Scout camp. The Medford High School yearbook records that in 1960 he was president of the Slide Rule Club. He was also active in the debating society, and was described by classmates as "argumentative."

In college, at Johns Hopkins, Bloomberg majored in engineering. He got mainly C's, and was popular. He became one of the first Jewish members of Phi Kappa Psi and, later, president of the university's interfraternity council. Despite his grades, he managed to get into Harvard Business School, where again he failed to make much impact academically.

He graduated in the spring of 1966 with no particular plans, expecting, he has said, to get drafted. If the war in Vietnam, or the civil-rights movement, or the Kennedy assassinations, or any of the other extraordinary events of the decade moved Bloomberg in any way, he has never let on. When the draft board classified him 1-Y—he has flat feet—he took a job at Salomon Brothers. It was there that he seems to have discovered himself.

In those days, Salomon was a second- or even third-class firm, not in financial terms but in social ones. It was a trading house, known primarily for its bond business, while the more genteel firms, like Morgan Stanley, were investment-banking houses. (One of Salomon's unofficial mottoes was "Dress British, think Yiddish.") Risk-taking of all sorts was celebrated, and so were most forms of aggression—screaming, cursing, bullying, backstabbing. To succeed on Salomon's trading floor, one of the managing partners once declared, a person had to come to work each morning "ready to bite the ass off a bear."

Everyone at Salomon worked hard, and Bloomberg worked hard to outdo everyone else. His first assignment was in "the cage," an un-air-conditioned bank vault where he stood around in his underwear, counting out stock and bond certificates by hand; his next was filing in the Purchase and Sales Department. He used to get to the office earlier than anyone except the head of the firm, Billy Salomon, and stay later than anyone except Salomon's heir apparent, John Gutfreund. When Gutfreund got into a cab to go home, he would often give Bloomberg a lift.

Bloomberg eventually worked his way onto the equities desk, where he called himself a trader, though really he was a salesman. He specialized in block trades, buying tens or even hundreds of thousands of shares from one institutional client and then turning around and selling them to another. "We could sell anything to anybody," he observes in his 1997 autobiography, "Bloomberg by Bloomberg," referring to himself and the head of Salomon's block-trading operation, Jay Perry. "We just did what all great salespeople do: We presented everything we had, and then highlighted whatever facts enabled customers to convince themselves they were getting a good deal. 'It has a strong specialist behind it,' I'd tell one buyer who might not have the slightest idea why the specialist mattered. . . . 'The chart pattern looks like a breakout,' Perry would declare for those who believed 'The trend's my friend.'" Block trading was at the time a relatively new—and lucrative—enterprise, and Bloomberg loved everything about it: the newness, the riskiness, the money. "I was the fair-haired boy, the block-trading superstar," he writes. "I was the pet of its two top executives. I greeted all important visiting customers, got interviewed by every newspaper that mattered, and had a great social life playing the role of Wall Street power broker to the hilt. More than a 'legend in my own mind.'"

Not everyone at the firm was quite as impressed with Bloomberg as he was. When Bloomberg rose to partner, in 1972, at the age of thirty, he became the third-ranking man on the equities desk, working under Perry and another legendarily smart—and also legendarily difficult—senior partner, Richard Rosenthal. For several years, the three men engaged in a round-robin power struggle—in one particularly raw moment, Perry dumped the contents of Bloomberg's desk onto the floor while he was off attending a breakfast meeting—until finally, in 1979, Bloomberg lost out. He was forced off the equities desk and given the job of running the firm's information systems. Wall Street was at that point in the very earliest stages of computerization—traders were still working out bond yields on oversized desk-top calculators—and the move was recognized by everyone at the firm as a demotion. "It's the kind of job where, when you hear someone getting it, you're not going to be surprised if two days later they leave," Richard Grand-Jean, a Bloomberg admirer and former colleague, told me. For whatever reason, Bloomberg stayed on. Two years later, he was fired.

Bloomberg has always attributed his dismissal to his candor: he used to declare openly, he says, that he could run the "goddam company" better than Gutfreund. Others explain it in more prosaic terms: Salomon was in the process of merging with Phibro, a publicly traded commodities company, and Bloomberg, as the head of information systems, was not producing any revenue. (When I asked Gutfreund for his version of events, he refused to comment; a few years ago, he told the Boston *Globe* that he did "not intend to engage in fine-tuning the myth of Michael Bloomberg.") Bloomberg claims to have been mostly concerned about how his then wife, Sue Brown, would react to his change in status—the couple, who have two grown daughters, divorced in 1993—and so he paid a visit to a furrier: "A sable jacket seemed to say, 'No sweat. We can still eat. We're still players.'" His next move was to found his own firm.

Bloomberg L.P. has its headquarters in a black glass box of a building on Park Avenue at Fifty-ninth Street. On the ground floor, facing out onto the sidewalk, sixteen screens show fluctuating stock and commodity prices, bond yields, and exchange rates. Inside the lobby, there are six more screens showing much the same information. Upstairs, every receptionist stands behind her own screen, and in every direction there are more screens, big ones and little ones, displaying all Bloomberg, all the time. Even in the ladies' room, there are screens set into the mirrors above the sinks.

Not long ago, I went to the headquarters to get a demonstration of the firm's proprietary data system from a salesman named Ken Napolitano. On my way to meet him, I passed hundreds of cubicles with two and sometimes four computer screens; a food court loaded with fresh fruit and candy; and a zipper display running an announcement in red lights: "Amy Johnston sells four more terminals at American Express to their Equity Research Department." (The Bloomberg system used to be available only over a dedicated terminal; today, it is offered through subscribers' P.C.s.) Napolitano led me into a small conference room that had a large projection screen on one wall and, on the table, a keyboard. Much like a pianist practicing scales, he began with a demonstration of some of the system's basic functions. He looked up some bond prices and, for the fun of it, pulled up some historical data. On January 4, 1955, I learned, the Dow Jones Industrial Average stood at 406.16 points.

Bonds, and more particularly the curious subjectivity involved in pricing them, are at the heart of Bloomberg's business, just as they were at the heart of Salomon's. Many factors affect a bond's value, including the interest rates it offers, the time to maturity, and the going rate for government issues, but since there is nothing like the New York Stock Exchange or Nasdaq for bonds, there is no way to know exactly what a bond is worth. John McConville, the editor of *Inside Market Data*, remembers Bloomberg's recounting to him a conversation he had once had with a bond trader. Bloomberg asked how the price had been set for a particular bond; the trader replied that he had made it up.

The data Bloomberg offers its subscribers are intended to put a limit on such inventiveness. To show me how, Napolitano chose a corporate bond issue from A.T. & T. with a maturity date of May 15, 2025. The first screens he pulled up showed the bond's ratings by Moody's and Standard & Poor's, and its average and current yields compared with those of a treasury note. Next, Napolitano produced a graph showing how telecommunications-company bonds in general stacked up against treasury notes. Then he pulled up a figure called the "Bloomberg Fair Value" for the A.T. & T. bond, which was based on prices for similar bonds and represented the firm's best estimate of its worth. Napolitano then looked up A.T. & T.'s stock and, clicking through more screens, created a chart showing how it had performed against that of other telecommunications companies. Finally, he performed what is called an "option-adjusted spread analysis," which somehow factored out the risk that the A.T. & T. bond would be called before its maturity date, and allowed its value to be compared directly with that of so-called "bullet" bonds. Napolitano was a good salesman, and as the numbers flashed by, sometimes in spreadsheet form, sometimes as a graph, it was easy to see why someone investing, say, a few billion dollars would consider the service's monthly fee of twelve hundred and eighty-five dollars per workstation money well spent.

Bloomberg's first customers, outside of Merrill Lynch, which still owns a one-fifth stake in his company, were large institutional investors, like pension funds. Initially, the service simply allowed them to make better-informed decisions; later, it began to change the world it was describing. As it became more difficult to exploit customers' ignorance, bond spreads—the gap between what a firm is willing to pay for a particular issue and how much it is asking to sell it—narrowed. This, in turn, cut down on profit margins for traders, meaning that, in a roundabout way, Bloomberg's success came at the expense of the very group of people who had fired him. Bloomberg has always maintained that he came up with the idea for Bloomberg L.P. only after his dismissal, but it is hard to imagine that the notion hadn't at least crossed his mind prior to that. In his last years at Salomon, after all, he had been working on organizing stock and bond data electronically for the firm. "In the eighties, Bloomberg built his business and sold the services he had developed at Salomon back to Salomon," Gutfreund told me. "We paid for it twice. I congratulate him."

In February, 1990, in honor of Bloomberg's forty-eighth birthday, one of his top staff members, Elisabeth DeMarse, put together a book entitled "The Portable Bloomberg." Dedicated to the president of "The Greatest Company in the World," it contained thirty-two pages of his collected "wit and wisdom" and was illustrated with pen-and-ink drawings of Bloomberg in, among other outfits, gladiator gear. In a prefatory note, DeMarse, who is now the president of an Internet consumer-finance firm, Bankrate.com, wrote, "Yes, these are all actual quotes. No, nothing has been embellished or exaggerated. And yes, some things were too outrageous to include."

A lot of "The Portable Bloomberg" consists of off-color jokes, and when *New York* published excerpts last summer, shortly before the mayoral primary, it created a brief sensation. There are quotations on Merry Old England: "There's only one queen in Buckingham Palace, the rest are in Trafalgar Square." On women: "If women wanted to be appreciated for their brains, they'd go to the library instead of Bloomingdale's." And on marriage: "Sex with someone you love . . . is sex with someone you love. The plusses are you don't have to buy dinner and the only thing you catch is calluses." In the section on the Bloomberg terminal, Bloomberg is quoted as saying, "It will do everything, including give you a blowjob. I guess that puts a lot of you girls out of business." On the campaign trail, Bloomberg characterized the remarks as "Borscht Belt jokes" and said he didn't remember having made them.

Also surfacing in the booklet is a business philosophy: "Whenever one of my employees designs a form or writes a memo, I walk out into the hallway and make a big deal of tearing it up. The last thing we need are lots of forms and procedures and policies."

"How do you motivate someone?" Bloomberg is quoted as asking. "Simple. Are they addicted to three meals a day?"

Bloomberg gave up day-to-day responsibility for Bloomberg L.P. last year in order to campaign for mayor. Until then, he ran the firm according to a strong, if quirky, set of management principles—Frederick Taylor meets B. F. Skinner. Bloomberg himself sat at a desk in the middle of a sea of other desks, an arrangement that he called an "open plan." He limited elevator service between floors, so that everyone would have to come in by the same entrance and climb the same stairs, and provided free food, so that his employees would be less inclined to leave the building. There were no titles or individual offices, and anyone who wanted privacy had to reserve a conference room. Bloomberg had these made out of glass. He also had saltwater aquariums installed at key locations, because fish, he said, provide "relaxation." (Bloomberg is still awaiting a ruling from the city's Conflicts of Interest Board on his continued ownership of the firm and, theoretically at least, could be told to sell it.)

The "open plan" was intended to inspire teamwork—"You're part of the Borg or you're not" is how one former employee described it—and, at the same time, cut down on pointless formalities. Anybody at the firm could walk right up and speak with Bloomberg; those who were too shy to approach him were likely to bump into him when they were picking up a free bag of Doritos. "He was constantly in touch," Doug McGill, a former London bureau chief for Bloomberg News, told me. "I could literally call him up at any time, and I always got right through to him." Every summer, there was a picnic for the entire staff at Bloomberg's Westchester estate, with a petting zoo for the kids. Bloomberg encouraged his guests to come in T-shirts and shorts, which is what he wore.

The company's strategy was relatively straightforward: offer the best and charge for it. As a matter of principle, Bloomberg never gave volume discounts, and he was constantly adding new features to the data service, which every subscriber was obliged to finance. "I follow the trader's adage: if you can't move something, mark it up, not down," he is quoted as saying in "The Portable Bloomberg." He paid his own employees well and, in return, expected them routinely to put in eleven-hour days. "What you cannot question about this guy is his dedication to high quality and to winning at any cost, or almost any cost," observed Thom Calandra, a former Bloomberg News reporter who is now editor-in-chief of CBS MarketWatch. "He's an overreacher. He's an achiever. And so far nothing he's done has resulted in tragedy."

Throughout the nineties, Bloomberg L.P. expanded rapidly. At the start of the decade, it had ten thousand subscribers and estimated annual revenues of under a hundred and fifty million dollars; by the end, it had a hundred and sixty-four thousand subscribers and annual revenues of $2.3 billion. In the process, it crushed several of its competitors, including Dow Jones's Telerate service. Whether or not Bloomberg himself was entirely responsible for this success—he did not, for example, do any of the technical work—he invariably received all the credit. "When you get hired, you get this whole stack of publicity," Calandra recalled. "Every single article is about Mike Bloomberg. Every article. And it's been like that for ten years. It's all about Mike, and it always has been about him."

Bloomberg played such a big role that even his personality tended to be viewed as corporate policy, including his bluntness. His favorite jokes were of the "What's the difference between pussy and parsley?" variety, and he told them pretty much without regard for who was listening. He freely discussed his own sexual exploits and those—real or imagined—of his employees. At least some of his staff members joined in. Around the office, the phrase "I'd fuck that in a minute" was voiced so routinely that, to save time, it was shortened to "In a minute."

The atmosphere at Bloomberg L.P. was cited in three sex-discrimination suits filed against the firm. One case was brought by a saleswoman, Sekiko Sakai Garrison, who alleged that she had been repeatedly harassed and then forced to leave after complaining about it. Among her accusations was the charge that Bloomberg had greeted the news that she was pregnant with the remark "Kill it!" Bloomberg has denied saying this, and during the mayoral campaign produced the results of a polygraph to back up his assertion; nevertheless, he settled the suit out of court for an undisclosed but by all accounts substantial sum. In a second suit, a saleswoman named Mary Ann Olszewski charged that she had been raped by a colleague while the two were out of town together on a business trip. Eventually, this suit was dismissed, after the plaintiff missed various filing deadlines, but not before Bloomberg had been deposed by her lawyer. An excerpt of the deposition was published in the *Village Voice:*

LAWYER: What would constitute satisfactory proof to you that the allegation was genuine?

BLOOMBERG: I guess an unimpeachable third-party witness.

LAWYER: Do you think that's possible in most instances of date rape?

BLOOMBERG: I don't know whether this was date rape.

LAWYER: Describe for me your conception of how there could be a third-party witness to confirm or deny the truthfulness of her allegations.

BLOOMBERG: There are times when three people are together.

LAWYER: Other than those circumstances when a woman claiming rape was in the presence of more than one man, what other?

BLOOMBERG: Why does it have to be a man?

LAWYER: Have you ever read any psychosocial literature about the subject of rape?

BLOOMBERG: There was a cover story in one of the weekly news magazines last month. I'm sure I glanced through it.

LAWYER: Which one?

BLOOMBERG: *Time*, *U.S. News*, or *Newsweek*. For all I know, it was all three. They all do the same things.

Bloomberg's budget presentation, in February, was the longest sustained public address of his mayoralty so far, and it wasn't so much an address as a lesson in municipal finance. The Mayor spoke for nearly two hours in City Hall's Blue Room as various charts and graphs were projected on a screen behind him.

"What we're going to do is show you how this next year, fiscal 2003, which starts July 1st, we are going to have a deficit of approximately 4.8 billion dollars," he started off. "Now, whether it's 4.7 or 4.9, 4.6 or 5.0 isn't material. There's no way you can tell exactly. It is very hard to predict the future. And when you talk about whatever gaps we're going to see in 2004 and 2005, you get less and less confidence in the numbers. The economy may get better; the economy may get worse. We may have one-time terrible events like 9/11; we may have nothing but good times. You can't predict."

The Mayor went on, "So we are going to show you how to balance a 4.8 billion-dollar deficit with no new taxes. We are going to have reductions and efficiencies. We are not going to rely on one-time things. We can't rely on one-time shots. We don't have a budget deficit for just 2003. The deficit that we think we're going to have in 2003 is about 4.8 billion dollars; 2004 has a bigger one; 2005 has an even bigger one than that. If you try to balance the budget by one-time shots and postponing your expenses, it is just going to make the next year even worse. So we have to face reality."

Bloomberg's preliminary budget was, in fact, somewhat less realistic than he claimed—it included, for example, several projected "savings" of the sort that are never realized, as his own administration later tacitly acknowledged. It also featured a billion and a half dollars in borrowing to cover current operating expenses, a practice that has quite possibly been justified by recent events but that under ordinary circumstances would not be allowed. Still, his budget was much praised, especially for its even-handedness. The Mayor proposed more or less across-the-board cuts, even in normally hallowed programs like senior citizens' centers. "The budget that we're going to show you hurts everybody," he said. "We don't think it hurts anybody fatally." Except for higher taxes, which he ruled out not so much on philosophical grounds as on practical ones—"You would scare people away and you would scare the rating agencies"—he professed himself willing to consider any reasonable alternatives. "I do not have all the good ideas," he observed. "A PRAGMATIC APPROACH TO A BAD-NEWS BUDGET" was the *Times'* assessment.

Bloomberg switched parties before the mayoral election in order to avoid a crowded Democratic primary. The change took place at the last possible moment allowed by New York election law, and it might have caused more controversy had he ever shown an interest in ideology of any sort. In office, Bloomberg has remained strikingly noncommittal. He has appointed his commissioners apparently without regard to political orientation—it is likely that several didn't even vote for him—and, by all accounts, has given them a great deal of latitude. (One told me that the Mayor's instructions to him could be summed up as "It's your agency—don't screw it up.") In contrast to Giuliani, who took his principles so seriously that he didn't speak to anyone he disapproved of, Bloomberg makes a point of meeting with everyone. When, for example, the verdicts against three officers convicted in the Abner Louima case were thrown out, Bloomberg appeared first at the 70th Precinct house, in

Flatbush, where the torture had occurred, to show his solidarity with the police. Then, that same afternoon, he went to a black church in Brownsville to show his support for the community that had felt betrayed by the police. On the morning of the St. Patrick's Day Parade, he held a celebratory breakfast at Gracie Mansion, and invited both the parade's organizers and members of a gay group that the organizers had excluded from the parade. Bloomberg has not only visited the Reverend Al Sharpton's headquarters, in Harlem, but he has promised, if invited, to come back every year. "The greatest thing he's done is he's changed the climate of the city so that people are no longer frightened of the mayor," former Mayor Ed Koch told me.

Aptly enough, since he seems to see his primary role as managerial, Bloomberg's inaugural gesture was to rearrange City Hall. He abandoned the traditional executive offices across from the Blue Room and instead installed himself and his deputies, open-plan style, in cubicles upstairs. (He also brought in free food, and fish tanks.) His current priority is winning control over the city's school system, a goal that previous mayors have also pursued, unsuccessfully. Bloomberg maintains that he is ultimately going to win this battle—the final decision rests with Albany—and has already announced his intention to move the school bureaucracy out of its current headquarters, in Brooklyn, and into the Tweed Courthouse, in lower Manhattan. Though the old courthouse has just been renovated, at a cost of ninety million dollars, and had been promised to the Museum of the City of New York, Bloomberg has proposed turning it back into offices, complete with cubicles.

That Bloomberg rarely addresses the emotional or moral complexities of life in the city is, undoubtedly, a rhetorical failure. He seems, at least in public, almost incapable of expressing strong feelings or beliefs, or of eliciting them from others. After the Mayor had delivered a particularly perfunctory address—this one to a group of schoolchildren—I heard one City Hall reporter joke, "It's his thank-you-for-inviting-me speech, which consists of 'Thank you for inviting me.'" At the same time, this limitation is one that, given Bloomberg's priorities, may not be all that significant. As far as he is concerned, the only reason to talk about a problem is to solve it, the corollary of which is that only problems that can be solved are really worth talking about. "I am going to show you how we got into this situation," the Mayor said matter-of-factly when he presented his budget, "and a solution to work our ways out of this situation."

Every year, the National Lesbian and Gay Journalists Association holds a benefit in New York to support, among other programs, the group's national convention, its style book on gay and lesbian terminology, and its student-outreach effort. This year, Bloomberg L.P. was one of the event's "gold level" sponsors, and the Mayor was a featured speaker at the cocktail reception, which took place at the offices of MTV, in Times Square.

Often, Bloomberg is described as a "media mogul," and this is at least partially accurate. In addition to the financial-data service, which generates nearly all the firm's profits, Bloomberg L.P. comprises a wire service, Bloomberg News; Bloomberg Television; Bloomberg Radio; and a consumer-magazine division, which publishes titles like *Bloomberg Markets*, *Bloomberg Wealth Manager*, and *Bloomberg Personal Finance*. (The company also has a books division, which publishes, among other things, *New Yorker* cartoon collections.) All in all, the firm employs seventeen hundred journalists in eighty-five bureaus around the world, and at the cocktail reception several Bloomberg reporters were in attendance. "Thank you for having me," the Mayor told the journalists, who were gathered at little round tables. "I was here last year. Since then I have come out of the closet. It's true. I have finally admitted that I'm a Republican. And the press has cut me a lot of slack since then, particularly on weekends. They really do leave me alone."

Speaking, as usual, without notes, he continued, "Oscar Wilde once said we are dominated by journalism. And that is both the good news and the bad news. The good news is that journalism is what keeps us a free society. If it wasn't for a free, aggressive, investigatory press, we really would have totalitarianism, and we should never forget that, no matter how many times we get annoyed with the press for intrusiveness, or whatever. And I do think sometimes, and this is my personal experience—you have a right to ask, but the great thing about the First Amendment is I have a right not to answer. You have a right to write it; I have a right not to read it. And that was the way I got through my campaign. I basically said I wasn't going to read any of this stuff anymore, and it's amazing, if you don't read it, life goes on." He concluded, "Anyways, congratulations to all of you."

In general, Bloomberg has a hard time masking his feelings toward the journalists who now trail him. Not long ago, he went record shopping, to demonstrate his support for merchants in lower Manhattan, and flipped through a rack of CDs as the cameras clicked away furiously. I happened to be standing nearby when he muttered, to no one in particular, "The dumbest things in the world, they're taking pictures of." (He bought two CDs by Crosby, Stills and Nash.) On another occasion, he was heading into a routine press conference at a Manhattan middle school when he ran into someone he knew. "You're not joining this gaggle!" he exclaimed.

Doubtless it *is* aggravating to be covered by the New York press, and while Bloomberg has been widely praised for his budget, his appointments, and his restructuring of City Hall, he has also been taunted. The first time he suddenly dropped out of view for the weekend without letting reporters know his whereabouts, the *Post* ran a picture of a milk carton with his face on it, asking "HAVE YOU SEEN ME?" The next weekend he disappeared, a *Post* photographer showed up at the home of the deputy mayor for operations, Marc Shaw, in Queens. The paper ran a picture of a dishevelled-looking Shaw, who appeared at the door in jeans and a T-shirt, above a caption identifying him as "the man in charge when the mayor's gone." The conceit was then picked up by David Letterman, who broadcast Shaw's photograph as the lead-in to a Top Ten list of the "Ways New York City Is Different When This Guy's in Charge." No. 1: "First city official since Koch to take a leak in the Hudson."

Yet Bloomberg's disdain for the press clearly goes beyond the missing-person gags. "If I had a heart attack in the sales department, everyone would come around and immediately give me CPR," he once announced to a group of reporters at Bloomberg L.P. "If I had a heart attack in the newsroom, you assholes would stand around and scribble notes." During the mayoral race, I asked him for his reflections on the campaign, and his response was to reflect on the stupidity of reporters. "I don't know whether it's just that they're not all that smart, or maybe they just don't think it sells," he told me. "But there is a focus on finding something wrong."

His own media empire notwithstanding, Bloomberg clearly doesn't like to focus on what is wrong. In my conversations with his associates, a recurrent theme was his lack of interest in any kind of self-criticism, or even analysis. This quality, several friends of his insisted, was essential to his success. "In his own mind, he really doesn't feel there's anything that he can't accomplish," Morris Offit told me. "He has these God-given talents—why not take advantage of them? It's very straightforward. If someone told me that Michael was getting some kind of therapy, I'd be the most surprised person in the world."

Matthew Winkler is the editor-in-chief of Bloomberg News and wrote Bloomberg's autobiography with him. He told me that during their collaboration Bloomberg kept trying to add exclamation points to the manuscript. "He's his own hero," Winkler said of his old boss. "As a result, he doesn't have to be that introspective. Life is a series of goals to be achieved. He defines the goals and then does everything he can to achieve them." He went on, "So it's relatively uncomplicated, and that's why it works. That's why *he* works—because he doesn't spend a lot of time wondering if it's all meaningless."

Bloomberg devotes the last chapter of his autobiography to philanthropy. Entitled "Wealth, Wisdom, and Work," it reads like a self-help manual for the fantastically wealthy. "After you've gotten used to living like a king, what do you do?" Bloomberg asks at one point. "First, forget worrying over taxes," he answers. "Second, don't spoil your family. . . . Third, be selfish! Buy yourself enormous pleasure. Give most of your wealth to charity!"

Bloomberg has been enormously generous, contributing to everything from his mother's synagogue, in Medford, to the Harlem Opera. A list of donations released by his campaign last summer showed that in the previous twelve-month period he had made gifts totalling more than a hundred million dollars to nearly six hundred groups. Though he is not much of a museum-goer, and by his own account sleeps at the opera, he was until recently on the board of the Metropolitan Museum of Art and of Lincoln Center. (Bloomberg himself underwrote the museum's renovation of its arms-and-armor gallery, and his company underwrote Lincoln

Center's summer season.) Bloomberg has even endowed a fellowship at Harvard for the professional study of giving. "Every two years this 'chair' passes from one school at Harvard to another," he writes. "And so, every twenty-four months, a new person will study, teach, research, and write from a new perspective about my interest, philanthropy. Will they make great contributions to society? You bet. Will there be great leverage to continue the work I love by teaching many? For sure. Will my family get enjoyment, satisfaction, admiration? Absolutely."

Bloomberg's view of philanthropy—upbeat and uncomplicated—matches, perhaps not surprisingly, his view of himself. Giving to others is not about guilt, or ethical obligation, or even identification with those who are suffering; it is, rather, another form of self-realization—in his words, "the greatest satisfaction available for cash today." Even as he was preparing to run for mayor last spring, Bloomberg was quietly at work on his most ambitious philanthropic project to date. The Mayor is the chairman of the board of trustees of Johns Hopkins, his alma mater, and for years has been a major benefactor of the university. His largest donations have been to Hopkins' school of public health, which is now named after him. Last year, he held a series of discussions with the school's dean, Dr. Alfred Sommer, in which he expressed interest in making a further contribution to public health that would change the world. Sommer travelled to New York with half a dozen other eminent research scientists from Hopkins. The group stayed at the Algonquin and sat at the "round table" trying to come up with a proposal. When the scientists presented their ideas to Bloomberg in a conference room at Bloomberg L.P., none of their suggestions seemed to him quite big enough—except for one, which was to eliminate a deadly disease. Sommer declined to specify which disease, but last May, Johns Hopkins announced an anonymous hundred-million-dollar gift to set up a malaria research institute.

"Wouldn't it be great to say you saved more lives than anybody in the history of the world?" Bloomberg asked shortly before the institute was announced. Six months later, he made another anonymous donation, of ten million dollars, to the Carnegie Corporation, to assist cultural institutions hurt by the September 11th attack.

A hundred days into his mayoralty, Bloomberg is still introduced as someone who did not need to run for office, and clearly this is the case. He already had a great life. "Let me put it this way," he once said. "I am a single, straight billionaire in Manhattan. What do you think? It's a wet dream." New York, meanwhile, even before September 11th, was headed toward hard times. In the months since the attack, ninety-eight thousand jobs have left the city, many of them never to return, and the very future of downtown as the world's financial center has been cast in doubt.

Bloomberg didn't run for mayor despite the difficulties of the job but, one has to assume, because of them. He has always been drawn to new challenges, to munificent gestures, and to danger. "Did I want to risk an embarrassing and costly failure?" he once observed about his decision to start Bloomberg L.P. "Absolutely."

While he was still at Salomon Brothers, Bloomberg took up flying. One weekend, he set off up the Connecticut coast in a rented helicopter. He was just off of Norwalk, over a tiny island in Long Island Sound, when his engine conked out. Black smoke filled the cockpit, and the helicopter began to tumble out of the sky. Bloomberg just barely managed to maneuver it onto the island, the tail dangling over the water, and bail out. More recently, when Bloomberg was taking his nephew on a sightseeing flight to Manhattan, a propeller on his private airplane failed. He was forced to make an emergency landing at Westchester Airport, but, as he later informed his sister, any landing you walk away from is a good one.

The Fellowship of the Ring

May 2002

O N DECEMBER 12, 1870, the New York *Sun*, a newspaper that had been hostile to Boss Tweed, suddenly proposed that a monument be raised in his honor. Whether the suggestion represented a change of heart or was just a joke—the paper recommended that Tweed be cast in a nautical pose, repairing the lines on his steam yacht in the midst of a hurricane—is difficult to say. In any case, Tammany Hall embraced the *Sun's* idea. The Tweed Testimonial Association was formed, and a circular was printed—at public expense—to solicit donations for the erection of a statue of Tweed "in consideration of his services to the Commonwealth of New York."

Tweed was at that point at the height of his power, and few were the projects that he didn't have a hand in. It was Tweed who pushed through the bill that legalized millions of dollars' worth of watered Erie Railroad stock, and also Tweed who arranged for the Albany legislature to incorporate the Metropolitan Museum of Art. Among the many posts he held simultaneously were that of New York state senator, head of the city's Department of Public Works, president of the County Board of Supervisors, and Grand Sachem of Tammany Hall. Not surprisingly, the Testimonial Association made rapid headway, collecting nearly eight thousand dollars by the middle of March. Meanwhile, unsolicited suggestions for the design of the monument poured in. The *Herald* recommended that the Boss be rendered in Indian garb, the city charter in one hand and a peace pipe in the other. The virulently anti-Tammany *Times* proposed that the statue of George Washington in Union Square Park be taken down and replaced by one of Tweed, to illustrate the progress of history. Finally,

Tweed himself graciously refused the honor. "Statues are not erected to living men, but to those who have ended their careers," he wrote. "I claim to be a live man, and hope (Divine Providence permitting) to survive in all my vigor, politically and physically, some years to come." The *Sun* printed Tweed's demurral under the headline "A GREAT MAN'S MODESTY," with the subhead "The Hon. William M. Tweed declines the Sun's Statue—characteristic letter from the great New York philanthropist—he thinks that virtue should be its own reward."

In the end, of course, Tweed still got his monument, albeit an unintended one. Situated on Chambers Street, just behind City Hall, the building that started out as the New York County Courthouse but eventually became known as the Tweed Courthouse features a neoclassical façade, a five-story Romanesque Revival rotunda, and thirty courtrooms, the most ornate of which are resplendent with granite columns and polychrome brick. It is among the most sumptuous public buildings in the city and, on a constant dollar basis, without question the most expensive. The final bill for its construction, which stretched over twenty years, exceeded fifteen million dollars—more than four times the cost of the Houses of Parliament, as outraged observers pointed out, and twice what the United States had recently paid to purchase Alaska.

Sometime in the next few days, painters and floor-layers will put the final touches on the job of restoring the Tweed, a monumental undertaking in itself. The project, begun in 1999, involved, on any given day, more than two hundred construction workers, along with brass smiths in India, tile-makers in England, foundrymen in Alabama, and stonecutters in Georgia, and it proceeded at a near-record pace. Perhaps inevitably, given the building's history, the success of the project has been glossed not just in architectural terms but in moral ones as well. Speaking at the courthouse back in December, Mayor Rudy Giuliani boasted that the restoration would "purify the building and remove the stench of Boss Tweed and corruption." As is so often the case with such high-minded enterprises, however, the real lesson has proved less edifying. Completed at a cost of nearly ninety million dollars, the Tweed restoration is shaping up into a second municipal debacle—one that, although quite different from the first, is not quite different enough.

*   *   *

William Marcy Tweed, who was not actually named William Marcy Tweed, was born on April 3, 1823, in lower Manhartan. In all likelihood, his middle initial stood for his mother's maiden name, Magear, and Marcy was another joke perpetrated by the newspapers. (In the eighteen-thirties, William L. Marcy served three terms as governor of New York, and is credited with adapting to political use the motto "To the victor belongs the spoils.") A contemporary of Tweed's described him as a good-looking young man, "with dark brown hair and clear, gritty eyes"; however, photographs show that by middle age he was bald and stout. In the famous Thomas Nast cartoons, he is inevitably pictured bursting out of his waistcoat—at his heaviest, Tweed weighed close to three hundred pounds—with a huge diamond glittering on his shirtfront.

Both in his strengths and in his limitations, Tweed was a quintessential Tammany man—or, at least, what we have come to consider one. He was not particularly eloquent—"I can't talk, and I know it," he once said—or even clever, and his early years were devoted to a series of ventures that mostly ended badly. For a while, Tweed worked with his father-in-law manufacturing brushes, before following his father into chairmaking. He was active as a volunteer fireman, and in 1850 ran—and lost—his first campaign, for assistant alderman. Two years later, he was elected to Congress, where he served, without distinction, as a member of the Committee on Invalid Pensions. He passed no legislation, made one speech, and according to one of his biographers, Leo Hershkowitz, the author of "Tweed's New York," was not renominated. In 1861, his chair business failed. Filing for bankruptcy, Tweed offered the following list of his worldly assets: "Three Hats, Two Caps, Two Thick Overcoats, One Thin Overcoat, Three Pair Pants, Six Vests, Two Dress Coats, One Business Coat, Three Pair Boots, Two Pair Shoes, Ten Pair Socks, Thirty Collars, Twelve Linen Shirts, Twelve Cotton Shirts, Ten Handkerchiefs."

Tweed's one substantial talent seems to have been a grasp of city politics, which is to say, of human frailty. In 1863, he was appointed deputy street commissioner, and as another of his biographers, Alexander B. Callow, Jr., points out in "The Tweed Ring," over the next four years he proceeded to quadruple the department's payroll. In 1864, he bought a controlling interest in a printing company, which quickly became the city's supplier of vouchers and stationery. As a member of the Board of Supervisors, Tweed organized his first ring, which took a neat fifteen per cent off the top of every city contract. (A "ring," in the words of one of Tweed's henchmen, was "a collection of men united for some common object.") Five years after declaring bankruptcy, he owned a brownstone in Manhattan and a home in Greenwich, Connecticut. In 1871, when his daughter Mary Amelia got married, the *Sun* reported that the scene in Tweed's Fifth Avenue mansion was so splendid that it "beggared description." The *Herald* estimated the value of the wedding gifts at seven hundred thousand dollars—roughly ten million dollars in today's money.

As an exercise in graft, the courthouse has been described as Tweed's masterwork, and the brazenness of the self-dealing is almost unimaginable today, Enron notwithstanding. The original, fairly modest appropriation stipulated that the entire courthouse, construction of which began in 1861, should cost no more than two hundred and fifty thousand dollars, including all its furnishings. But Tweed convinced his colleagues on the Board of Supervisors that this was too niggardly. First, they added a million dollars to the project, then an additional eight hundred thousand, and so on. It is estimated that less than twenty-five per cent of expenditures went toward actual construction. A carpenter named George Miller, also known as Lucky, was paid three hundred and sixty thousand dollars for one month's work. Andrew Garvey, a plasterer, received five hundred thousand dollars for a year's work, and then a million dollars to repair that work. (He became known as the Prince of Plasterers.) For three tables and forty chairs, the city paid nearly a hundred and eighty thousand dollars; for "brooms, etc.," forty-one thousand dollars. One check, in the amount of sixty-four thousand dollars, was made out simply to "T.C. Cash." The marble for the building was quarried near Tuckahoe, New York, until Tweed and his cronies acquired a quarry in western Massachusetts.

Five years into the project, after millions had been disbursed with little to show for it, a group of outraged citizens demanded an inquiry, and the Special Committee to Investigate the Courthouse was formed. It acted quickly, and found no justification for concern, even as it ran up a bill of more than eighteen thousand dollars for twelve days' work. Nearly half that amount went to Tweed's printing company, which published the committee's official report.

Jack Waite is the architect who oversaw the Tweed's restoration, and on a spectacular spring morning not long ago I arranged to meet him on the courthouse's front steps, which lead up to three sets of giant walnut doors. As I waited, people kept coming up to me and asking when the building would be open. I told them I had no idea.

The courthouse is now strictly off limits, closed to the general public, to the press, and even, in the company of a reporter, to its architect. Waite arrived, and the best we could do was take a walk around the outside. "If there's one building that really encapsulates the history of New York during the second half of the nineteenth century, when the city became the capital of the world, it's this one," he told me. "Tweed liked fine things." As we circled the block, Waite pointed out how the original ruddy-hued marble from Tuckahoe had weathered and could be distinguished from the paler, Massachusetts stones.

Thanks to its associations, the Tweed was neglected and unloved almost from the moment it was completed. For half a century, it served as a county court; then it was converted into a city court and then a family court. Eventually, many of its soaring chambers were partitioned into offices for use by second-tier city agencies. The building's polychrome brick was painted gray, its entry foyer walled off to make space for rest rooms, and its intricately molded cast-iron steps encased in concrete. In 1974, a task force appointed by Mayor Abe Beame described the Tweed as "one million cubic feet of unusable space" and recommended that it be demolished. Architecturally speaking, neglect may have been the best thing for the building. "It's all intact, because everyone was afraid to spend any money on it," Waite observed.

When the city began work on the renovation, it had only the sketchiest idea of what the building might be used for. This was either idealism or folly, or both. There was still no firm plan midway through the project, even after *Newsday*, invoking Tweed, reported on how much the work was costing. Finally, the Giuliani administration hired an architectural consultant to study the matter, at a cost of a hundred and fifty thousand dollars. The consultant considered everything from high-end condos to a boutique hotel before concluding that only a museum made sense for the building, both because of its splendor and because so much public money was going into restoring it. Not long afterward, Giuliani offered the Tweed to the Museum of the City of New York.

The museum's board of directors was attracted by the idea of being given, gratis, a fine new home for its collections of antique toys and silverware. But it turned out that the board didn't want quite the same building that the city was working on. The Tweed has enormous windows, which the city had had refurbished at a substantial cost; from the museum's perspective, these windows let in too much light. A ventilation system for a restaurant had been installed on the east side of the building, but the museum's consultants wanted to put the restaurant on the west side. Even as the city was ordering high-tech glass panels for the doors etched with beavers and Indian braves, the museum's architects were drawing up plans to have the doorways modified. The Giuliani administration agreed to a second round of renovations—much of it aimed at undoing the work of the first—and, what's more, agreed to foot half the bill. The remodelling was expected to take two years and to cost more than forty million dollars.

Mayor Michael Bloomberg held his inaugural party in the Tweed, but he made it clear early on that he was not entirely happy with the deal Giuliani had struck. His objections—at least the ones that he voiced—ranged from the effects of the museum's move on its current uptown neighbors to technical concerns about the Tweed's landmark status. Then suddenly, in March, while talking to a group of schoolchildren from Staten Island, he scuttled the museum plan in favor of a brand-new one that seemed entirely of his own devising. Instead of bestowing the building on the Museum of the City of New York, or any other museum, he announced his intention to turn it back into city offices. He said he wanted to move several hundred of the city's school administrators into the top floors of the Tweed and turn the ground level into a demonstration school. The justification he offered for the move was that, since the courthouse is so close to City Hall, it would show his commitment to education. "Symbolism is important," he told the children.

Even many members of Bloomberg's own staff seemed taken aback, and reaction to the plan in the rest of the city ran from outrage to disbelief. "Ludicrous" was the assessment of John Dyson, the former deputy mayor who had overseen the renovation. One city official covered his face with his hands when I asked about Bloomberg's idea. "I can't even talk about it," he said. "My feelings are too strong."

The nature of municipal government is such that it is possible that Bloomberg will have his way, but unlikely. Location aside, there is nothing about the Tweed that suits it to the use the Mayor has in mind. To accommodate a school full of children, not to mention hundreds of bureaucrats, much of the renovation would have to be gutted, again at considerable expense. In the meantime, the courthouse just sits there— magnificent, but empty—guarded at a cost of fifteen thousand dollars a month.

Ultimately, Tweed's masterwork proved to be his undoing. On July 22, 1871, the *Times* ran a front-page story headlined "THE SECRET ACCOUNTS," with the subhead "Proofs of Undoubted Frauds Brought to Light." In it, the paper provided what it claimed was incontrovertible evidence of the Boss's swindles. (One of the *Times'* sources is believed to have been a young man named James O'Brien, who worked his way into the Tweed ring's favor by serving as a trustee of the Tweed Testimonial Association.) In the weeks that followed, one account after another related in monstrous detail—$404,347.72 spent on safes, $565,713.34 on carpets—the extent of the thievery. An often repeated story from the period is that one of Tweed's cronies, Richard (Slippery Dick) Connolly, the city comptroller, tried to buy the *Times* off—in one version offering five hundred thousand dollars, in another five million. "I don't think that the devil will ever make a higher bid for me," the paper's publisher, George Jones, is said to have replied. That November, Tweed still managed to get reëlected to the State Senate, but in December he was indicted.

From that point on, Tweed suffered a rapid, if colorful, descent. The first of his trials, which took place in his own, half-finished courthouse, ended in a hung jury, amid rumors, never substantiated, that the jurors had been bribed. At his second trial, Tweed was convicted on two hundred and four counts of auditing failures. (Before heading off to a cell in the Tombs, he is reported to have had dinner sent over from Delmonico's.) Tweed appealed his sentence, and nineteen months later he was released, only to be hastily rearrested on different charges. Bail was set at three million dollars, a sum that even Tweed's friends couldn't muster. His incarceration was lightened, in the quaint fashion of the time, by frequent trips home for dinner. On one such jaunt, Tweed went upstairs and never came back down. Six months later, he was sighted in Cuba. A few months after that, he was arrested in Spain, where he was discovered posing as a seaman. Tweed had supposedly been recognized on the basis of a Thomas Nast cartoon.

Initially, Tweed's ruin was heralded as a victory for the cause of reform. Among the celebratory verses written at the time was a poem, "The House That Tweed Built," which cheerfully proclaimed:

> Let us hope
> The Boss and his gang will have plenty of rope
> Till they swing,
> The whole Ring,
> To Sing-Sing.

Samuel Tilden, a lawyer who took much of the credit for pursuing Tweed, became, on the basis of that pursuit, governor of New York, and almost, in an Al Gore sort of way, President of the United States.

But the reformers' achievement soon proved to be a hollow one. The Tweed ring had been a huge operation, involving, among many others, the mayor, "Elegant" Oakey Hall; the president of the Department of Public Parks, Peter (Brains) Sweeny; and Slippery Dick Connolly. Some of the members fled after the ring was exposed, some made partial restitution, and many more continued on in government service. When Tweed, suffering from heart trouble and diabetes, finally realized that there was no other hope, he approached the state attorney general, offering to provide a full account of his misdeeds, and to hand over all his property, in return for his release. Tweed wrote out his confession, even providing checks from various associates as evidence, only to have the attorney general reject the offer. The problem was not, as Alexander B. Callow, Jr., points out, that

Tweed had provided too little evidence but that he had provided too much. Implicated in his various schemes was half of official New York. "Could even Mr. Tilden afford to have Tweed's story told?" the *Times* wondered.

Tweed spent the last months of his life in the Ludlow Street jail, on the Lower East Side, which he had, in his official capacity, also helped to build, in a room where he kept a piano and a servant. Ill and disheartened, he was down to a hundred and sixty pounds. On April 12, 1878, his daughter came to visit and stepped out to fetch her father some ice cream. Tweed died while she was gone. He was fifty-five. His last words are reported to have been "I hope they will be satisfied, now they have got me."

Postscript: In 2002, the New York City Board of Education moved its headquarters into the Tweed Courthouse. The old Board of Education Building, 110 Livingston Street in Brooklyn, is being converted into apartments.

Everyone Lies

August 2002

P EOPLE OFTEN ASK Esmond Anderson where he goes to eat. The truth is he rarely eats out. During seven and a half years as a restaurant inspector with the New York City Department of Health, Anderson scrutinized some two thousand commercial kitchens. Five years ago, he started teaching at the city's Health Academy, in the basement of a clinic on West 100th Street. His classroom is decorated with posters detailing, in Spanish and in English, the risks posed by dented cans, leaky vacuum-sealed packages, and careless thawing. One chronicles an outbreak of botulism traced to "killer potatoes." Anderson, who is fifty-three years old, is a trim man with very little hair and an almost imperceptible gray mustache. He speaks in the accent of his native Guyana, and manages to convey a respect for the gravity of his task and, at the same time, an appreciation of its futility. He likes to tell his students—pushcart venders, sous-chefs, restaurant managers, bartenders, and short-order cooks—that he thinks of them all as potential murderers.

"The things that you're going to learn, some of them are going to shock you," he informed his class one recent afternoon. "You might say, 'I never knew this! How is it I've been preparing food and serving it all this time and no one ever died?' As a matter of fact, how do you *know* that your customers have never died? If they died, they don't come back to you to complain."

Anderson's weeklong course costs a hundred and five dollars. It consists of five three-hour sessions and ends in an exam that is offered in twenty languages. The take-home quizzes have questions like "People, both food workers and customers, pose the greatest risk to food safety. True or False?"

and "List three situations when hands must be washed thoroughly." The week I attended, I sat in the back row. On my right was a woman from Queens who managed a Blimpie; she had already had, she acknowledged to the group, an unhappy encounter with a city health inspector. On my left was a man who operated a fleet of ice-cream trucks in the Bronx. (When I suggested that this ought to be pretty safe, he countered that, on the contrary, ice cream was a "bacteria magnet.") At a later session, one of my neighbors was a Russian man who used to work at a hair salon near the World Trade Center but was planning to get into shish kebab. He took copious notes on tiny sheets of paper, and enthusiastically yelled out the answers to all of Anderson's questions. ("Vayrmin!" he declared, more or less correctly, in response to one of them.) In front of us, a man in an Auburn University baseball cap spent most of the class bent over his desk, asleep.

"Anybody glad to be here?" Anderson asked at the start of the course. A solitary hand went up. "That's a nice general consensus," he observed.

By law, every "food service establishment" in New York City must have on duty at all times at least one worker with a course certificate from the Health Academy. The explicit purpose of the class is to address the many technical hazards of meal preparation. Among the topics it covers are the life cycle of microörganisms, the sources of cross-contamination, and the best ways to prevent foodborne illnesses, from listeriosis and shigellosis to staphylococcal food intoxication and scombroid poisoning. "After today, anytime you see poultry or eggs, this is what should come to your mind: salmonella," Anderson announced midway through the first class.

The real subject of Anderson's curriculum, however, is not so much bacteriological as moral: how do you persuade someone to care about food that someone else is going to eat? In principle, New York City's health code regulates everything from the minimum allowable cooking time for roast beef to the proper procedure for dealing with drinking straws. In reality, of course, dining out in the city is an act of faith that could be described as taking your life on your fork. The city does not keep statistics on the number of cases of foodborne illness contracted in restaurants; since most victims never go to a hospital, or even to a doctor, such a figure would be impossible to obtain, but almost certainly it is a large one. Eleven years ago, for example, a worker with hepatitis A at a corporate cafeteria in lower Manhattan managed to pass on the disease to sixty people. New York City, which has an estimated twenty thousand restaurants, employs just sixty-six "public health sanitarians," who spend a quarter of their time on tasks like checking for window guards on apartment buildings and testing chlorine levels at public pools.

At one point, Anderson posed the following hypothetical question to the class: "It's lunchtime, and you've got a big pot of chili on the countertop that you're supposed to serve for your lunch special. You have it open and up comes a fly zooming in, kamikaze style, and it lands in this pot of chili. What do you do? Ladle him out and then continue serving? How many of you would dump the whole pot?"

"Oh, boy, wow," he said, as the class started guffawing. "We've got some honest people here."

One morning not long after I visited the Health Academy, I arranged to meet Nicolle Woods and Bryant Washington in Greenwich Village. Woods, who is thirty-three, is an attractive woman with almond-shaped eyes and a friendly, no-nonsense manner. She has been a restaurant inspector since 1998, and was recently promoted by the Health Department to the position of senior sanitarian. Washington, who is twenty-eight but looks about eighteen, has also worked as a restaurant inspector for the past four years. In his spare time, he sings tenor in a doo-wop band. Their first stop of the day was a diner where, as it happened, I had eaten several times. Woods and Washington flashed their badges, and before they had a chance to pull out their pads half the staff had disappeared. I saw this reaction—mice scurrying before the approaching cat—at every restaurant we visited.

The inspectors began with the dining room. The fruit salad in the dessert case was covered, and the pastries laid out on the counter were individually wrapped, obviating the need for a "sneeze guard." The ice-cream freezer was clean. There was no thermometer in the refrigerator underneath the counter, but when Woods took the temperature of a quart of milk with a metal probe it was cold enough to satisfy her. The necessary permits, including the owner's food-protection certificate, were posted by the door, next to a sign advertising the availability of a C.P.R. mask.

The inspectors headed into the kitchen. Among the disappeared was the cook, and several vats of soup were boiling away unattended. Nearby, sandwich fixings were piled on a cooling unit called a lowboy. Woods stuck her metal probe into a mound of tuna salad. The reading was fifty-five degrees, ten degrees above the legal limit. She summoned the owner, a slight man with a pompadour. He wore the sickly, stricken smile of the damned.

"See the temperature?" Woods asked him, passing him the bin of tuna fish. "What temperature should it be?"

He hesitated. "Why it is fifty-five?" he finally asked, in a tone of exaggerated surprise.

"I don't know why," Woods replied. "But it's garbage now." She repeated this process remorselessly with a pile of sliced ham (fifty-five degrees), a container of cut-up chicken (also fifty-five), and a tray of raw eggs (sixty-two). The eggs, she concluded, had been left out on the counter and only shoved into the lowboy after we arrived.

From this point on, things began to deteriorate rapidly. The kitchen skylight, coated with bird droppings, was broken. Inside the walk-in refrigerator, stacks of raw hamburger patties were dripping their juices into pans of precooked noodles. Downstairs, in the storage room, blocks of mouse poison were lying around uncovered. A fly was swimming, or perhaps just floating, in a large pan of raw chickens. Several cans had dents in them, including a container of cranberry sauce that looked as if it had been run over. The owner rushed to rearrange the cans, pushing the defective ones off to the side. "Always I give them back," he said. Finally, the cook appeared. He was wearing a spattered apron and ostentatiously pulling on a pair of disposable latex gloves. Just then, Washington yanked a toilet seat out from next to the refrigerator.

"It broke last night," the cook wailed, by way of explanation. He rolled his eyes. "My luck today," he said.

The inspection lasted about half an hour. After it was done, Woods and Washington sat down at a banquette in the back to fill out the requisite paperwork. Violations of the health code fall into two categories—Class A, or "critical," and Class B, C, and D, which are "general." (Each instance of a critical violation is counted separately; general violations are grouped more leniently.) It takes either four criticals or five generals to fail an inspection.

With six critical violations and six general, the diner had, in effect, flunked twice. Woods, who has tiny, astonishingly neat handwriting, filled four pages with descriptions of its many shortcomings. Washington, meanwhile, went to make sure that the condemned food had been disposed of. He found the chickens still in their pan with the dead fly. He had the owner throw them out and, for good measure, pour bleach over them. Without this extra precaution, he told me, the chickens probably would have wound up under gravy. "As soon as we go, they'll be dragging stuff out of the garbage," he said. When their paperwork was complete, Woods and Washington summoned the owner to the banquette.

"I call already the refrigerator man," he said.

"What temperature should your cold food be at?" Woods asked.

"Under the forty-five."

At the very least, the inspection was going to result in several hundred dollars' worth of fines—the precise figure would be assessed by an administrative tribunal—and, at worst, it had set in motion a process that could eventually close the diner down. The city tries to inspect every restaurant once a year; last year, it performed some eighteen thousand inspections and failed about two thousand five hundred establishments on the first round. Restaurants that fail one inspection are given a second, and often a third, chance, and those that still fail are padlocked. In the twelve-month period that ended in June, three hundred and seventy-eight establishments were shut down by the Health Department.

Sitting next to the owner on the banquette, I suddenly felt depressed, though whether this was out of sympathy for him, exactly, I wasn't sure. I tried not to think about the chickens slowly blanching in the basement. The cook wandered over. He shook our hands, still wearing his latex gloves. It seemed to me unlikely that he would put on a new pair before returning to his lunch preparations—another health-code violation. "Don't work so hard," he said.

The next stop was a Chinese place, also in Greenwich Village, where illuminated photographs of elaborate dishes hung above the counter.

Woods charged in, explaining to me over her shoulder, "In Chinese restaurants, you have to move at the speed of light." Still, she wasn't fast enough. The chef, who also seemed to be the owner—this issue was never resolved to the inspectors' satisfaction—saw her coming and immediately pulled a five-gallon vat of fried rice off a shelf and dumped the entire contents into a steaming wok. Whether the rice had been "out of temperature" was now impossible to determine, and that was almost certainly the point.

The inspection turned up mouse droppings under the counter, among the plastic utensils, and, somewhat more mysteriously, in the freezer—a critical violation. In the basement, Washington discovered raw and cooked food heaped together—a general violation—and cleavers stuck behind sewage pipes that were being used as a makeshift knife rack, also a general violation. I found it hard to keep track of how things were going because I spent most of the inspection trying not to be scalded by the pots of oil boiling on the stove while avoiding the hole in the floor that served as the entrance to the basement. Ultimately, the place failed, but it scored better than the diner, with a total of two critical and five general violations.

City health-department officials are reluctant to generalize about what sort of food-service establishments tend to be the least hygienic. One day, I raised this question over lunch with the director of the Bureau of Food Safety and Community Sanitation, Robert Edman. I had invited him to Bouley, the restaurant with a four-star chef, now situated on West Broadway. "Mom-and-pop restaurants might have a very limited menu," he said. "Your fancy restaurants have a much more elaborate menu. By the laws of probability, more can go wrong here than can go wrong there." Edman told me that he thought that Bouley was well run, having recently seen its inspection report. Still, just by sitting in the dining room he noted one possible general violation—he could not see a poster showing how to perform the Heimlich maneuver—and one potential critical one: the menu advertised an entrée containing "wild mushrooms," which, if actually wild, are illegal. "Everybody claims to be a mushroom expert," he observed dryly. "But every year an expert dies."

The day I went out with the inspectors, we had lunch at Benny's Burritos, on Greenwich Avenue, which was chosen mostly on the ground that neither Woods nor Washington had ever been inside the kitchen. Woods volunteered that she had sworn off Chinatown, noting that "any sane New Yorker wouldn't eat there," while Washington said he could no longer eat from pushcarts: once, inspecting a vender commissary in midtown, he had seen something revolting involving cat feces and a large open bin of pretzel salt. Washington also recalled an Indian restaurant in the East Village whose sewage pipes had backed up in the basement, driving the rats upstairs. (The restaurant had continued to use the flooded basement for storage, and all the workers tramped around in rubber boots.)

As we finished our burritos, I asked the two what they had learned from their years on the job. Without hesitating, Woods said, "Everyone lies." She still seemed saddened by this revelation. Referring to a Hebrew day school where she had recently inspected the cafeteria, she added, "The rabbi is lying." Great cooks are said to be naturally generous; it occurred to me that to be a restaurant inspector it probably helps to be a born misanthrope.

The last stop of the day was a funky, vaguely pan-Asian restaurant. It was two-thirty in the afternoon, but a few stray diners were still lingering over lunch. Woods pulled on her Department of Health jacket, and the usual vanishing act ensued. The only person left in the kitchen was the cook, who was frying something that looked like tofu. A bowl of hard-boiled eggs was sitting on the counter.

"Garbage," Woods announced.

"Garbage?" the cook said. "No problem." Woods asked to see a food-protection certificate, and a certificate issued to the owner was produced. The cook said that the owner typically arrived at the restaurant around three o'clock. Woods was about to register a critical violation—no certificate holder on the premises—when the owner suddenly appeared. He was wearing a red baseball cap and carrying a copy of the *Post* under his arm. He insisted that he had been there all along but, overcome by an urge to read about J. Lo and Ralph Fiennes, had just stepped out to buy the paper. Woods made it clear that she didn't believe a word of this, then nevertheless struck the violation.

We headed downstairs. Four or five workers were cleaning furiously, sweeping up and moving boxes. The freezer checked out satisfactorily, as did the dishwasher. Woods asked to see the thermometer that the restaurant used to monitor food temperature, but none of the workers could come up with one. Meanwhile, Washington noticed an infestation of flies in the basement.

Back upstairs, Woods and Washington sat down in the dining room to fill out their report. As they were writing, a young man, smiling sheepishly and clutching his shirt, walked into the restaurant. Woods and Washington exchanged looks. After a few minutes, another young man emerged from the back, waving a thermometer. Woods examined it.

"Where'd you buy that from?" she asked the owner.

"I had it," he said, as if wounded by her skepticism. He sat down at the table and watched as the inspectors continued to write. He was wearing flip-flops, which he kept clicking against his soles. Finally, Woods and Washington handed him their report. The restaurant had two critical violations—the warm eggs and the fly infestation—and three general ones, meaning that it had passed. The owner was still facing fines, but he was relieved enough to start joking. He said he already had a plan to get the fines reduced. "I go in and cry," he said cheerfully.

Woods and Washington began to pack up their things. It had been a long day, and, from a public-health standpoint, not a particularly encouraging one: they had issued twenty-four violations. On the other hand, they had made it through three inspections without being physically threatened, or even verbally abused. (Washington told me that an irate restaurateur had once hurled a bug zapper at his head.) Around us, a handful of diners were still finishing lunch. They must have suspected what was going on but continued to chat, to argue, and to eat. I had noticed this pattern at the diner, and also at the Chinese place, where customers had kept right on ordering despite the commotion. Perhaps they were confident enough in the food they were being served not to worry, or perhaps—and this seems more likely—they just didn't want to know.

Six Billion Short

January 2003

T HE CITIZENS BUDGET Commission, a watchdog group funded by some of the city's major businesspeople, describes its goal as "influencing constructive change" in civic life. To this end, it holds periodic seminars and issues papers with titles like "A Proposal to Increase the Productivity of Non-Managerial Civilian Municipal Workers." All mayors find the C.B.C.'s high-minded efforts an irritant—some more than others. Rudolph Giuliani refused even to deal with the group, and one year went so far as to try to organize a boycott of its annual fundraising dinner.

Last month, Mayor Michael Bloomberg agreed to be the keynote speaker at a weekend conference that the C.B.C. was holding. He began, characteristically, with a joke: "If you don't mind, I'd like to take a few minutes off and call Rudy and ask him whether this was an intelligent thing to do." He went on to acknowledge some of those present, including the New York public advocate, Betsy Gotbaum, whom, he said, he often met on Saturday mornings anyway, at the hair salon, and also the City Council speaker, Gifford Miller, who, he speculated, got his hair done someplace different—"cheaper, probably." Then he said, "All kidding aside, we are in the middle of some very tough times."

Bloomberg put the size of the city's budget gap for the next fiscal year at $6.4 billion. Depending on how you calculate, this shortfall represents a sixth of the city's budget or a quarter of it. The lower figure is the gap expressed as a proportion of all city revenues, the higher as a proportion of only those revenues raised from city taxpayers. Measured another way, the gap corresponds roughly to the total annual expenditures of New York's

Police, Fire, Sanitation, and Corrections Departments combined, or, alternatively, more than the entire 2002 budget for the city of Houston and its surrounding county.

"The law requires us to close the gap," the Mayor declared. "Our expenses and revenues have to be the same, and, regardless of the pain, we will make them the same." He praised the City Council for having recently approved the largest property-tax rate hike in New York history— eighteen and a half per cent—saying that members of the Council had acted "dramatically and courageously," and he alluded to a series of spending cuts that his administration has in the works. Nevertheless, he insisted, to the surprise of many in the audience, that the city should not be called on to reduce expenditures any further.

"The fact of the matter is we have cut as much as I believe we can," Bloomberg said. "More cuts risk adversely affecting New York City's quality of life and reducing the ability to grow our way out of this problem."

How the city does get out of its problem—or fails to—will be settled sometime in the months ahead. In a few weeks, the Mayor will present his financial plan for the upcoming fiscal year, and Governor George Pataki will present his proposed state budget, in Albany. (In his inaugural address last week, Pataki described the fiscal problems facing the state as "historic, grave, and daunting.") At issue in an immediate sense is how to fill the city's budget gap—whether through additional spending cuts, higher taxes, state aid, or creative accounting. At stake in a larger sense are New York's prospects five, ten, perhaps even twenty-five years from now. As Bloomberg observed, "Someone once said that the holidays are when kids get what they want and adults pay for it. A budget shortfall is when adults get what they want and their kids pay for it." Then he caught himself. "We're not going to do that."

The last time New York experienced a shortfall of this magnitude was during the fiscal crisis of the seventies—a parallel that is not, of course, terribly reassuring. That shortfall, which was the result of genuine idealism, calculated generosity, and extremely bad bookkeeping, several times brought the city to the edge of bankruptcy: The problems began in the late nineteen-sixties, when Mayor John Lindsay presided over an ambitious expansion of the city's anti-poverty programs at the same time that he was negotiating a series of beneficent contracts with its municipal unions. (One pension "sweetener," for the teachers' union, was later described as "the largest unconditional commitment of city funds in the history of American city government.") During Lindsay's first term, spending grew by an average of more than fifteen per cent a year, and in his second term by more than ten per cent a year. The city imposed an income tax, raised the property tax, and doubled the subway fare, but revenues still could not keep pace. The Lindsay administration dealt with this inconvenience by issuing debt. As the notes came due, the city covered them by issuing more debt, until a recession hit and the whole house-of-cards arrangement finally collapsed.

When it did, Mayor Abe Beame was standing under it. He was a year into his term, and his first reaction was to temporize, either because he genuinely believed that the problem was being overstated or because he couldn't think of anything else to do. At one point, he invested fifty thousand dollars of his own money in New York notes, declaring, "The economic strengths of this city are unparalleled." When, in May of 1975, the banks refused to underwrite any more borrowing, Beame continued to insist that New York's fiscal condition was sound. He denounced the financial houses, the editorial boards, the State Legislature, and the federal government, all of whom, he charged, were "more concerned with numbers than with people."

Beame and the city got through that summer on a series of increasingly arcane financing schemes, but by early fall just about every source of money that could be tapped had been. At last, in mid-October, the Mayor presented an austerity plan aimed at bringing the budget back into balance in three years. In a cover letter to Governor Hugh Carey, Beame complained that he was being forced, in effect, to destroy New York in order to save it. "We can take no pride in the plan, because it places a higher priority on the grim realities confronting the city, rather than on the needs of our citizens," he wrote. The bitter tone of the letter, combined with the cuts that the Mayor was proposing, seemed to suggest that, in his opinion, at least, things couldn't get any worse. He was wrong. Just two days later, several hundred million dollars' worth of short-term notes came due, and the city didn't have enough cash to redeem them. Angry note-holders crowded the Municipal Building, and bond trading on Wall Street ground to a halt. Aides to the Mayor drafted a statement for him to read at the appropriate moment: "I have been advised by the comptroller that the city of New York has insufficient cash on hand to meet debt obligations due today." Default was averted—by hours—only when the teachers' pension fund agreed to loan the city a hundred and fifty million dollars.

The consequences of the fiscal crisis were nearly as dire as Beame had predicted. The crisis cost thirty-five thousand municipal workers their jobs, brought an end to free tuition at City University, forced the suspension of countless public construction projects, and generally ushered in one of the bleaker periods in the city's history. A quarter of a century and two stock-market booms later, New York is, in a very real sense, still paying for it. Every year, the first five hundred million dollars the city collects from its sales tax goes toward retiring bonds issued to resolve the crisis, and this will continue until 2008, when those bonds finally mature.

Bloomberg is not the type to find fault, either with himself or with others. When he discusses the city's fiscal problems, as he is obliged to do just about all the time these days, he pointedly tries to avoid assigning blame. "No one's at fault, or maybe, in a different sense, we all are," he said recently. "Let's today not look to the past and say what might have been if we knew what was going to happen."

As a matter of record, no great clairvoyance was required, and many groups, including the C.B.C., forecast what was going to happen quite accurately. In the late nineties, New York's economy boomed, and then the boom ended. During the first half of the cycle, cash flooded into the city treasury; every time Goldman Sachs handed out a round of bonuses, or a Silicon Alley start-up went public, New York, thanks to its income tax, took a percentage. Thus, even as the city was cutting its hotel tax, its commercial-rent tax, and its sales tax on clothing, total tax revenues were steadily growing.

Giuliani, who had always cast himself as a fiscal conservative, had to decide what to do with this embarrassment of riches. On reflection, he chose to spend it. He increased the education budget by half, and the police budget by nearly three-quarters. The number of city employees, which had declined significantly during the early nineties, swelled back up to a near-record figure of two hundred and fifty thousand. Meanwhile, the bill for debt service in New York rose by two-thirds, and, owing largely to actions in Albany, the city's pension costs almost doubled. The increased spending certainly made New York a nicer place to live, but it was the civic equivalent of counting on the Pick-6 to meet your mortgage payments. Even before Giuliani left office, the economy was clearly turning. Nevertheless, in his final budget, which the City Council approved just three months before the World Trade Center attack, he increased expenditures by nearly two and a half billion dollars. By the end of that fiscal year, in June, 2002, tax collections had dropped by more than a billion dollars.

Immediately on taking office, last January, Bloomberg had to deal with this shortfall and, more fundamentally, with a government that had once again grown beyond its means. He argued that because of September 11th, which cost the city some hundred and twenty thousand jobs, it was not the moment to raise taxes or drastically cut spending, and he announced plans to balance the budget by borrowing $1.5 billion. This subsequently became $2 billion. The borrowing bought time, but at the cost of a hundred and eighty million dollars a year in added debt-service charges.

Since then, the city's fiscal situation has only deteriorated. Tax revenues have been lower than anticipated, and savings that Bloomberg had been counting on, including two hundred and fifty million dollars in unspecified "productivity increases," never materialized. The property-tax increase and the cuts that the Mayor pushed through in November will probably get the city through the current fiscal year, which ends in June. But even according to Bloomberg's own figures they barely go halfway toward filling the $6.4-billion gap projected for the year after.

When the Mayor makes his budget presentation, he will, presumably, give a detailed account of how he plans to close the rest of the gap. One proposal that he has floated involves lowering the city's top income-tax rate while extending the tax to a million or so commuters. (As the tabloids pointed out with delight, those who would fare best under this plan are the city's wealthiest residents, Bloomberg included, who would save tens of thousands of dollars a year.) The Mayor's justification for the plan is that commuters use city services, too. "Last time I checked, when the firefighters went into the World Trade Center they didn't ask anybody where the hell they lived," he has said. Although there may be an argument here, in a practical sense it's almost beside the point, since the only group that has the power to extend the tax is the New York State Legislature.

In fact, until a few years ago, when the legislature chose to meddle in the matter, New York had a commuter tax, which brought in three hundred and fifty million dollars a year. The tax was repealed in the spring of 1999, in a nakedly partisan effort to influence a special election in Rockland County. ("God forgive you all," Tony Seminerio, a Queens assemblyman who voted against the repeal, told his colleagues. "You don't deserve to be elected officials.") Bloomberg is hoping not just to revive the recently killed tax but to quintuple it. As the New York State Financial Control Board, a relic of the last fiscal crisis, delicately put it in December, his plan "relies on actions outside of the city's control and seems unlikely to elicit an entirely favorable response from its intended partners."

Bloomberg is, in general, an optimist. As a candidate, he used to warn against driving people out of New York. "Raising taxes is not an option!" he declared. Now that he has done just that, he cheerfully asserts that there's nothing to worry about: "I don't believe that people will leave this city because of higher taxes. I do believe they would leave this city very quickly because of lower services." Bloomberg maintains that another boom is just around the corner, and that the important thing is not to overreact to temporary setbacks. "I think New Yorkers expect me to run city government in much the same ways I ran my company," he observed a few weeks ago. "Fair enough. I didn't build the most successful media company in the world with layoffs." A little solicitude, he seems to believe, will be enough to win over the State Legislature. Not long ago, he flew the Assembly speaker, Sheldon Silver, and the Senate majority leader, Joseph Bruno, down to his house in Bermuda for a few rounds of golf.

Optimism is a reassuring quality in a mayor, and Bloomberg's successes so far—gaining mayoral control of the school system, pushing through tough new smoking restrictions—probably would not have been possible without it. But, unchecked, hopefulness can start to sound uncomfortably like evasion. "Now it's time, since we've done what we can, for others to step up to the plate," he told the C.B.C.

In 1975, a different mayor could probably have averted the fiscal crisis, or at least softened its worst effects. Abe Beame, a product of Brooklyn clubhouse politics, was too timid and, eventually, found himself sidelined. A few months into the crisis, the State Legislature created a new agency, the Municipal Assistance Corporation, or MAC, to, in effect, run the city's finances. Its chairman was the investment banker Felix Rohatyn, who, along with Governor Carey, is generally credited with saving New York from insolvency.

Not long ago, I went to visit Rohatyn at his apartment on Fifth Avenue. Rohatyn is now seventy-four, with white hair and salt-and-pepper eyebrows, and heads a financial-consulting firm. "There are similarities in the surrounding ethos, if you will, of today and the seventies," he told me in his distinctive low murmur. "In the seventies, there was a war in the Middle East, we had the stock-exchange collapse, we had Nixon going into Cambodia, and we had a recession economy." Taking into account the national economy, which is weak, and the state's fiscal condition, which is precarious—during the boom, Governor Pataki, too, spent everything that came in, and then some—Rohatyn said it was hard to judge whether New York is any better off than it was in the mid-seventies: "We had a situation which is not present today, which is bankruptcy, although there are other issues that are maybe worse than what we had." He noted that, perversely, one disadvantage now is the absence of inflationary pressure: "I have never said publicly that we owed our balanced budget to the Arab oil embargo, but it certainly helped. It's very difficult to do this if you don't have some inflation that drives your revenues."

As chairman of MAC, Rohatyn oversaw the restructuring of the city's debt. MAC paid off the city's short-term notes—the source of its continual cash-flow problems—by issuing thirty-year bonds. Part of the complicated

arrangement that persuaded the banks to underwrite these bonds was a
thorough overhaul of the city's books. New accounting standards were
imposed that make it all but impossible for the city to hide its deficits or
issue debt to pay for routine expenses. Now, if it ends the fiscal year with
even a relatively modest shortfall, the Financial Control Board automa-
tically takes over its finances.

During the twenty-five years that these rules have been in effect, they
have probably prevented a good deal of chicanery; still, as the city's current
difficulties demonstrate, they have their limits. "It was obvious that the
market was going to crash at some point," Rohatyn told me. But as long as
money was pouring in there was nothing in the rules to prevent the city
from spending it. "Maybe the accountants could have said, 'You cannot
treat this windfall as recurring revenues,'" Rohatyn said. "Or the rating
agencies could have said, 'You can't borrow against these revenues as if they
were permanent.' Or the Control Board. But that's introducing outsiders
into the system. You can do that when there's a crisis. When I served on the
Control Board and was chairman of MAC, we did some of these things, but
immediately people would say, 'Well, who elected Felix?' And they were
right."

Rohatyn described the choices facing the city today as "pain or more
pain," and he urged Mayor Bloomberg and Governor Pataki to appeal to
Washington for some form of revenue-sharing aid to get through this
difficult time. "The Mayor and the Governor have to try to create a national
coalition and go to the federal government for temporary assistance to state
and local governments. If we have to close these deficits at the local level,
it's all taxes and cuts, which is very deflationary and recessionary. Frankly,
other than that, I don't see anything that is likely to give us any significant
relief."

How well or how badly the city fares in the coming year will depend on
a lot of things, including the amount of aid the federal government does
provide, the direction the stock market takes, and the outcome of events in
Iraq. Ultimately, though, it will be up to the Mayor and the City Council
to balance the budget—"regardless of the pain," as Bloomberg put it—
because under the current rules the only alternative is to hand that task
over to the Financial Control Board. In the seventies, the city's political

culture failed, and it wasn't until after the bankruptcy papers had been drawn up that the necessary austerities were accepted. Perhaps this time around the city will act in time to avoid a full-blown crisis. The worry always is that it can't act without one.

Accountants in the Sky

May 2003

B EFORE I WORKED in Albany, I had always wanted to be a political
reporter, perhaps because I had no real idea what the job entailed. I
arrived there on December 31, 1986, the eve of Mario Cuomo's second
inaugural, and almost immediately was assigned to cover a scandal
involving an assemblywoman named Gerdi Lipschutz. A sixty-three-
year-old former dental assistant from Queens, Lipschutz had served in
the Legislature for six terms and had risen to the chairmanship of the
Assembly Majority Steering Committee. At the behest of her county's
Democratic organization, she had also, prosecutors revealed, maintained
two "no-show" employees on her legislative payroll. First, her indignant
colleagues shunned her; later, they voted to strip her of her seniority and
deprive her of her legislative stipend—or "lulu"—and collectively called
on her to resign. On her last day in office, it fell to me to follow her out to
her car in the Capitol's underground garage. I can still recall the baleful
look that she shot me when I asked her if she had any final observations to
share about her situation.

In principle, Albany is a state capital much like any other, with
struggles that are no more or less edifying; as a practical matter, anyone
who has ever spent much time there knows different. (William Kennedy,
Albany's Virgil, who has described the city as "a state of mind," notes that
"wickedness has been our lot for more years than any man alive can
remember.") I ended up reporting on Albany for five legislative sessions.
During that time, the State Senate Minority Leader, Manfred Ohrenstein,
was indicted on five hundred and sixty-four counts of grand larceny and
conspiracy, and the Assembly Speaker, Mel Miller, was indicted on

nineteen counts of conspiracy and mail fraud. Both cases were eventually dismissed. (Shortly after I left, the state's chief judge, Sol Wachtler, was charged with extortion after demanding a payoff from his ex-girlfriend and threatening to kidnap her daughter.) The commanding officer of the New York State militia was discovered not only to have accepted bribes and falsified official documents but also to have been a bigamist, and two janitorial workers were reprimanded for having had sex—repeatedly—on a desk at the headquarters of the New York State Department of Transportation. The state's drug-treatment commissioner was forced to resign after allegations that he had steered contracts to friends who failed to provide any actual drug treatment. He became a pushcart vender and on warm days sold hot dogs in front of the Capitol. He called himself the Knishener.

Late last month, I went back to the Capitol to see how Albany would handle this year's twelve-billion-dollar budget gap, the worst since the Great Depression. On the first day I spent in the city, the state's legislative leaders emerged from a meeting with Governor George Pataki to say that they still hoped to reach an agreement with him on a spending plan, which was interpreted to mean that they had reached an impasse. On the second day, the Governor asserted, "In times of challenge, New Yorkers have always stood together in making the right decisions," which was understood to signal a complete breakdown in negotiations. By the end of the week, the Legislature had approved a ninety-three-billion-dollar budget that violated just about every condition Pataki had laid down. The Governor has labelled it "patently unconstitutional." At one point, standing in the Capitol's Red Room, he declared, "I will do everything in my ability to prevent this plan from becoming law, including exercising my veto powers." Depending on how things play out, the struggle between the Governor and the Legislature will either merely prolong the state's fiscal problems or, more likely, compound them.

Such are the ways of Albany that when things seem to be proceeding in an orderly, democratic fashion it is an almost sure bet that they are about to spin out of control. Thus, the first sign that the budget process had broken down last month came when it began to move forward. Members of the

State Senate and the Assembly returned to work after a ten-day spring recess to find that budget bills had been printed and were being distributed by the clerks who sit on either side of the Capitol. Lobbyists wandered through the hallways, clutching legislation with titles like "An act to amend the general business law, in relation to allowing the department of correctional services' division of correctional industries to purchase inmate-made goods," and grinning like kids who have just discovered their dad's stack of *Juggs*.

In general, the only way to make sense of what goes on in the Capitol is to turn things on their head. The Assembly meets in a grand chamber with red granite columns and carved sandstone pilasters. The Senate convenes in an even more splendid room, with walls covered in embossed Spanish leather, Mexican onyx, and 23k. gold leaf. Meanwhile, all the decisions that matter occur elsewhere. Of the two hundred and twelve members of the Legislature, two hundred and ten are, for all intents and purposes, superfluous, like so many extras from "Gangs of New York." ("What's the difference between a state legislator and a welfare recipient?" ran a joke that recently made the rounds in the Capitol. "At least the welfare recipient has a work requirement.")

The two legislators who do count are the Senate Majority Leader, Joseph Bruno, and the Assembly Speaker, Sheldon Silver. Bruno, a Republican from the city of Troy, made a lot of money selling telephone systems and now owns a horse farm. He dresses well—Mario Cuomo used to make fun of his good looks—and radiates geniality. Silver, a Democrat from lower Manhattan, is by training a trial lawyer and by temperament a misanthrope. He speaks in a lugubrious baritone, and generally gives the impression of having just returned from a funeral.

Partly because of the New York State constitution and partly because of the way the constitution has been exploited, these two men are, in their own spheres, virtually omnipotent. The Legislature has an elaborate committee structure, which is supposed to insure that every bill can be debated, in public, by lawmakers who are knowledgeable in the subject area. In reality, if a bill is of any significance it is Bruno and Silver who determine, independently of the committees, whether or not it will advance. The same is true once a bill gets to the floor. In Albany, except under total-eclipse-of-the-sun-like circumstances, votes have only one possible result.

David Paterson, a Democrat from upper Manhattan, is the Minority Leader of the State Senate, which sounds like a position that has considerable authority but, because of the way the Legislature is organized, has very little. Paterson has been in the Senate for eighteen years, and in this time has watched some seventy-five thousand pieces of legislation come to the floor. He told me that in only four instances had there been any uncertainty about the outcome of the vote, and in only one, involving a constitutional amendment to allow casino gambling, had the measure actually failed. He recalled the event wistfully: "Then you start to feel like you're a real senator, on TV.

"How do you get such uniformity of voting from such individual people from different regions of the state, diverse populations, and different income groups?" Paterson went on. "Because everybody's afraid of the leader. And if you don't coöperate you may go back to your office and find that the lights are off and the computers are shut down. Sometimes you go back to your office and the door is locked."

So well established is the leaders' dominance that, by now, even keeping up the pretense of deliberation is regarded as a waste of effort. When I was in the Capitol recently, I happened in on a meeting of the Senate Committee on Veterans, Homeland Security, and Military Affairs. Only two members had bothered to show up—the eleven others were voting via proxy—and neither had a word to say in defense of or opposition to any of the five measures under consideration. It took about ninety seconds for the chairman to call the meeting to order, run through the agenda—one bill was held in committee and four were reported out—and adjourn. Later that afternoon, the Assembly took up the first two budget bills, worth more than ten billion dollars. The debate, such as it was, lasted less than fifteen minutes. As legislators went through the motions of considering the second bill, a member of the Assembly's Republican minority, James Tedisco, of Schenectady County, rose to berate the members of the majority for their slavish behavior. "You're going to vote for whatever the Speaker tells you to vote for," he said. Tedisco pointed out, accurately, that lawmakers were being asked to vote on a spending plan before the bill laying out the tax increases intended to pay for it had even been introduced. "It is very clear that you don't give a rat's tail," he declared. No one in the room took the trouble to challenge Tedisco's account, although one Democrat stood to observe that the minority was really no different: "Could you just enlighten us what makes you so special?" (Two days later, in fact, the ranking Republican assemblyman on the Racing and Wagering Committee was stripped of his position by the Assembly Minority Leader for refusing to vote the party line.)

A particularly neat illustration of how Albany has reinterpreted the rules of democracy is provided by the so-called message of necessity. As its name suggests, the measure is supposed to be invoked only in emergencies. It allows the Legislature, with the approval of the governor, to introduce and vote on bills virtually instantaneously, with no time at all for public input. Such are the attractions of this arrangement that nowadays in the Capitol an emergency is declared whenever it's convenient. Not long ago, Eric Lane, a professor at Hofstra Law School, decided to try to quantify the phenomenon. He found that eighty per cent of the major bills that were approved in the past several years had been passed under messages of necessity.

This spring, the state was facing a genuine fiscal emergency, so, by the logic of Albany, the Capitol had to revert to actually observing the constitution. Since Bruno and Silver were at war with the Governor, they couldn't ask him for a message, and had to have the budget bills printed a full three days in advance of scheduling a vote on them. As one public-interest lobbyist I ran into observed with grim satisfaction, "This is practically open government."

On the same day the Legislature began to pass its budget, the Governor began to issue dire warnings about the consequences. In particular, he objected to the Legislature's plan to restore many of the spending cuts he had proposed and to raise the state's income-tax and sales-tax rates in order to do so. He presented the choice confronting New York in Manichaean terms. On one side were those who planned to "show the courage, the leadership, the fiscal restraint necessary to balance the state budget without gimmicks or taxes," and on the other were those who intended to "ignore the realities, revert to politics as usual and, in the process, prolong the fiscal and economic crisis." Although the Governor declined to name names, he made it clear that, in his view, at least, the former group had only one member.

New York's impending budget catastrophe had been evident for at least two years, and possibly longer. Between the bursting of the Internet bubble, in 2000, and now, the state lost an estimated three hundred thousand jobs. State tax receipts, after growing on average by more than seven per cent a year through the late nineteen-nineties, shrank by an average of nearly five per cent in 2001 and 2002. Pataki's immediate response to all this bad news, courage and leadership notwithstanding, was to ignore it. In 2002, a gubernatorial-election year, he crisscrossed the state insisting that things had never been better—"Our state remains firmly on the right track"—and, rather than trying to restrain spending, proposed a budget that increased it by four billion dollars. In an all but explicit deal for the support of 1199/S.E.I.U., the state's powerful—and politically active—hospital workers' union, he promised, for example, two billion dollars in salary increases. When, shortly before the election, his fellow-Republican Joseph Bruno acknowledged that the state was facing a ten-billion-dollar budget shortfall, Pataki dismissed this, telling the *News*, "I don't know where it came from. Joe is a wonderful leader. He doesn't always do thorough research before putting out an analysis." A few weeks later, while the voting machines were still being packed away, the Governor let it be known that Bruno had been right about the ten billion dollars, except that the figure was actually closer to twelve billion.

New York has always been something of a pioneer in the field of fiscal mis-management. The Capitol itself is a prime example. In 1867, when the building was commissioned, the anticipated cost was four million dollars; by 1874, only two out of five stories had been completed, but the estimated cost had tripled. New York was an early issuer of debt—it floated some of the nation's first state bonds to pay for the construction of the Erie Canal—and, since then, has borrowed against the classroom buildings at its state universities, a parking lot at the Aqueduct racetrack, and revenues that it hopes in a vague sort of way may somehow materialize in the future.

Governor Nelson Rockefeller, whose plans for the state invariably out-
stripped its ability to pay for them, was particularly innovative in this way.
In the nineteen-sixties, to build Albany's Brasília-like Empire State Plaza,
he transferred the land next to the Capitol to Albany County, had the
county pay for the plaza's construction, and then bought the whole thing
back for the state through an elaborate lease-purchase agreement. When I
was in Albany in the late nineteen-eighties, the Cuomo administration
came up with an arguably even more inventive scheme: "selling" Attica
prison to New York's Urban Development Corporation, for two hundred
million dollars. The arrangement ended up costing New York taxpayers
some two hundred and ninety million dollars in interest payments, but
from the administration's perspective it worked out so well that Cuomo
subsequently "sold" a section of I–84 to the Thruway Authority, which
also assumed the road's multimillion-dollar maintenance costs. "I did not
come into government to win an award as the great accountant in the sky,"
he once declared.

Even against such illustrious predecessors, Pataki has managed to hold
his own. (A recent piece in *The Economist* called him "the governor who
gave away the store.") Most of Pataki's first two terms coincided with one
of the longest economic expansions in American history. In that period of
enormous growth, he nevertheless managed to preside over an impressive
increase in state borrowing: New York took on ten billion dollars' worth of
new debt in less than eight years. Its outstanding obligations now amount
to thirty-eight billion dollars, making it—Excelsior!—by far the most
indebted state in the nation. (California, the runner-up, has obligations of
thirty-three billion.)

Pataki presented his own budget plan back in January. In contrast to the
Legislature's, it calls for significant cuts in state aid to education and health
care and no increase in the state's broad-based taxes. Still, to call it fiscally
responsible would be quite a stretch. Pataki has recommended that the
state create yet another authority, simply in order to borrow, in this case
against money that New York is set to receive as a result of the 1998
tobacco settlement. (He has also proposed using the money that is to be
raised this way—some four billion dollars—to pay routine operating
expenses, just the sort of move, fiscal monitors have pointed out, that

brought New York City to the edge of bankruptcy in 1975.) When, last month, it was revealed that the tobacco companies might not be able to make the payments that Pataki's plan is based upon, his response, rather than to reduce the amount of proposed borrowing, was to lament that the debt had not already been issued. "It would have been better to go in December, and that's why I was pushing it in December," he said.

A few days after the Governor and the Legislature stopped speaking to each other, Mayor Michael Bloomberg went up to Albany to discuss New York City's budget problems, which every month grow more severe. The state's job loss has been concentrated in the city—the unemployment rate here is now more than nine per cent—and, for obvious reasons, the city's treasury has been particularly hard-hit by the collapse of the stock market and the events of September 11th. Last month, when the Mayor issued his revised budget, he said that under the best-case scenario the city would have to lay off forty-five hundred workers in the coming year, and under the worst case fifteen thousand.

One of the most touching aspects of Bloomberg's mayoralty has been his enduring faith that Albany would act to help the city, if only because it was in everyone's best interests. The Mayor's fondest fantasy was a multibillion-dollar commuter tax on those who work in the city but live elsewhere—an idea he continued to push long after everyone else in New York politics had abandoned it, which was about ten seconds after he brought it up. Initially, Bloomberg seems to have believed that Pataki was going to be his ally in this quest. During the gubernatorial campaign, the Mayor held a fundraiser for Pataki at his town house on the Upper East Side, and, at significant political risk to himself, he waited until after the Governor had been safely reëlected to push through an eighteen-and-a-half-per-cent city property-tax increase. At just about every point, however, Pataki rewarded the Mayor's fealty with indifference. Not only did the Governor nix the commuter tax; when he presented his spending plan, he proposed cutting annual state aid to the city by nearly a billion dollars. (In one particularly treacherous move, the Governor suggested rejiggering the state's Medicaid formula in a way that would have saved most counties money but increased costs to the five boroughs.)

In the plan that the Legislature recently adopted, much of the aid to the city that the Governor had threatened to cut was restored. For the remainder, the Mayor won permission from the Legislature to raise the city's sales tax by an eighth of a per cent and impose an income-tax surcharge on city residents earning more than a hundred thousand dollars. These increases would come on top of the one-quarter-per-cent increase in the state sales tax and the surcharge on the state income tax that the Legislature has approved, and potentially place the city at a disadvantage vis-à-vis its suburbs. (This was what the Mayor had hoped to avoid with a commuter tax.) Then the lawmakers came up with a plan to refinance the debt the city is still paying off from the fiscal crisis of the nineteen-seventies. Short term, it will save the city half a billion dollars a year; long term, it means that in 2033 our children will still be paying for the sins of our fathers. Putting the best face on events, as he so often does, Bloomberg declared himself satisfied, saying, "It is painful, but it is the right thing to do."

Local taxes will be going up next year not only in the city but across the state. Already, for example, Nassau County has announced a twenty-per-cent increase in property taxes, and Rensselaer County has announced a twenty-eight-per-cent hike. Rising local taxes are the reason that Silver and Bruno were under such pressure to resist Pataki. Of the ninety billion-plus that Albany spends every year—debt service and pension costs excluded—nearly seventy per cent is distributed to hospitals and local governments in the form of payments like Medicaid and school aid. Thus, when the state cuts its budget, most of the savings come from simply shifting the losses onto county legislatures and school districts. These bodies can, in turn, cut services, but only up to a point: the state itself imposes very specific mandates about what services must be provided. Seen in this context, Pataki's insistence on not raising state taxes may represent a genuine fiscal policy decision or it may simply amount to so much political rhetoric. The latter interpretation is the more popular in Albany; it is generally taken for granted in the Capitol that the Governor's top priority these days is finding a new job for himself, perhaps in the Bush Administration.

What happens next in Albany is, at this point, anybody's guess. It is possible that the Senate and the Assembly will fail to override Pataki's promised vetoes, in which case parts of the budget will have to be negotiated all over again. Or it's possible that they will succeed, in which case Pataki may mount a legal challenge. Finally, it is possible that some sort of compromise will be worked out. Whatever the outcome, the conflict itself will have been extremely costly, generating yet more uncertainty at a moment when, as Governor Pataki put it, "we owe it to the people of New York to again rise and meet the challenges we face and demonstrate the courage to make the right decisions at the right time for the right reasons."

Not long ago, I went to a forum on Albany politics—"Three Men and a Budget: What's Wrong with New York's Legislative Process and How Do We Fix It?"—sponsored by the New York City Bar Association. Participants included both good-government types, like Blair Horner, the legislative director of the New York Public Interest Research Group, and industry lobbyists, like Lester Shulklapper, whose clients include the state Beer Wholesalers Association and R. J. Reynolds Tobacco Company. A good part of the evening was devoted to rehearsing the various ways in which ostensibly democratic procedures and institutions have been subverted. Eric Lane, the Hofstra Law School professor, noted that the staffs of legislative committees are hired not by the committee chairmen but by the legislative leaders. "If you understand the Albany mentality, that is done so committees can't function," he said. Horner pointed out that in Albany redistricting is controlled by those who stand to benefit from it the most, so "the system is rigged to begin with." Alone among the panelists, Shulklapper defended the ways of the Capitol, observing, "There have been wonderful debates in the Legislature." (He recalled one, on the topic of abortion, which took place in 1970.) The participants—again with the exception of Shulklapper—agreed that Albany was a fantastically inefficient place in all ways except one. For the last nineteen years, the Legislature has not managed to pass the state budget on time even once, but during that same period ninety-nine per cent of incumbent lawmakers held on to their seats in general elections. Viewed in these terms, Albany does what it does all too well. The key to understanding Capitol politics is knowing what matters and what doesn't.

At one point in the evening, I bumped into Andrew Cuomo, the former

U.S. housing secretary, who ran for governor of New York last year and lost. I first met Cuomo when he was building housing for the homeless in Brooklyn and I was covering his father. He asked me what I was doing, and I told him that I was planning to write a piece about Albany. He laughed. "But who would read it?" he asked.

The Student

October 2003

O N JANUARY 26, 1993, six days after becoming First Lady, Hillary Rodham Clinton paid a private visit to Jacqueline Kennedy Onassis. The encounter took place at Onassis's Fifth Avenue apartment, where lunch was served in the living room, overlooking Central Park. The two women had met only a few times before, but Clinton had sought out Onassis as one of the few women in America who could understand what she was going through. They talked for two hours about, among other things, the dangers faced by charismatic leaders and the challenge of raising children in the public eye. Eventually, the conversation turned to clothes. Nearly everything that Clinton had done in her first days in the White House had been criticized, from her decision to move into an office near the President's to her choice of hats. (The derby-like creation that she wore to her husband's swearing-in made her look, according to one news account, as if a flying saucer had just landed on her head.) Clinton asked Onassis whether she should hand herself over to a team of fashion consultants, as many had urged. Onassis responded with horror. "You have to be you," she told the First Lady.

The advice seemed obvious, but no sooner had Clinton returned to Washington than she ignored it. She had already been named to head the President's task force on health-care reform, an unprecedented appointment for a First Lady, and dozens of journalists were competing to land the first interview with her in her new position. Instead of granting it to a political columnist, or even to a medical reporter, Clinton chose to sit down with a food writer, Marian Burros, of the *Times*. The *Times* ran Burros's piece, which focussed on the First Lady's decision to shift the emphasis of the White House menu from French to American-style cuisine, on the front page. Clinton posed for the accompanying photograph in a high-fashion, shoulder-baring Donna Karan evening gown.

There are not supposed to be any second acts in American politics. Either because voters are impatient or because they are simply inattentive, a perception, once fixed in the public imagination—Michael Dukakis in a tank, Gary Hart on the *Monkey Business*—tends to crowd out the possibility of all others. A reputation for disingenuousness would seem to be particularly damaging, since any attempt to dislodge it is bound to be construed as another piece of insincerity.

Depending on how you reckon, Clinton's second act began either three years ago, with her election to the United States Senate, or somewhat further back, with the revelation of her husband's infidelity. It reached a triumphant peak this summer, with the publication of "Living History," her extended meditation on the tribulations of being First Lady. Such is Clinton's treatment of her subject, which is to say herself, that when trouble arises it is almost always from a surfeit of good intentions. "With Jackie's tacit permission, I determined to continue having fun," Clinton writes of her encounter with Onassis, and she ascribes the flap over her dress to the narrow imagination of her critics: "I cared about the food I served our guests, and I also wanted to improve the delivery of health care for all Americans." The memoir has sold nearly a million and a half copies in the United States alone, more than recouping the eight million dollars that Simon & Schuster paid for it. (It has also been published abroad in thirty-five languages.) In a circular sort of way, its sales have no doubt benefitted from, and at the same time contributed to, the recent state of speculation about Clinton and the Presidential race.

How Hillary Clinton, whom many members of her husband's Administration still credit with some of the worst decisions of his tenure, could have pulled off such a remarkable recovery is mysterious in many of the same ways that her earlier difficulties were. One possible explanation is that Clinton has far better judgment when it comes to her own career than when it comes to her husband's. Another—the one Clinton proposes in "Living History"—is that her troubles as First Lady were all just the result of a terrible misunderstanding.

*   *   *

Senator Clinton and her staff occupy the same L-shaped suite, on the fourth floor of the Russell Senate Office Building, that her predecessor, Daniel Patrick Moynihan, and his staff worked out of for twenty-two years. Clinton's office, which is at one end of the L, is spacious and airy, with a marble fireplace that holds four decoratively stacked logs. The room is painted a pale shade of daffodil, with drapes and upholstery to match, and projects what might best be described as reserved femininity. On the chairs, there are little needlepoint pillows, one stitched with a copy of the cover of Clinton's 1996 book, "It Takes a Village," another with the words "Senator Hillary." Like most politicians' offices, Clinton's is filled with photographs, but instead of the usual shots of the senator posing with luminaries, her collection includes a picture of Robert Kennedy, who also served as a senator from New York even though he wasn't from the state; a moody portrait of her husband, with his back to the camera, gazing out the windows of the Oval Office; and a composite picture of her sitting with Eleanor Roosevelt. The suite is not considered particularly desirable— Moynihan had many opportunities to upgrade, but chose not to—and Clinton ended up with it because, under the elaborate rules governing seniority, when she first entered the Senate she ranked below several other lawmakers who had entered on the same day. (Extra points go to those who have previously served as governors or congressmen, but the system gives no credit to former First Ladies.) After Moynihan retired, he came back to visit the office and pronounced the place a lot more yellow.

One morning in late May, I went down to Washington to spend a day with Clinton. When I met up with her, at around 9:30 A.M., she was sitting in her office, sipping some sort of frozen coffee concoction through a straw. Clinton is not at her best early in the day, and she looked as if she were struggling to wake up when a group of entrepreneurs-cum-environmentalists called E2 was ushered in. The group included Robert Fisher, a former president of the Gap, and its concerns ranged from overfishing of the world's oceans to the Bush Administration's legislative agenda. Clinton, sipping her coffee, agreed with the group's gloomy views about aquatic life and the President's proposals—"The Administration is taking every opportunity they can to weaken the Clean Air Act and the Clean Water Act," she said—and, finally, voiced the hope that "this will be the first of many such meetings." Then she excused herself to attend a press conference outside the Capitol.

The press conference dealt with the 2004 defense authorization bill, which was still working its way through Congress. A few months earlier, Clinton had won a seat on the Senate Armed Services Committee. When I asked her why she had wanted the assignment, she said, "I concluded that the war on terrorism is a long-term challenge, and that it will be important to understand what our military response will be and to satisfy myself we're as well defended as we need to be. It's also clear that this Administration has a strategy to starve the federal budget of everything but defense. I think that it's a mistake to turn our backs on so many of our important domestic and international priorities, but since that is the direction that these deficits and this huge debt load are taking us, I wanted to have some understanding and influence over how that money was going to be spent." Others, including many other Democrats, put the matter more succinctly. Clinton, they say, is trying to fill the gap in her résumé under national defense.

Because she is so junior, Clinton usually speaks last at Senate press conferences, and at the conference on the defense bill, which dealt with an amendment to allow National Guard members and reservists to buy into the military's health-insurance system, she had to wait through remarks by the amendment's co-sponsors, Senator Patrick Leahy, of Vermont; Senator Tom Daschle, of South Dakota; and Senator Lindsey Graham, of South Carolina. Experienced politicians often seem to zone out while their colleagues rehearse the inevitable platitudes, in this case about doing right by the men and women risking their lives to serve their country; Clinton, in contrast, always seems to be paying rapt attention. She nodded vigorously as Daschle and Leahy and Graham emphasized and reëmphasized the importance of assuring Guard members and reservists access to health care. When, finally, it was her turn to speak, she said, "What this bill basically says is that 'you're too valuable a resource for our country for us to treat you like this.'" Then she thanked her colleagues, especially Graham, the quartet's only Republican, who, she noted, had himself served in the National Guard.

By the time the press conference broke up, it was almost noon. Clinton had three events in three different parts of Washington to attend over lunch—a surprise party for a friend, a meeting with the Senate's Democratic caucus, and an awards ceremony organized by a group called Girls Inc. That afternoon, there was going to be a vote on the defense-bill amendment, and while Clinton was being ferried around the city her press staff was trying to arrange another news conference, this one with Graham alone. In 1999, Graham, then a congressman, served as one of the thirteen House managers who presented the case against Bill Clinton to the Senate during his impeachment trial. ("He was told to abide by the rules of litigation, and he cheated, and you've got to put him back in bounds," Graham said at the time, referring to the President. "Remove him.") From a public-relations perspective, there was an obvious appeal in bringing the old antagonists together, and after the amendment had been approved, 85–10, Clinton and Graham climbed up to the Senate Press Gallery and plopped down next to each other in a pair of leather chairs. About a dozen reporters wandered over. One woman was wearing a bright-pink outfit. Clinton, who was dressed in one of her trademark black suits, called out, "Love the fuchsia, girl!"

Clinton's extraordinary celebrity is the unspoken but determining condition of all her interactions. Sitting next to her, Graham seemed at once excited and vaguely embarrassed, like a kid who has been caught showing off. "Well, this is, I think, the first thing I've ever had passed," he announced. "I'm going to try to talk more with the senator from New York." He appeared to be at a loss for what to call the former First Lady, at one point referring to her simply as "she." Clinton, for her part, kept referring to Graham as "Lindsey." She seemed completely relaxed, and if she was aware of Graham's discomfiture—presumably, she was—she apparently found it gratifying. One reporter asked about the amendment's prospects in the House.

"We're about to start working on that," Clinton said. "I think both of us are a little surprised that we got it through here in a week."

"I'm shocked," Graham interjected. "I'm awed and shocked."

Clinton laughed. "That's right," she said. "I think it's because people were so awed and shocked by us working together that they just basically threw up their hands, you know, and said, 'O.K.!' "

When Clinton was first elected, she was often asked how she thought she would fare in the Senate, given her and her husband's history with that body. Clinton professed herself unconcerned. "I think I will get a very positive reception," she asserted at her first post-election news conference, in Manhattan. "I have worked with a number of the Republican members in the past. I'm looking forward to working with them on a bipartisan basis on issues that affect their states, as well as New York, and of course our entire country." The same day, speaking in Mississippi, Senator Trent Lott, then the Majority Leader, declared, "I tell you one thing, when this Hillary gets to the Senate, if she does—maybe lightning will strike, and she won't—she will be one of a hundred, and we won't let her forget it."

To a large degree, Clinton's confidence now appears to have been justified. In addition to the amendment to the armed-services budget that she sponsored with Lindsey Graham, Clinton has co-sponsored measures with Gordon Smith, Republican of Oregon, to promote careers in nursing; with Don Nickles, Republican of Oklahoma, to extend unemployment benefits; and with John Warner, Republican of Virginia, to assist people caring for elderly or disabled relatives. (A measure that Clinton co-sponsored with Senator Kay Bailey Hutchison, a Republican from Texas, to establish a program to recruit professionals as teachers, was approved as part of the education bill that passed the Senate in 2001.) Some former Clinton detractors, like Senator James Inhofe, Republican of Oklahoma, now go so far as to refer to her as a friend. At the top of a voluminous pile of documents that Clinton's staff sent to me was a compilation of flattering quotes, including several from congressional and Senate colleagues, many of whom had wrangled with her in the past or voted in favor of throwing her husband out of office, or both.

"I think she's doing fine," Senator Lott was now quoted as saying. "I think she's trying to dig in and do her homework, trying to lower her profile a little bit."

As it happened, Clinton's next meeting of the day was with Asa Hutchinson, Under-Secretary for Border and Transportation Security at the Department of Homeland Security. Hutchinson, who is from Arkansas, is a former congressman and, with Graham, served as a manager in Bill Clinton's impeachment trial. Senator Clinton had requested the meeting, which took place in her office, to discuss topics like security at small airports. As it was breaking up, Hutchinson turned to her and said, with what seemed to be genuine admiration, "Congratulations. It's just an amazing feat what you have done."

"I'm having the time of my life," Clinton responded. "I pinch myself every morning."

Clinton's journey to the Senate began, more or less officially, on July 7, 1999, with the announcement that she was forming a campaign committee. As the site for the announcement, Clinton chose Daniel Patrick Moynihan's farm, in the tiny upstate New York town of Pindars Corners. She conferred with the Senator in a one-room schoolhouse, then walked down the road with him to a newly mown hayfield where risers had been set up for the cameras. Clinton pronounced herself "very humbled and more than a little surprised to be here." She raised the concerns that, she supposed, were on everybody's mind—"Why the Senate? Why New York? And why me?"—and, finally, she took a few questions from the press, which she didn't so much answer as try, not always successfully, to parry.

The consensus on the hayfield that morning was that Clinton would have her work cut out for her—the sort of judgment that has a tendency to be self-fulfilling. I had brought along a friend who lived near Pindars Corners, and, as one of the few locals available for comment, he immediately found himself besieged. A television reporter asked him whether New York "needed" the First Lady. Not understanding where things were heading, he replied, "New York doesn't need Hillary Clinton, but I think most New Yorkers welcome her candidacy." He appeared on the evening news delivering only the first half of his remark.

Beyond the obvious blunders—the donning of a Yankees cap, the embrace of Suha Arafat—Clinton's campaign was, from the beginning, troubled by the old, unresolved questions of identity. On the one hand, the First Lady was clearly running on who she was; on the other, who she was was precisely what was at issue. To a surprising degree, Clinton's public image had been improved by the Monica Lewinsky scandal and the subsequent impeachment of her husband. Still, many, including some of Clinton's closest friends, argued that the sympathy extended to a long-suffering wife was a treacherous basis on which to build a candidacy. The Senate race seemed sure to prompt a reëxamination of the multifarious scandals associated with the Clinton Administration, starting with White-water, and to summon up all the most unflattering impressions of the First Lady. ("Lady Macbeth in a headband" was a much-repeated formulation.) At one point, Clinton's campaign staff, disturbed by her lack of support among suburban women, convened a series of all-female focus groups in Westchester County. (Tapes of the sessions were leaked to a columnist, Michael Tomasky, who subsequently published a book about the campaign, "Hillary's Turn.") Among the words that the participants used to describe Clinton were "cunning," "savvy," "pushy," and "cold." One woman complained, "She's afraid of showing a weakness to us." Another said, "We really don't know who Hillary Clinton is."

The Clinton campaign's response to the question of "who Hillary Clinton is" was to turn the question on its head. With her "listening tour"—an elaborate show of humility to the citizens of New York—she offered the inverse of a typical campaign; instead of presenting a set of positions to voters, Clinton travelled around the state soliciting views from others. (As a former campaign aide put it to me, explaining the theory behind the tour, "People wanted to know that it was about them, and not about her.") When, eventually, the First Lady began to put out position papers—something that toward the end of the campaign she took to doing almost every day—she continued to focus on topics of local (and profoundly noncontroversial) interest, like rural communities' need for better Internet service.

While journalists fumed about the anodyne nature of her agenda—one reporter accused her of having undergone a "controversectomy"—voters seemed unfazed. They were usually flattered, which clearly was the point. Here was a woman who could be doing anything, and what she wanted to do was to expand broadband access in Cattaraugus County. In the course of the campaign, I followed Clinton to at least a dozen events. One trip to Buffalo began with her being asked on live radio whether she had ever slept with Vince Foster. The interview left her staff deeply rattled, but Clinton proceeded to work the lunch crowd at a local senior center, pausing at every table to shake every hand, as if nothing out of the ordinary had happened. One woman rambled on incoherently to her about something having to do with a house foreclosure; Clinton listened patiently, then thanked the woman for bringing such an important matter to her attention. A second woman complained about the difficulty that young people had finding jobs in the area, a lament that Clinton had doubtless heard hundreds, if not thousands, of times before. "While you're talking, she's actually listening to what you're saying," the woman remarked to me afterward. "She doesn't just want to get away."

Whether this sort of attentiveness would, in the end, have been enough to defeat Mayor Rudolph Giuliani is hard to know. During his phase of the tagteam campaign, Giuliani never really bothered to engage Clinton as a serious rival. When he mentioned her at all, it was usually to make fun of her—for pretending to be a Yankees fan, a New Yorker, a sincere person. The Mayor implied, and many others explicitly stated, that Clinton's only interest in the Empire State was as a stepping stone to further power. "If she wins in New York, it will only be a matter of time before she announces for President," William Powers, chairman of the state G.O.P., declared.

Rick Lazio, the Long Island congressman who replaced Giuliani in the race after the Mayor was found to have prostate cancer, tried to adopt a similar approach—"I put my Mets hat on when I was six years old," he declared in his announcement speech—but, lacking Giuliani's stature, and his instinct for savagery, he never could quite pull it off. Even many Democrats believe that it was Lazio's weakness as a candidate, more than Clinton's appeal, that finally decided the race. In an obviously scripted confrontation at a debate in Buffalo, Lazio marched over to Clinton and demanded that she sign a pledge to ban so-called "soft money" contributions from the campaign. "When Lazio walked across that stage, that was every husband walking across that kitchen with a threatening tone in his voice" is how one prominent New York Democrat recalled the incident. "They did for her what she couldn't do for herself. They made her sympathetic."

The Senate is a body governed by laws and by traditions, to the latter of which belongs the freshman visit to Senator Robert Byrd, the West

Virginia Democrat. Byrd has served in the Senate for fifty years—longer, as he likes to point out, than all but two of the members who have passed through the chamber since it was created—and is widely acknowledged to be the world's reigning expert on its rules. By the time of Clinton's election, she and Senator Byrd were already well acquainted—too well, one might say. Their most consequential encounter occurred in 1993, during Clinton's disastrous tenure as head of the President's task force on health-care reform. The First Lady wanted the legislation that the task force had drafted, which ran to more than thirteen hundred pages, tacked onto the so-called budget-reconciliation bill. The justification for this was, substantively speaking, thin, but procedurally it offered a critical advantage. The budget-reconciliation bill practically has to pass—if it doesn't, the entire appropriations process gets bollixed up—and debate in the Senate is limited. Clinton needed Byrd, who was then the chairman of the Senate Appropriations Committee, to approve the move, something he refused to do. His decision had the effect—intentional or not—of killing off the legislation and, with it, Clinton's hopes of introducing universal health insurance.

"I had seen her a few times through a glass darkly, as the Scripture says," Byrd told me recently when I met with him in his office in the Capitol. "I would say she did not necessarily start out as one of my favorites, if I might use that term. But she is one of my favorites now, because I like her approach. I like her sincerity. I like her convictions." Byrd said that he was particularly impressed by Clinton's hard work and deference, which, he had advised her on the occasion of her freshman visit, in November, 2000, would be among the qualities her fellow-senators would judge her on. "I think she has been the perfect student," he said.

The first piece of legislation that Clinton introduced in the Senate was a package of seven bills designed, in her words, "to spur job growth in upstate New York and around the nation." The package, which fulfilled a campaign promise, called for, among other things, the creation of "technology bonds" to promote broadband access in rural communities. When Clinton introduced the package, on March 1, 2001, she handed her colleagues customized briefing packets with color-coded maps showing how each of their states would also benefit from her initiatives.

In general, Clinton has received high marks for her inaugural legislative efforts. This is not because they are particularly far-reaching, or even original—on the contrary. Like most junior senators, Clinton has spent her first years in office largely trying to funnel federal dollars to her state. She has, for example, successfully worked to maneuver a new, hundred-million-dollar border-crossing station in Champlain, New York, through the Senate's Environment and Public Works Committee, of which she is a member.

"People thought, Well, gee, she's the First Lady, she's probably going to be very insulated," Garry Douglas, the president of the Plattsburgh-North Country Chamber of Commerce, who worked with her on the project, told me. "But not only does she take our phone calls—on occasion she calls us." Douglas also said that he was "remarkably impressed" with Clinton's staff, an assessment that I heard repeated from many sources. Other officials observed that there was almost no economic-development project too small-bore for Clinton to show an interest in. Last year, for instance, in an effort to promote local agriculture, she organized an event in the Capitol called New York farm day. At the event, which she repeated last month, she served only New York-grown products. "She is a true missionary for New York food and wine," Jim Trezise, president of the New York Wine & Grape Foundation, told me.

All the lawmakers who spoke to me on the record about Clinton—a self-selected group, to be sure—praised her in much the same terms as Senator Byrd. They noted her faithful attendance at committee hearings, her deference to more senior colleagues, her general willingness to fade into the background. "When she goes to meetings—you know, we have New York delegation meetings—she just sits there, the same as anybody else," Peter King, a Republican congressman from Long Island, told me. "She's not trying to jump out front and grab an issue from you, because she knows she's going to get the coverage anyway. Now, that may sound almost self-evident: of course Hillary Clinton can get her face in the paper. But the thing is, a lot of people, no matter how much publicity they get, they still don't have the confidence to know they can get it."

A few weeks after Clinton and Graham's amendment was passed, I went down to Washington again. The day was given over to the Homeland

Security Appropriations bill for 2004. Ever since the September 11th attacks, Clinton has, for obvious reasons, devoted a great deal of time to homeland security and, in particular, to obtaining more funds for New York. Working with the state's senior senator, Charles Schumer, with whom she does not always enjoy the best relations—the pair have had at least two semi-public shouting matches—Clinton was instrumental in getting twenty billion dollars for New York in the days immediately following the disaster. This past winter, after months of lobbying, Clinton helped secure an additional ninety million dollars to track the health effects of the attacks on rescue workers.

"This was an issue where she might have said, 'Listen, this is bogged down someplace,' but she stayed with it," Peter Gorman, the president of the Uniformed Fire Officers' Association of New York City, which represents the F.D.N.Y.'s superior officers, told me. "That's the amazing thing about her. She's really a woman who is not afraid to get involved in any issue that's important to us."

The Homeland Security Appropriations Act finances the Department of Homeland Security. It also provides the states with security funds, using a formula based almost entirely on population. Clinton wanted to change this formula, by directing the Secretary of Homeland Security to take other factors into account, such as the risk of attack. To explain her proposal, she had had a series of charts made up. At one point, she went down to the floor of the Senate, propped the charts up on an easel, and was about to launch into her spiel when she was informed that a vote on two other amendments had been scheduled, and she would have to wait. She trekked back to her office to meet with members of the New York Farm Bureau, who were concerned about dairy prices and Canadian imports, then walked back to the Capitol to await her turn to speak. It came at about six in the evening. There were only two other senators on the floor, not an unusual number for a routine legislative matter.

"Now, this is obviously a bit confusing and arcane, because it has to do with formulas and percentages, but it is a very important issue," Clinton began, speaking to the mostly empty chamber. "There is an absolute clear consensus among security experts that a better formula must be devised," she went on. "I said the other day that if we were to determine our defense posture, our projection of force around the world, on some kind of per-capita basis, we would be placing soldiers in Canada and Sweden, because, after all, they are there. Well, obviously, it is nonsensical. We don't do that. We look at the threats. We try to design our weaponry and other responses to take account of all of the threats that military forces might encounter, and we should be doing the same here." Midway through Clinton's remarks, Susan Collins, the chairman of the Governmental Affairs Committee, rushed onto the floor; evidently, she had been advised that it would be unwise to let Clinton's comments go unanswered. After Clinton was done, Collins, a Maine Republican, stood to oppose her amendment, pointing out that the Governmental Affairs Committee had been trying to draft legislation to deal with precisely the same issue. She offered to work with the senator from New York on this legislation, because, as she put it, "I'm very sympathetic to what a high-risk, high-vulnerability state the Senator so ably represents"—at which point Clinton withdrew her proposal from consideration. Although it might have appeared that she had wasted the entire afternoon waiting around to offer her amendment, only to drop it at the crucial moment, Clinton was upbeat. By the unwritten rules of the Senate, she told me, the exchange with Collins had been filled with significance.

"Actually, it turned out better than I expected," she said as we walked back to her office. "When she said, 'You have a lot of good points, you have a special concern about New York that I want to work with you about,' that is a wonderful invitation to pull down your amendment and engage in a discussion based on that kind of comity. It's really the way things get done around here."

Clinton wrote "Living History"—with a team of ghostwriters—nights and weekends when her senatorial schedule allowed. Once, I asked her how she had managed to remember everything she recounts in the book—whether she had kept some sort of diary she could refer back to. She turned to me and said, matter-of-factly, "No. Because it would have been subpoenaed."

"Living History" begins with Clinton's childhood in the quiet town of Park Ridge, Illinois—"My dad was a rock-ribbed, up-by-your-bootstraps, conservative Republican and proud of it," she writes—and briefly describes her falling in love at Yale Law School with a fellow-student who "had a vitality that seemed to shoot out of his pores." Most of the book's five hundred and thirty-four pages, though, are devoted to Clinton's years as First Lady, in chapters that discuss, in turn, her efforts to overhaul the nation's health-care system, to improve the lives of women around the world, and to deal with the various scandals that were constantly cropping up. Clinton addresses virtually every allegation, usually in order to point out where her actions were misconstrued. Discussing the ten-thousand-per-cent profit she made during her nine-month foray into cattle-futures trading, in the late seventies, for example, she writes, by way of explanation, "I was lucky enough to lose my nerve and get out before the market dropped."

Whitewater takes up one whole chapter and parts of several others. The story of the Clintons' land deal with Jim McDougal, who was later imprisoned for ransacking a savings and loan, Madison Guaranty, that Clinton herself had done legal work for does not lend itself to an edifying telling. "I've been asked how I could have been so ignorant of McDougal's actions," she writes. "I've asked myself that too." What is arguably the story's climax—the discovery of Clinton's Madison Guaranty billing records, which had mysteriously gone missing—becomes, in Clinton's version, simply a matter of poor housekeeping: "It was difficult to convey the disarray we had lived with ever since moving into the White House."

By far the most often cited section of the book, of course, is the section dealing with the Lewinsky scandal, and with Clinton's reaction to her husband's confession of infidelity. The story of the President's affair with Lewinsky broke on January 21, 1998, and on that day, Clinton relates, the President woke her up early to say, "There's something in today's papers you should know about." Bill denied that there was any truth to the charges, and six days later Hillary went on the "Today" show. "The great story here for anybody willing to find it and write about it and explain it," she told Matt Lauer, "is this vast right-wing conspiracy that has been conspiring against my husband since the day he announced for President." For the next seven months, despite mounting evidence to the contrary, Clinton continued to believe, she maintains, that her husband was the victim of politically motivated slander. Then, on the morning of August 15th, the President woke her up early again, this time to inform her that, as she puts it, there had in fact been "inappropriate intimacy."

"Gulping for air, I started crying and yelling at him, 'What do you mean?' " Clinton recalls. " 'What are you saying? Why did you lie to me?' " A week before the book was released, the Associated Press got hold of a copy and put Clinton's recollection of this scene out on the wire, guaranteeing the book huge publicity in the days leading up to its hugely publicized release.

To an extent unusual for an author in her position, Clinton actively marketed "Living History"—first, in appearances in New York, Washington, and Philadelphia, and later, during the summer recess, in appearances in cities like Little Rock and Seattle. (By the end of the tour, she had autographed some forty-five thousand copies.) I went to an early book signing, in the Clintons' adopted home town of Chappaqua, in Westchester County. The event, which took place at the local public library, was limited to those with tickets, but more than a hundred people had shown up without them and were waiting in the parking lot. Also hanging around outside was a man in a bright-red devil's suit, waving a sign that said "I sold my soul to Hillary." Inside, Clinton recognized several people she knew and waved to them enthusiastically. She read a few excerpts from the book—one about a trip she had taken to South Asia as First Lady, and one about dropping Chelsea off at Stanford. Then she turned to the book's penultimate chapter, "Dare to Compete," which deals with her decision to run for the Senate.

It is the peculiar conceit of "Living History" that this decision was not in any way an expression of—or even influenced by—personal ambition. Clinton portrays herself as drawn into a candidacy entirely as a result of the efforts of others, among them Charles Rangel, the Harlem congressman, who suggested the idea in a phone conversation, and Senator Bob Torricelli, of New Jersey, who was asked about it on "Meet the Press." Nita Lowey, a congresswoman from Westchester, gave her another nudge by dropping out of the race, Clinton says, neglecting to mention that Lowey dropped out only because Clinton had made it clear that she wanted in. By Clinton's account, the decisive push came from, of all unlikely people, a high-school basketball player named Sofia Totti. Clinton had agreed to a promo appearance for an HBO special entitled "Dare to Compete," at which Totti had the honor of introducing her:

> As I went to shake her hand, she leaned toward me and whispered in my ear. "Dare to compete, Mrs. Clinton," she said. "Dare to compete."
> Her comment caught me off guard, so much so that I left the event and began to think: Could I be afraid to do something I had urged countless other women to do? Why am I vacillating about taking on this race? Why aren't I thinking more seriously about it? Maybe I should "dare to compete."

For all its traffic in intimate material—the scandals, the early-morning bedroom encounters, the self-doubts—"Living History" is not, finally, a record of a life; it is a political act. It offers an account of Clinton's actions that, however bowdlerized, she can refer back to if, as seems almost inevitable, questions about them arise on a future occasion. Like the "listening tour," it is a response to constraints that to any ordinary person would have been paralyzing.

On the Friday before Labor Day, Clinton had just wrapped up the last phase of her book tour and was midway through an upstate swing when a rumor about her began to circulate. According to this rumor, which surfaced online in the Drudge Report, Clinton had called a meeting with her top advisers, among them her husband, to discuss whether she should run for President. At a press conference in the Finger Lakes, Clinton denied that any such meeting was planned—she said that she was simply hosting a "thank-you dinner" for supporters—and insisted that, "for the nine-hundred-and-seventy-fifth time," she was ruling out the Presidential race. A few hours later, she denied the report again. This did not do much to dampen the speculation, which continued over the weekend and by Monday had made its way onto the front page of the *Post*. In a story headlined "My Girl" and labelled "exclusive," the *Post* quoted former Governor Mario Cuomo saying that if Clinton did decide to run he "would support her in a flash." The dinner, a week later, turned out to be as

Clinton had described it; nevertheless, it set off a whole new round of rumors. Clinton told her supporters—jokingly, she later insisted—how important their help would be for her next campaign, "whatever that may be."

The recent surge of interest in Clinton's plans is in part a response to the weakness of the current Democratic field. Voicing a widely held view, Cuomo has referred to the candidates vying for the Party's nomination as a "babble," and Bill Clinton is reported to have told his wife's supporters that there were "two stars" in the Democratic Party—General Wesley Clark and Hillary. When Clark subsequently announced his candidacy, there were so many reports that the Clintons were backing him—perhaps as a "stalking-horse" for Hillary—that Bill reportedly felt compelled to call several of the other candidates to deny this. (Hillary, for her part, told reporters at a breakfast sponsored by the *Christian Science Monitor* that claims that the Clintons were supporting Clark were "an absurd feat of the imagination.")

At the same time, the speculation is clearly being driven by the old assumption that Clinton didn't come to New York just to work on broadband access. Notwithstanding her sedulous attention to local issues, she has made several moves over the last year or so—including writing her memoir—which, if they do not conclusively demonstrate Presidential ambitions, are certainly open to that interpretation. (According to a Marist College poll taken just before the book was published, twenty-eight per cent of New York voters thought that Clinton's primary motivation for writing "Living History" was to set the stage for a national race, while twenty-seven per cent believed that she just wanted to tell her side of the story.) This past January, after only two years in office, Clinton assumed the chairmanship of the Senate's Democratic steering committee, a position that officially makes her part of the Senate's Democratic leadership and gives her a prominent role in shaping the Party's message. Clinton has emerged as one of the Democrats' most active—and successful—fund-raisers, hosting events for fellow Democratic senators at her Washington residence, a fifty-five-hundred-square-foot house near Embassy Row, and also writing checks to Democratic officials around the country from her political-action committee, HILLPAC, which, in the first six months of 2003, raised more money than any other Democratic leadership PAC. Just recently, Clinton launched a Web site-cum-fund-raising operation (friendsofhillary.com), which chronicles how "Hillary is making a difference" in areas ranging from "agriculture" to "women" and has prominently featured letters importuning her to run for President. As Clinton likes to point out, she is the first New York senator ever to serve on the Senate Armed Services Committee, an appointment for which she had to give up her seat on the Senate Budget Committee. When I asked one longtime New York political operative whether he could think of an explanation for this choice aside from national aspirations, he claimed to be stumped: "You got me. For the Long Island defense contractors who all moved to Texas years ago?"

Clinton has also been influential in setting up a new liberal think tank called the Center for American Progress, headed by Bill Clinton's former White House chief of staff John Podesta. The institute is not supposed to be explicitly partisan, but many Democrats are clearly hoping that it will come up with a more compelling agenda for the Party—if not by 2004, then at least by 2008. (One friend of the Clintons told me that Hillary would not run for President next year, although, as he noted, she has "very pointedly not ruled out" running in any other year.)

I asked Clinton about the state of Democratic politics one day when she was waiting to go onto the Senate floor. "I think it's been hard for our party to deal with both the loss of the White House and the loss of Congress," she told me. "That hasn't happened in the memory of anyone here." She went on, "I'm fundamentally optimistic, because I think that the policies of this Administration are distinctly wrongheaded, and that, after the photo ops are over, the facts and evidence actually count as to how people are experiencing their lives. And I believe that time and evidence are on our side."

Clinton voted in favor of authorizing the use of force against Iraq, and she has been careful not to question Bush's military judgment. On just about every other issue, though, including the handling of the aftermath of the war, she has been critical of the President. Referring to Bush's request for a supplemental appropriation to finance ongoing operations in Iraq, she said recently, "For me, the eighty-seven billion dollars is not just a bill for Iraq—it's a bill for failed leadership." Last week, in spite of her own experience with special prosecutors, she called for the appointment of one to investigate Administration leaks revealing the identity of the covert C.I.A. operative Valerie Plame. Clinton frequently faults Bush for his stewardship of the economy. "I'm absolutely convinced that the Administration's policy is the wrong medicine," she told me. "They have the same diagnosis and treatment for everything: it's tax cuts, tax cuts, tax cuts." Meanwhile, she argues, the Administration's shortsightedness on domestic security has left the country deeply vulnerable to another September 11th-like attack. "I alternate between frustration and outrage mixed with head-slapping amazement that we're not doing more," she told me. "Maybe we'll get really, really, really lucky and nothing bad will ever happen again. But I can't in good conscience operate from that assumption."

Clinton's criticism of the Bush Administration parallels that of most other Democrats, including most of the Democrats running for President. Occasionally, though, she veers off in a direction of her own.

One afternoon in the spring, I went to hear Clinton give a speech to a group of nurses at Roosevelt Hospital, in Manhattan. "You know, some of us need more help and guidance and support than others," Clinton told them. "Some of us are born healthy and others are not. Some of us have traumatic, terrible accidents or events or diseases that affect us. None of us know what will happen to any of us tomorrow, and therefore I think we are all bound together in a web of relationships where we do—not only for religious reasons or moral reasons but practical reasons—have an obligation and opportunity to support one another."

Clinton went on to say that she was worried that the nation's priorities were "getting misplaced." She emphasized the importance of sacrifice—"I think that's what makes a stronger country"—and introduced the concept of "future preference," under which tomorrow takes precedence over today. By the end of her speech, she was calling into question that most basic of American values—self-reliance. "I hope we don't forget that the idea of the rugged individual is a great idea for films, for books, but there are very few people who go through life without needing anyone, without having to make any sacrifice for anyone else," she said. "In fact, it's kind of an impoverished life, if that's the attitude."

At the same event, Clinton referred to the hospital's interim president.

"I like the name 'interim president,' " she said. "I like the name 'president' even better."

As it happened, I was supposed to interview Clinton the day after the item on her Presidential plans appeared in the Drudge Report. The interview, the second of two that she agreed to, was scheduled to take place in her car, during a drive from the town of Skaneateles to the New York State Fair, just outside Syracuse. I spent the night before the interview in a hotel, and when I was about to check out I couldn't find my room key. After rummaging under the bed and through my suitcase, I still couldn't find it, so I told the man at the desk that I was sorry, but I had to go because I had an appointment to interview Hillary Clinton. He asked if I meant *the* Hillary Clinton, and I said yes.

"Now, don't get all nervous and competitive," he told me. "Just be yourself."

By Clinton's reckoning, "millions of words" have been written about her; her memoir adds another two hundred thousand to the total. Even the best and most exhaustive of these accounts seem somehow incomplete— and this is certainly true of "Living History." One of Clinton's own pieces of campaign literature from the Senate race put the problem this way: "We know everything—and nothing—about her."

In our first conversation, I tried to talk to Clinton about how her life had changed since she left the White House. A friend of hers had told me that she thought Clinton felt "liberated" by having her own political office. I asked Clinton if it was true.

"I wouldn't use that," she said. "You know, before Bill ran for President I had my own office, I had my own job." She went on to say, "There's nothing comparable to being First Lady. It's not a job; it's a role or a position. It is remade every time someone fills it, because of the election, up until now, of a husband as President.

"It was a hard adjustment for me," she said. "So for me this is more like a return to what I had done before those eight years. It has a definition; it has responsibilities. There are certain things you are expected to do. You do them to the best of your ability. So I'm very comfortable having this job, which it is. It's a job. The other is not."

I asked her how her views had changed since she moved from the White House to the Senate. "I feel like I've been really lucky to have those different perspectives, because it has informed my understanding of a lot of issues and how to approach them," she told me. "I learned so much about Washington and national politics and the legislative process during the eight years of my husband's two terms. I made a lot of mistakes. I learned from those mistakes. At least, I hope I did." Then she steered the conversation back to the complexities of her former role. "I don't know that anything can prepare you for ending up in the White House," she said. "It is just so many light-years apart from any other experience."

The ill-defined demands of the First Lady's office are a recurring theme in "Living History." "I was navigating uncharted terrain—and through my own inexperience, I contributed to some of the conflicting perceptions about me," Clinton writes at one point. "I was still learning the ropes and still discovering what it meant to be America's First Lady," she observes at another. While it is probably true that every First Lady has to tinker with the role, Clinton was the first to imagine that it fell to the President's wife to reinvent the American health-care system. What is missing from her account is, not coincidentally, what is left out of her account of the Senate race—any mention of her own ambition.

The closest Clinton comes to acknowledging what was really at issue is some broad generalities about gender roles. "We were living in an era in which some people still felt deep ambivalence about women in positions of public leadership and power," she writes. Even in these self-abstracted terms, though, she doesn't carry the argument nearly as far as she could. Surely it is unfair that the same ambitions that are admired in a man are in a woman considered repellent. But to complain about this double standard would be to acknowledge precisely what Clinton has worked so hard— and, as the Senate seat she now occupies demonstrates, so successfully—to repress.

The second time I interviewed Clinton, I decided to try to see if I could push beyond her vague statements about women in power. First, I asked her if she would give different advice to a young woman entering politics from what she would give to a young man. "There are lots of little inconsequential but apparently important matters, like hair style and wardrobe and the height of one's heels on marble floors, that you have to be aware of," she said.

Would she advise Chelsea to go into politics? "I would never talk about what I advise my daughter to do."

Was she treated differently in the Senate because she is a woman? "I really have been impressed at how collegial the atmosphere is," she replied.

Shortly before the interview, I spoke to Dwight Jewson, a marketing consultant who had been hired by Clinton's Senate campaign to investigate why she was polling so poorly among certain groups—particularly suburban women—that she needed to win. "When you're a strong, powerful woman, you're seen as one of two types of person," Jewson told me. "You're either our mother, because our mothers are strong powerful women we love, or you're a manipulative, opportunistic bitch." I asked Clinton what she thought of Jewson's assessment.

She paused for a split second. "I think we're getting beyond that," she said. "I'm sure there are some people, just as there are people who have never accepted the civil-rights revolution and the equality of all kinds of human beings, who live with and act on stereotypes, but I just don't see that as pervasive anymore."

Finally, as we were pulling up at the New York State Fair, I asked her whether she ever wished she wouldn't have to read another word about Hillary Clinton. She smiled. "That does cross my mind."

Ever since entering the Senate, Clinton has hosted an annual invitation-only lunch at the State Fair. Her guests include community leaders and elected officials from central New York, along with an assortment of people who somehow fit in with the lunch's annual theme. Last year's was agriculture, and the guests included several dairy farmers. This year's was the military. Clinton had a private meeting beforehand, so I went over to the lunch ahead of her. It was a steamy day, and many of the guests, especially those in uniform, had arrived early to escape the heat on the fairgrounds. Rhea Jezer, the former chairman of the state's Sierra Club, was sitting with her husband, Daniel, a rabbi. "When my mother died, when I had a foot operation that got infected, Hillary called," Jezer told me. "She really cares. Yet the press says that she's cold. I don't understand that."

Jezer introduced me to the Onondaga County executive, Nick Pirro, a Republican, who apparently had been invited out of a spirit of bipartisanship. He looked as if he were having second thoughts about his decision to show up. "There's no middle ground on Hillary," he told me. "People are either very for or very against her. There are a lot of people who believe she really is in this to run for President."

That morning, in a brief item, the Syracuse *Post-Standard* had announced that Bill Clinton would be accompanying his wife to the State Fair, as he had done several times in the past. Hundreds of fairgoers began to line up in the heat outside the building where the lunch was being held. Hillary's staff had expected Bill to show up, but the former President had decided that he was too busy working on his own memoir to make the trip upstate.

Just how much of a role Bill plays in Hillary's career at this point is hard to say. The two appear together in public only occasionally; I saw them both just once, at a book party for Hillary at the Four Seasons, in Manhattan. Bill told the crowd at the party that "Living History" was "an accurate, true account of the person I believe did more good for more people in the position of First Lady than any person who ever served in that position." Hillary said, "At the end of the day, I would not have lived the life I've lived or become the person I am, for all that means, without my husband." I made repeated efforts to interview Bill Clinton for this article, finally sending him a list of questions via e-mail. Several weeks later, the answers arrived, also via e-mail. To a query about whether he was surprised in any way by his wife's Senate career, the former President wrote, "My only surprise is that she's doing even better than I thought she would, which is saying something." In response to a question about what his wife brought to the Senate, he offered the following list:

1. She likes people and cares about their problems;
2. She knows how to make good policy;
3. She's brilliant and works very hard;
4. She fights for what she believes in and doesn't give up;
5. She's always reaching out for new allies, including Republicans;
6. She loves her country and her state;
7. She's always thinking about what life will be like for our children and their children.

By the time Clinton got to the lunch at the State Fair, there was not a single empty seat in the room, which had been set up for more than four hundred people. Clinton began her remarks by saying that it was a "great honor" for her to serve on the Senate Armed Services Committee, and she related how she had teamed up with Senator Graham to try to provide health insurance for members of the National Guard and reservists. "Some of you may recall Senator Graham and I have some significant differences," she said, prompting titters from the audience. "But on this we are absolutely united." Finally, to much cheering from the crowd, she vowed to fight the proposed closing of a V.A. hospital in nearby Canandaigua.

"That really raises an over-all issue, and that is: What are our priorities as a nation?" Clinton continued. "What is it we are going to focus on and value, and what is it we are willing to pay for? I am very disappointed that in just two and a half years we have gone from surplus back into huge and growing deficits. And I just have to respectfully disagree that the economic policies pursued by the Administration are working. I don't see the jobs being created; in fact, we have the worst job-creation record since Herbert Hoover, and that was not exactly a good time for our country."

After the lunch, Clinton made her way over to a neighboring building for a press conference. The place was packed with people, many of whom still seemed to be under the impression that they were going to see both Hillary and Bill. A microphone had been set up behind a display of apples and apple products, and a girl in an orange taffeta gown with a sash that said "Williamson Apple Blossom Queen" was waiting beside it. It was so hot that people began to help themselves to the apple-juice boxes. Clinton announced a program under which General Mills, in return for labels from New York apples, would donate money to the state's schools.

"We have the most delicious apples in the world, and we have the best students and kids in the world, so it's a perfect combination," she said. She took a few questions from the press, including one about her husband— "He just couldn't make it this year," she said curtly—and then began to work the crowd. People kept asking her to pose for pictures or to sign things—mostly copies of "Living History," but also baseballs, brochures from the fair, and scraps of used paper and envelopes. One man handed her an old copy of *Time* magazine with a menacing-looking picture of her on the cover and the headline "The Truth About Whitewater." Clinton looked nonplussed, but signed it anyway. "When am I going to get to vote for you for President?" one woman asked her. "You are such an inspiration," another one said.

Eventually, Clinton worked her way over to a building known as the Center of Progress, where her Senate office had a booth of its own, next to a booth for the state comptroller. It consisted of tables covered with pamphlets, including one for kids that asked, "Did You Know . . . New York has the longest Toll Expressway in the entire world? (Governor Thomas E. Dewey Thruway is 559 miles long.)" Hundreds more people had lined up to see her, and they grabbed the pamphlets and handed them to her to sign.

Unlike her husband, Clinton does not appear to draw energy from huge crowds of people. Such is her self-discipline, though, that, as she is beaming into the camera or scribbling her name for the umpteenth time, she is almost always able to convey the sense that there's nothing on earth she'd rather be doing. The effort she puts out doesn't resolve the contradictions of her career—ambition and self-sacrifice are never fully interchangeable—but it can make them blur together. One woman I met at the "Living History" reading in Chappaqua put the point this way: "Anyone who is willing to do what she's done to be in public service is a hero."

After about half an hour at her booth, it was time for Clinton to head over to a Friends of Hillary fund-raiser. On her way out of the building, she paused at the comptroller's booth, where she posed for a picture with the staff and signed more autographs. During her time at the fair, in addition to her Secret Service detail, Clinton had been guarded by a dozen or so state troopers, and they lined up to say goodbye to her at the door. She thanked them and, before getting into her car, shook hands with every single one.

PART II

Impolitics

Stormin' Norman

May 1999

I T TAKES A certain asceticism, not to mention an abstracted sense of self, to work for the American Civil Liberties Union and get a kick out of it. The pay is modest, the hours are long, and if things go right the reward may well be the satisfaction that comes from having made it possible for a particularly pathetic band of Nazis to march through a Jewish neighborhood. Almost by definition, the work strains against common decency, or, at least, common sense, and taking it on means committing oneself to the life of a perpetual contrarian: the majority, after all, has more effective ways of defending its interests than a lawyer from the A.C.L.U.

Norman Siegel has headed the organization's New York branch, the N.Y.C.L.U., for the past fourteen years. He is fifty-five, has wiry brown hair and a craggy face, and, as much as anyone, has helped promote the group's post-Skokie image. He has fought, on principle, against police racism and has defended, also on principle, police who are racists; he has championed gay rights and the rights of groups to exclude gays. Around City Hall, the mere mention of his name elicits groans, and in the office of the corporation counsel, among the attorneys who are obliged to defend the city against his innumerable lawsuits, he has long been regarded as an overzealous litigant, a publicity hound, and a colossal pain in the ass. In the terse assessment of one of the city's lawyers, "Norman Siegel has the worst sense of humor of anyone I've ever met."

As Siegel likes to point out, though, he often prevails in court, as he did recently on behalf of the black Hebrew Israelites and their amplified prophecies of doom. The city had effectively tried to banish the group from Times Square, where for years its members had been ranting against whites, in the process making the lives of tens of thousands of people just a bit more miserable every day. Siegel argued that inflicting such misery was constitutionally protected, and he is now pursuing damages for the group from the city.

Until recently, Siegel's public image consisted largely of this kind of dubious, if high-minded, achievement. In the press, he was often parodied as a gadfly for all seasons, the one person in New York who could be counted on to rail against a policy that everyone else was embracing, or to defend the indefensible. But gradually, after City Hall was cordoned off, and then more rapidly, after the slaying of Amadou Diallo, the state of civil liberties in New York ceased to seem a joking matter. Almost every day now, somewhere in the city there is some kind of protest organized around the N.Y.C.L.U.'s favorite themes of due process and equal protection. Already several congressmen, the state comptroller, and assorted celebrities have got themselves arrested to signal their concern about these issues, and many others probably would have done so if it weren't for the fact that it takes several hours to get booked by the cops. The scale and the duration of the public outrage, which is entering its fourth month, have surprised even those who have helped promote and direct it.

Such is the enfeebled state of Mayor Rudolph Giuliani's opposition that, although he has clearly been hurt by the protests, one would be hard-pressed to find another elected official who has been helped. Neither the public advocate, Mark Green, nor the city comptroller, Alan Hevesi, nor the City Council speaker, Peter Vallone, has had anything very forceful to say about the Diallo shooting, though all have mayoral ambitions. The city's best-known civil-rights leader cum ambulance chaser, the Reverend Al Sharpton, has, of course, tried to make up for this, but there are only so many times that the same man can be rehabilitated.

Almost by default, then, Siegel has emerged as one of the Mayor's most vigorous and credible antagonists. From the start of the Diallo protests, he has acted as a de facto lawyer for the demonstrators, and he is increasingly sought out by protest organizers as the person who can articulate the principles they are fighting for. For Siegel, it appears that the vigils and the marches and the arrests represent an unlikely gift from history. As is rarely the case for a true believer, he has made his way from the margins of civic life to the center, without so much as adjusting his rhetoric or even trying to mute his obsessions.

One day toward the end of March, I arranged to join Siegel at a meeting of the city's Taxi and Limousine Commission, in lower Manhattan. Siegel was planning to speak during the public-comment period, to demand that the commission's administrative hearings, which are the functional equivalent of court proceedings, no longer be conducted in private. When he arrived, however, he found that the agenda offered no opportunity for public comment, and, since he is quite a stickler for procedure when it comes to making a fuss, he decided to leave without speaking. I met him in the lobby, where he was waiting with a leader of one of the cabdrivers' associations, Vijay Bali, who was trying to convince him that the agenda had been rewritten expressly to thwart his plans.

Siegel, as I subsequently learned more fully, has a great deal of patience for activities that many other people would consider a waste of time, and he seemed unfazed by the fact that we had all travelled downtown for nothing. Bali, for his part, seemed happy just to be along. Ever since last spring, when Siegel rushed into federal court to win permission for the city's yellow-cab drivers to demonstrate against new taxi rules, they have held him in enormous regard, and nowadays some refuse to accept payment for his fare. "We were treated not like human beings," Bali told me. "Norman gave us a semblance of self-respect."

Siegel's next stop that day was Police Headquarters, where those protesting the Diallo shooting were staging tightly choreographed acts of civil disobedience. A buzz went through the crowd when Susan Sarandon, surrounded by cameras, made her way to the front of the line to get arrested. While I waited with Siegel in the brilliant early-spring sunshine, he kept darting over to speak to various members of the N.Y.P.D. brass, to make sure that the arrests were going smoothly and that the cops weren't planning to bump up the charges, because if they did he was planning to challenge them in court. A lot of people approached him, mostly to offer thanks or congratulations. One man, who was white, said, "You deserve a lot of credit, Norman," and another, who was black, said, "I just want to tell you, as long as people like you are around, I think there's some hope for our country."

Siegel was obviously pleased by the praise, and by the whole festively angry multiracial scene, which reminded him, he said, of some of the great demonstrations of his youth. Still, he had some nagging concerns that prevented him from entering fully into the spirit of the event. Periodically, the crowd would shout for the cops accused of killing Diallo to be arrested, but since at that point a grand jury was still investigating the case, Siegel pointed out to me, such a move would be a clear violation of due process. And when the chant "No Justice! No Peace!" went up, Siegel told me that he could not really condone it, because the second phrase seemed to imply a threat of violence. Thus, when others yell "No Justice!," Siegel will join in, but he remains silent when they scream "No Peace!"

"That's the problem when you think through all these slogans and try to be consistent," he said.

Siegel's role model is Chuck Morgan, who gave him his first job in the A.C.L.U. when he was fresh out of New York University School of Law, in 1968. By that time, Morgan had become a legendary figure in the civil-rights movement. A white Southerner, he had delivered a famous speech to businessmen in Birmingham, Alabama, accusing them of silent complicity in a church bombing, and he had sued to get Julian Bond seated in the Georgia House of Representatives. Several times in our conversations, Siegel quoted Morgan to me, trying to twist his Brooklyn accent into something approaching a Southern drawl. Morgan "taught me stamina," Siegel said at one point. "He would always say to me, 'It's great if you're smart. Went to Harvard or Yale? That helps. But stamina's the key. Outlast the bastards, Norm, that's the key.'" While Siegel was working for Morgan in Atlanta, most of the famous figures in the civil-rights movement, as well as most of the famous journalists covering them, passed through the A.C.L.U. office, usually, it seems, at the cocktail hour, and they would gather around Morgan's desk to schmooze and drink bourbon. Siegel used to sit in the corner, just taking it all in. To this day, a poster of Bond, looking very young and melancholy, hangs in Siegel's Manhattan office.

After a few years in Atlanta, Siegel moved back to New York, and ended up working on the N.Y.C.L.U.'s campaign to impeach Richard Nixon. He met the woman he lives with, Saralee Evans, when he hired her to coördinate the many volunteers the campaign attracted. (She is now a civil-court judge in Manhattan.) It was a heady time for Siegel, and for the A.C.L.U. as a whole, which picked up more than twenty-five thousand new members the years before Nixon resigned. A few years later, in 1977, when the A.C.L.U. took on the case of the Nazis who wanted to march through Skokie, Illinois, the group proceeded to lose about the same number of members, but by that time Siegel had left the organization and was working with Morgan in private practice in Washington, D.C.

Siegel returned to the group in 1985 to head the N.Y.C.L.U., and soon the New York affiliate had its own Skokie-like experience. Although the N.Y.C.L.U. depends on the national organization for much of its funding, it has almost complete discretion in cases, and the first major case Siegel took was that of Joyce Brown, a.k.a. Billie Boggs, a homeless, mentally disturbed woman who lived next to a heating grate on the Upper East Side. The city had Brown committed to Bellevue under a new and ostensibly humanitarian policy; she called the N.Y.C.L.U. to come and get her out. The case dragged on for weeks, becoming not just national but international news, and when it was over Siegel was regarded in many circles as just as nutty as she was.

In the mid-eighties, as the connection between the deinstitutionalizing of the mentally ill and the city's homelessness problem was becoming ever more apparent, New Yorkers, for reasons both selfish and not, were growing increasingly distressed by the recumbent bodies they had to step over on the way home. The Joyce Brown case played to these complicated emotions in a way that Siegel never seemed to fully appreciate. Even as he argued that the city had an obligation to provide Brown with housing, he maintained that it had no right to keep her in an institution. He received a lot of hate mail, some of which he has kept. Eventually, though the key legal issues were not resolved, Brown was released, and Siegel took her to speak at Harvard Law School, further infuriating his critics. As the coup de grâce, he hired her to work at the N.Y.C.L.U.'s office, a move that even some of his own board members found inappropriate. The arrangement didn't last long, but Siegel still keeps in touch with Brown, and he brings her back a T-shirt from each of his trips.

The case Siegel made for Brown was, in legal terms, unremarkable, but it was easily parodied as promoting the right to freeze to death on the street. In the years since, Siegel has been a favorite target of ridicule, especially in the city's tabloid newspapers, which have called him, among other things, a "kneejerk naysayer," a man "who never met an anti-social behavior he didn't defend," and "New York's pre-eminent civil-liberties zany."

Yet it is precisely the cases that are most easily lampooned which Siegel seems to remember most fondly. Take, for instance, the case of the Ancient Order of Hibernians and the Irish Lesbian and Gay Organization. The Hibernians organize the city's annual St. Patrick's Day Parade, and, even though it now seems to be cherished mainly as an excuse for public drunkenness, the group's leaders say that it is a religious event, and on religious grounds they will not allow gays and lesbians to march as a group. In 1993, the city tried to deal with this problem by giving the parade permit to an organization that promised to be more inclusive. Siegel went to court on behalf of the Hibernians, arguing that the city could not award a permit based on a parade's message, an argument that eventually prevailed. But at the same time Siegel advocated that the Hibernians' rivals should also be allowed to hold a parade, just one block over. (No one ever took him up on this suggestion, for fairly obvious reasons.) Recounting the whole tortured saga to me recently, Siegel was still convinced that his position—or positions— made absolute sense, and he concluded by saying, "I loved that case."

Siegel grew up in Brooklyn, in Borough Park, at a time when the neighborhood was almost totally Jewish and Italian. His father, who died when Siegel was twenty-five, was a foreman in a printing shop. Siegel's mother is eighty-three, and she now lives in a neighborhood that some like to call West Brighton, because it sounds tony, but that Siegel prefers to call Coney Island, because it doesn't. Siegel says that he can tell a lot about a person just by knowing where he went to high school, and he goes back to his own high school, New Utrecht, every Friday morning to teach a class on the dangers of stereotyping.

Inside the N.Y.C.L.U. there are many raps against Siegel—that he is a lousy fund-raiser, that he is a not much better administrator, and that he is too focussed on New York City at the expense of upstate. Outside the organization, the major complaint is that he is an insatiable publicity seeker. "I think that a part of Norman is driven to be on television," the city's corporation counsel, Michael Hess, told me. "I find that more and more he runs to the press." Even some of Siegel's allies said that they sometimes cringe to see his face, looking just a little too eager, on the tube once again. "He really needs to say 'no' to certain media requests" is how one of them delicately put it.

As a reporter, I can attest that Siegel is, indeed, almost always available to the media, from early in the morning until late at night, on weekends, and even when he is out of the country on vacation. Many of the stories he recounted to me included not only the way the event had been covered in the *Times* but also the names of the various reporters who had called him about it. Yet all this attending to the media, I discovered, represents a relatively small part of Siegel's typical, very long day. Practically every evening, I could have accompanied him to some obscure community-board meeting or forum where he would be trying to persuade some group to pass some resolution that was, eventually, supposed to lead to some sort of action on a cause he holds dear. Ira Glasser, the executive director of the A.C.L.U., who has known Siegel for years, told me that he has never met anyone who goes to more neighborhood meetings, and more willingly. "He not only tolerates it," Glasser said. "He loves it."

The class that Siegel teaches at New Utrecht, with Galen Kirkland, a black lawyer, is another good example of his many less glamorous projects. Siegel got the idea in 1989, after a black teen-ager, Yusuf Hawkins, was killed in a racially motivated assault not far from the high school, whose student body is still significantly Italian but is now also part Russian, Hispanic, Asian, and black. The course is supposed to challenge the students to examine their own tendency to stereotype, but, when I visited it, many of them seemed quite comfortable with the inevitability of stereotyping, and there were several moments of hilarity when they explained to Siegel just what racial or ethnic profile they themselves fit into. A hulking kid in a white T-shirt and gold chains, for example, was persuasively described by his peers as looking like someone who just "threw a body into the Hudson River."

*   *   *

Among the few people in New York City's public life who can match
Siegel for intensity is Mayor Giuliani. The two share an unwavering faith
in their own causes and a willingness to pursue fights beyond the point
where most other people, with less stamina, would simply give up. As it
happens, they are the same age, and they even went to law school together,
at N.Y.U., though, while Giuliani was in the library making law review,
Siegel was outside protesting.

Siegel is outspoken in his dislike for the Mayor: at one point he
described Giuliani to me as a "weirdo" and at another as "half human."
But he is also—in an ironic sort of way—openly grateful to him.
Starting last spring, when the Mayor tried to prevent the cabdrivers from
tying up traffic in protest, then tried to deny a permit to what was
optimistically called the Million Youth March, and then banned
demonstrations in front of City Hall, Giuliani has provided the
N.Y.C.L.U. with high-profile cases almost on a monthly basis. "He
was a gift to us," Siegel said. "The issues remined me of when I was in
the South, they were so clear-cut."

For one brief moment, Giuliani tried to reach out to Siegel, and for this,
too, Siegel is grateful. In 1997, after Abner Louima was allegedly brutalized in a Brooklyn precinct house, the Mayor appointed Siegel to a task
force charged with finding ways to improve police-community relations.
The appointment, Siegel now says, was "a big mistake" by the Mayor,
because it gave Siegel more credibility.

Siegel dates his own interest in police misconduct back to 1988 and the
Tompkins Square Park riot, during which police were caught on videotape
beating up ordinary citizens. Scandalously few of the cops were ever
disciplined, and Siegel became convinced that the N.Y.P.D. could not
be trusted to police itself. Over the next few years, he schlepped from
community-board meeting to community-board meeting, pushing for the
creation of an independent Civilian Complaint Review Board, which was
finally established in early 1993. By the time Siegel was appointed to the
Mayor's task force, however, he had already lost faith in the board. "It was
probably one of the most frustrating things I've experienced," he told me.

Once on the task force, Siegel quickly became Giuliani's goad, claiming
publicly that the Mayor wasn't taking the group's efforts seriously. The

Mayor, for his part, denounced Siegel for leaking to the press. In the end, the task force issued a majority report, calling for, among other things, a residency requirement for city cops and a strengthening of the complaint board. Siegel and two other members issued a dissenting report, written in a sustained tone of high dudgeon, calling for those things plus a special prosecutor to investigate police brutality. But the Mayor, instead of just rejecting the minority report as another example of Norman's being Norman, openly mocked the majority report, too—a move that, with the Diallo shooting, proved to be extremely shortsighted.

These days, Siegel is very much at the center of the post-Diallo civil-rights coalition, and is being sought out by a lot of people who not long ago would barely return his phone calls. He is constantly shuttling between meetings with the police and the protest leaders, who include the head of the city's powerful health-care workers' union, Dennis Rivera; former Deputy Mayor Bill Lynch; and, of course, Sharpton. Rivera, who recently woke Siegel up at around six o'clock in the morning to help draft a set of goals for the coalition, told me, "In fifteen minutes with him on the phone, I learned more about police brutality than I did sitting in meetings with other people for days." Not surprisingly, the goals ended up echoing the task force's dissenting report, so when several thousand people marched across the Brooklyn Bridge recently one of the things they said they were demonstrating for was the appointment of a special police prosecutor. Just last week, Siegel took on the case of a New York City policewoman who learned that she had been fired after testifying—supposedly anon-ymously—about abuses in the unit whose members killed Diallo.

Siegel has been around long enough to know that the outrage generated by Diallo's death will eventually dissipate, and he is already planning for that day. Currently, his pet project is what he likes to call New York Summer 1999—a sort of reverse twist on the Mississippi Freedom Summer of 1964—during which Southerners would come North to register voters and learn about New York's civil-rights problems. It is Siegel's contention that New York City today is in some ways just as segregated as the South was thirty-five years ago, and he is hoping that the Southern Christian Leadership Conference will help sponsor the project.

The whole idea is quintessentially Siegelian, and when he explained it to me it struck me as at once admirable and hopelessly misguided. Although it is moving to find someone who still adheres to the fundamentally optimistic, we-shall-overcome message of the civil-rights movement, somehow when you are working with Al Sharpton instead of the Reverend Martin Luther King, Jr., the history-repeating-itself-as-farce adage seems only too apt. "Norman is a believer," Michael Meyers, the executive director of the New York Civil Rights Coalition, told me. "He believes in people even when he knows better."

When I asked friends of Siegel's about him, several used the word "naïve" to describe him, which, given his extensive list of media contacts and his near-ubiquity on local television, at first sounded preposterous to me. Eventually, though, after sitting with him while he waited more than two hours to testify at a City Council committee hearing, the description began to make sense. Siegel not only believes that we are all better off with the Hebrew Israelites in Times Square and that the cops ought to be held more accountable and that testifying at excruciatingly boring City Council hearings is important; he also believes that all these things are connected, and that if he can just get to enough people and explain this to them it will make a difference. Clearly, he owes the prominence he enjoys today to the Mayor, but even after Giuliani moves on and the television appearances become less frequent Siegel, it seems safe to say, will still be doing what he has always done. He will still be fighting the good fight, or at least what he imagines it to be.

Common Man

September 2000

A MERICA LOVES REGIS Philbin, and Regis, I like to think, likes me. He has, at any rate, taken me with him to his gym on Columbus Avenue, across from the WABC studios, to work out. He is wearing a gray *Men's Health* T-shirt, black nylon shorts, and very white Nike sneakers. He has little flecks of pancake makeup stuck to his nose. At one of the many low moments in his career, in the early nineteen-eighties, Philbin had a fitness show on cable, "Regis Philbin's Health Styles," and now, at sixty-seven, he is still in dauntingly good shape. The first time we met, he stripped off his shirt in the dressing room of "Who Wants to Be a Millionaire," flexed in the style of Charles Atlas, and said, "You'll never see this from your English-professor husband!"

Philbin's gym routine is to concentrate on a single muscle group, working it with three different exercises, each repeated three times. Today, he is doing shoulders. He has just used an elaborate contraption with ropes and pulleys to lift a hundred and ten pounds. He resets it for me at twenty. Philbin has made a career of anatomizing human frailty without ever drawing blood, and the possibility that I might be not just a weakling but sensitive about it seems to leave him at a loss. "I thought you said you worked out," he says at one point, almost plaintively. Eventually, for lack of an alternative, he settles for a half-hearted joke about my physiognomy. "Betsy has an expressive face," he says to some imagined audience while I, grimacing, grapple with another machine.

As the new fall season gets under way, Philbin is, almost by an order of magnitude, the most watched man on television. ABC, in effect, no longer has a prime-time lineup; it just has "Millionaire," which it will run four evenings a week starting next month. Bill Carter, of the *Times*, has called the program "the most significant development in American television in ten years," which is actually a relatively modest claim compared with those of others, who have called it the most significant development in the history of the medium. Virtually every time it airs, "Millionaire" is the top-rated show for the night, and its popularity has, all on its own, lifted the ABC network from third place to first, boosted the stock value of its parent company, Disney, and inspired a wholesale rethinking of what makes a prime-time hit.

Meanwhile, a Philbin-based industry of "Millionaire" tie-ins and spin-offs has grown up on the side. There is Philbin's line of "Millionaire"-style shirts and ties to be promoted, a series of "Millionaire" computer games to be dubbed, a "Millionaire" musical CD to be plugged, and Philbin's most recent autobiography, "Who Wants to Be Me?," to be flogged. Everyone wants to get a piece of Regis, and when I first approached his publicity people, back in June, about getting mine they said he was too busy. Later, he relented, but not without first warning me, via voice mail, "You can't do this. You can't follow me around. You don't have this kind of stamina!" On the day we exercised together, I calculated that in the course of fulfilling all his obligations Philbin had had to get in and out of his clothes seven times.

As an index of individual talent, success on this scale almost never makes sense. Still, "Millionaire" is a special case. By Philbin's own account, he ended up hosting the show only because of his wife, who wanted him out of the house in the afternoon. He decided to look for a game show to fill his time, since, as he put it to me, "those are easy—usually you can do them five in one day." The executives at ABC, for their part, never thought of Philbin as a potential host until he suggested himself for the job, and even then they first offered it to several other people, who turned it down, presumably because the whole idea of a prime-time game show struck them as juvenile, or far-fetched, or both.

A week or two before I went with Philbin to the gym, I accompanied him to a taping for a new sports edition of the "Millionaire" CD-ROM game. He had just finished his morning talk show, formerly "Live! With Regis &

Kathie Lee," and now, since the departure of his co-host, Kathie Lee Gifford, just "Live with Regis," which has run five days a week for the last fifteen years. We took a chauffeured car down from the "Live" studio, on West Sixty-seventh Street, and when we arrived at the recording studio, which is on West Forty-second, we were on the wrong side of the street. The driver offered to make a U-turn to deliver us to the door. Philbin declined. "You sure?" the driver asked. "Yeah, sure," Philbin replied, though he should have known better. "Is that your final answer?" the driver asked. Philbin shot me a look of infinite suffering.

Inside the recording studio, half a dozen people were waiting. Philbin introduced me to them as a reporter who was doing a "very important piece" on him, an "exhaustive" piece, a piece that would be "a test" to read all the way to the end. We were ushered into a small soundproof room. Philbin sat on a stool in front of a large microphone. It soon became clear that the microphone wasn't working. No one seemed to be able to identify exactly what the problem was. "You understand?" Philbin told one of the technicians. "Eighty-five pages in *The New Yorker*. This is at least five pages."

After several minutes of bustle but no progress, Philbin asked his assistant to summon the managing director of the studio, Stephen Pinkus, who was apparently an old friend of his. Pinkus arrived almost immediately to inquire into the problem.

PHILBIN: The problem is I don't know what the hell the problem is. Pinkus, listen to me. *The New Yorker* magazine is doing an in-depth study.

PINKUS: Well, whatever he doesn't like we'll rip out. Get me construction!

PHILBIN: He's going to do a little show biz now. Pinkus, she's writing. She's writing things down. Let's go.

PINKUS: Ooh, ooh, I'm sweating!

PHILBIN: Steve Pinkus is a good name to slip in there. A lot of laughs, but no action.

PINKUS: What is the problem, so I can make it happen for you?

PHILBIN: We can't get audio.

PINKUS: Oh, well, you want audio also?

PHILBIN: He's very funny, Pinkus.

PINKUS: I must tell you something. Every time I walk in this building, they say, "You look just like Regis." And I say, "I taught Regis how to dress!"

The difference between watching Philbin on camera and off camera is, one quickly discovers, mostly just the camera. "Live with Regis" is unscripted and, to a large extent, also unplanned. Philbin doesn't believe in writers, and so no one, including his co-host, really knows what he's going to say during the twenty-minute stretch between the opening credits and the first commercial break. His shtick turns on the familiar devices of aggravation, insult, and bad luck—Why didn't Brad and Jennifer invite him to the wedding? "I should have been there!"—again and again.

As soon as the problem with the microphone was sorted out and Philbin got down to work, things proceeded swiftly. The producers had allocated twelve hours over three days for the taping, but Philbin read his lines, mostly a series of cheesy sports metaphors—"You're confident Answer B is a TKO," or "You're sure that Answer D won't drop you in a sand trap"—with so few glitches that he was finished in half that time.

At around one o'clock, the group broke for lunch. A lavish spread had been laid out just outside the sound studio. Philbin looked at the trays, heaped, in his honor, with baby vegetables, steak wraps, grilled chicken, and sautéed salmon, and started in again. He had, he told me, asked for a simple tuna-fish sandwich, and the sandwich, in its absence, became a preoccupation. "All I ever wanted was a tuna-fish sandwich. . . . Write this down. In New York City, you can't get a tuna-fish sandwich. . . . They want to give me sautéed chicken and salmon, and I don't want that. . . . Regis wanted to get a tuna-fish sandwich, but it's impossible in New York, delis being what they are." Eventually, someone went out to buy him the sandwich. It came wrapped in a piece of white paper, and Philbin ate it. Then he poured himself a cup of coffee, which was lukewarm. "That's O.K.," he said. "Regis doesn't deserve hot coffee."

Television, as a rule, humiliates the old, and there's no obvious reason that Philbin should be an exception. He may have a whole line of CD-ROM games, but he can't play them. "I'm computer-free, thank you," he once told me. The people he admires most—Dean Martin, Jack Paar, Perry Como—I could never remember if they were alive or dead.

Philbin got his first job in television, moving props at KCOP, in Hollywood, in 1955, the same year that "The $64,000 Question" premièred. TV was little more than a decade old, and almost everything on it, including the commercials, was broadcast live. Philbin recalls one particular ad, for a furniture store, which required schlepping entire roomfuls of dinettes back and forth from the prop house every time it aired.

Philbin grew up in the Bronx—his father was a personnel manager, his mother was a housewife—and appears to have enjoyed a classic, nineteen-forties stickball-and-soda-fountain sort of youth. He has no real explanation for his decision to work in television. "Why?" he once said when I pressed him on the subject. "I thought it would be fun. I don't know why." At Cardinal Hayes High School, and then at the University of Notre Dame, he had nothing to do with dramatics, or with performance of any kind. "I used to sit there in the auditorium and watch the band and watch the variety shows and the school productions," he told me. "I had no guts, no confidence. It was terrible." In this spirit, he dedicated his first autobiography, "I'm Only One Man!" (1995), to "any of you who have ever wanted to do something but feared you might not be good enough to do it."

For all his reported lack of confidence, Philbin rose quickly in L.A., from stagehand to writer to local newscaster. By the time he was twenty-eight, he had his own talk show, which aired Saturday nights at eleven-fifteen in San Diego, and when he was thirty-one Westinghouse tapped him to be the host of a nationally syndicated program. Entitled "That Regis Philbin Show!," the program was designed to compete against Johnny Carson's "Tonight Show." *Variety*, in a review of the show's première, called it "so low key it must have lulled a good portion of the audience to sleep." It was cancelled after just four months.

For the next twenty-five years, Philbin struggled, mostly unsuccessfully, to regain his early prominence. He went back to newscasting, hosted a series of local morning shows, and tried another nationally syndicated program; this one failed after five months. Tom Battista, who had been Philbin's director back in San Diego, had become the general manager of a station in St. Louis, and for three and a half years Philbin, commuting from L.A., did a once-a-week late-night show there. "All of us have to eat," Battista, who is still a close friend of Philbin's, told me. "And in this business it's sometimes tough to get a meal."

Recently, I went to look at a cache of old Philbin tapes that have been stored in boxes at ABC. A lot of his career was missing, either because no one had bothered to preserve the tapes or because no one had bothered to make them in the first place. I saw a very young Philbin milking a goat and getting attacked by a karate expert, and an older, grayer Philbin wrangling with baby lions in a cage, practicing pliés in a leotard and tights, and laughing uproariously while one of his co-hosts threw up. ("Put the camera on that man and shoot him! This is live television!") There was Philbin learning how to remove spots from stuffed animals with cornmeal, how to make dog biscuits at home, how to fight snoring, and how to do "sexergenics"; Philbin interviewing Dick Clark and Raquel Welch and Johnny Carson ("I don't know what my life would be without you at night to look forward to," he tells Carson, who responds, "Things aren't going that well, huh?"); and Philbin complaining—about his commute to the station, his inept bosses, his wife's eating habits, his reviews.

The conspicuous gap in the tapes was "The Joey Bishop Show," on which Philbin served as the abject sidekick. The show was yet another ill-fated attempt to go head to head with Carson, and lasted from 1967 to 1969. Whatever tapes still exist, Bishop has them and isn't sharing. I called him one day to ask about his recollections of Philbin, and the first thing he wanted to know was how he could be sure I was really a reporter. When he'd been more or less appeased on that topic, I asked whether he thought Philbin had changed, or grown, since his sidekick days. Bishop responded, "What are you looking for? Dirt?" He did, however, share with me, unsolicited, his thoughts about "Millionaire," which were that the prize money started too low. "I'm not rooting for some guy to win a hundred dollars," he said.

This summer, just before Kathie Lee Gifford left the morning show, she and Philbin performed a sold-out farewell concert at Westbury Music Fair, on Long Island. Gifford has a big, Broadway voice and a taste for songs about heartache, and "ordinary miracles," and change that "comes in on tiptoes." Philbin's voice—he himself is not sure whether it is a baritone or a tenor—probably wouldn't stand out at a neighborhood sing-along.

When the rehearsal for the show was finished, at about five-thirty, Philbin headed out to meet a publicity agent named Danny Frank for dinner at a local steak house. Philbin frequently complains that he has no entourage, but he obviously isn't interested in one, and he befriends, it seems, pretty much anyone who wants—or needs—his attention badly enough. One morning, I saw an elderly man greet Philbin at the door of his apartment building and then walk the hundred yards over to the studio with him. Later, I asked who that was, and Philbin told me it was just someone who seemed to like walking him to work and talking about sports. Similarly, Philbin told me that his friendship with Danny Frank dated back to a day in 1983 when Frank had spent several hours outside the studio waiting for him in the snow.

Frank, who used to book Henny Youngman into malls, has jowls and a fringe of gray hair and wears a diamond pinkie ring on each hand. During dinner, he and the steak house's owner, Gillis Poll, did most of the talking, a lot of it centering on trying to get Philbin to appear at a new restaurant that Poll's brother is opening in Central Park. Philbin just rolled his eyes, and cracked an occasional joke at Frank's expense. At one point, Poll's mother, Alexandra, a large woman in tinted glasses and a billowing white outfit, came in and sat down at the table.

"We had Vice-President Quayle and Pete Sampras here, and I have never come in, and this is the honest truth," she announced. "You are very loved. You really are very, very loved. I mean not only from me, but people love you. They really do. You are clever, clever with some of these contestants, and you make faces, and I am hysterical. You're not boring. You've got talent." Mrs. Poll then presented Philbin with a pocket-size holy picture in sterling silver, which, she said, she had brought back from Italy. Philbin thanked her: "It's the Virgin and—the baby Danny Frank!"

Until "Millionaire," Philbin's audience consisted mainly of women of a certain age—or older—and these are still, far and away, his most devoted fans. At the concert hall, there were easily four females for every male, and not a small number of them had trouble walking to their seats. Before the show, I spoke to some of these women about what had brought them to the concert and, more generally, their feelings about Regis and Kathie Lee. Most seemed well versed in the ups and downs of Philbin's life. (These include a first marriage, to the actress Kay Faylen, which produced a daughter, Amy, and a son, Danny, who was born without muscles in his legs and is confined to a wheelchair.) None made the slightest distinction between Philbin and his television persona. "He gets lost going to a restaurant," one woman, a piano teacher from Nesconset, told me. "He's totally down-to-earth, totally vulnerable. He didn't forget the mistakes he made in his life." About Gifford, sentiment seemed much more divided. One woman called her "a little too much"; another pronounced her "phony." Gifford has said that she left "Live" to pursue other opportunities, but some proffered the theory that she was really going because she couldn't deal with Philbin's "Millionaire" stardom.

My seat for the concert was in the front row and, as it happened, next to several members of Gifford's entourage. At one point, when she was working the aisles, vamping for a man who told her he had been married forty-eight years, Gifford noticed me taking notes. She asked what I was doing, and when I told her I was a reporter she snatched up my notebook and started reading aloud from it to the crowd. Just moments earlier, I had scribbled that her dress made her look like Bamm Bamm, but all she could discern from my handwriting was a transcription of her own words: "Let the next bimbo who works with him do that!" My presence became a running joke of her routine, and several times she turned to me, following one of her remarks, to shriek, "Write that down! That's funny!"

Gifford and Philbin have a standard act that they have refined over the years, the highlight of which is a classic put-down-the-audience stunt that ought to, but somehow doesn't, offend. Philbin invites onstage several hefty women, chats them up, and then serenades them with "Calendar Girl." This time, a woman who was determined to be included rushed the stage, flinging at Philbin a pair of red silk panties. "Thank you very much; that's a thrill," Philbin said while pantomiming terror. In honor of Gifford's departure, Philbin closed with a comic version of "Thanks for the Memories," and she called him "the bravest man" on television. "You can tell this man never had a writer," she declared, intending this, one had to assume, as a compliment.

After the show, there was a private party for the stars and the orchestra in a tent out in the parking lot. Since Philbin was with his wife, Joy, and involved in farewell toasts, I decided not to bother him on my way out. (The next day, I received a message on my voice mail: "Spend a whole day with you. Sing my guts out onstage for you. Do everything I can for you, and not even a goodbye.") As I was leaving, I went past a barricade behind which thirty or forty fans were waiting. Suddenly I found myself recognized as "the reporter," and, for no very good reason, the center of attention. One woman insisted on telling me a long, rambling, and completely unconvincing story about a date she had had with Regis in the early nineteen-fifties, when she was a teenager, and another wanted to tell me an even weirder and more irrelevant story, about her cousin's night out on the town with him. I found the whole experience disquieting; it gave me a faint inkling of what Philbin has to put up with all the time.

Just about the only claim Philbin makes with any passion for his forty-five years in television is on behalf of "host chat," the unscripted opening that he has used in a succession of talk shows, starting with his very first one in San Diego. Philbin claims to have got the idea for host chat from his idol, Jack Paar, in what amounts to a Gracie Allen-meets-Harold Bloom version of artistic influence. "Paar would come out, lean against his desk, and tell you what he saw," Philbin told me. It was only years later that he discovered that Paar's graceful, witty, off-the-cuff observations had, in fact, been composed for him by a staff of writers.

The subject matter for host chat is drawn partly from the morning's headlines but mostly from the flotsam and jetsam of Philbin's own experience, much of which, of course, consists of the making of the show. Philbin's on-air relationship with Gifford is, or at least was, central. When she joined the show, in 1985, Kathie Lee Johnson was a single woman whose career highlights included a stint on a TV comedy called "Hee Haw Honeys." She subsequently married Frank Gifford and went through two on-the-air pregnancies. Her stories about her children and her husband and her many home-improvement projects, while often hard to take, always gave Philbin something to work with. Both Michael Gelman, the executive producer of "Live," and Art Moore, WABC's director of programming, gradually became part of the routine as well; Gelman once bought himself a BMW and has never heard the end of it.

Lately, Philbin's own success has further narrowed his scope. He and Joy, who was Joey Bishop's assistant, live near his gym, on West Sixty-seventh Street. (They have been married for thirty years, and have two daughters, Jennifer and Joanna, who are both grown and out of the house.) The apartment is just across the street from WABC, where "Live" is shot in the morning, and down the block from the studio where "Millionaire" is taped, in the afternoon. During the week, Philbin spends most of his time inside this tiny triangle, and on the weekends he and Joy go to a house they own in Greenwich, where he likes to play tennis and watch sports on TV. Recently, Philbin was so strapped for material that a long stretch of host chat was given over to one of those annoying people whose legs are always blocking the aisle at the movies just when you need to go to the bathroom. (He needed to go twice.)

Philbin once told me that he thought host chat was "underappreciated," a valid claim, perhaps, but one that I was still a bit surprised to hear him make. To do live television of this nature requires a number of talents— among them flexibility, quickness, and an ear for the unexpected—but self-regard is not one of them. One day, after I had sat in the studio audience for "Live," I asked Philbin whether he thought that particular morning's program had gone well. "I don't even think about it anymore," he told me. "I never evaluate it afterward. It is what it is." The premise behind host chat, to the extent that there is one, would appear to be that people don't actually expect very much from TV. The worst that one could say about Philbin is that he has exploited this sad fact about the medium, and the best that he has recognized it for the wonderful opportunity it represents.

Not long ago, on "Who Wants to Be a Millionaire," Philbin put a question to a bouncer from L.A. named Rich Rosner:

What capital city is located at the highest altitude above sea level?

A. *Mexico City*

B. *Quito*

C. *Bogotá*

D. *Kathmandu*

Rosner had been a contestant on the first installment of "Millionaire," back in August of 1999, without ever reaching the "hot seat," and now he had got as far as the eight-thousand-dollar mark. He sat there sweating, talking to himself, rehearsing his reasoning, and eventually decided to use one of his "lifelines" to call his writer friend Michael. Michael was ninety-per-cent positive that the city was Kathmandu, but even after hearing this Rosner still couldn't make up his mind. He debated using another lifeline, pondered some more, and pronounced himself torn between Kathmandu and Mexico City. "It's really something, isn't it?" Philbin said. "You waited a year to get back here, and now you're here, and now we're waiting a year for your answer."

"Millionaire" has no time limits. Instead, it allows its contestants to stew over their responses indefinitely. This summer, one contestant, hoping to become the first woman to win the top prize, took forty minutes to answer the five-hundred-thousand-dollar question. (She answered wrong.) The very next week, a man surpassed her time by taking fifty-two minutes to wrestle with a two-hundred-and-fifty-thousand-dollar question. (He also answered wrong.) The "Millionaire" editors distill these tedious waits down to agonizing pauses, which they fill with the show's maddening telltale-heart sound effects and shots of the stricken contestants and their spouses. On TV, Rosner's ordeal lasted five minutes before he finally followed Michael's advice, only to learn that the correct answer was Quito.

All game shows are inherently sadistic. "Millionaire" is, in this respect, entirely typical—a familiar, even atavistic reprise of the original fifties formula. Yet still it manages to push the conceits to new heights of hamdom. Everything about it is overproduced and over the top, from the melodramatic pauses, throbbing sound effects, strobe lights, and hyperbolic prize money to the pan shots, fog machines, and campily futuristic set. To sit in the audience, with the lights underneath the Plexiglas floor swivelling in all directions and a huge camera boom sweeping overhead, is to feel as if one were inside a giant pinball machine.

Philbin says he recognized the potential of "Millionaire" immediately. In the spring of 1999, his agent sent him a tape of the British version of the show and, he told me, "As soon as I saw it, I said, 'Yeah, this is the one.' " He called executives at ABC who were considering importing the program to this country and made his pitch to be the host. "They weren't thinking of me," he said. "I wasn't on any list." (According to Philbin, people on the list included Phil Donahue and Montel Williams, neither of whom wanted the job.) He kept on pushing. His current contract with the network is reportedly worth twenty million dollars.

Philbin does not, in fact, represent a logical choice for the program's host. First of all, the job requires him to read most of his lines, something that he's never been terribly good at. (He still blames the failure of his Westinghouse show on the fact that he had to deliver jokes that had been written for him in advance.) Second, the show is in the wrong spirit for him. ABC licenses "Millionaire" from its British creators, who provide a set of specifications that run to a hundred and sixty-eight pages, and who insist on strict adherence to them whether the show is being produced in Italy or India. This is both the sort of rigidity that Philbin usually resists and the sort of self-seriousness he usually makes fun of.

The host of the British "Millionaire" is a large, voluble, ruddy man named Chris Tarrant. Tarrant clearly sees his role as compounding, whenever possible, the Sturm und Drang. "Are you positive?" he will ask, in a tone of voice that suggests you ought not to be. "Absolutely confident? Final, final answer?" Tarrant often treats a right answer as if it were wrong. "You had eight thousand pounds," he will say mournfully. Then, after a long pause: "You've now got sixteen thousand pounds!"

Philbin also teases his guests. In a moment that has become a "Millionaire" classic, Tom Colletta, who worked his way up to the eight-thousand-dollar question with Philbin stringing him along in the Tarrant manner, protested, "I'm a fat man, Regis, my heart can't take it." Philbin shot back, "I'm just trying to help you sweat off a few pounds." But Philbin is too benign to play torturer with the requisite gusto, and he generally seems more intent on diffusing anxiety than on generating it. When contestants

lose, even when they have done something incredibly stupid—especially
when they have done something incredibly stupid—Philbin appears to
feel genuinely sorry for them.

Michael Davies, the executive producer of the American "Millionaire,"
is himself British. He told me that at first he tried to encourage Philbin to
behave more like Tarrant. Now he is reconciled to, and even grateful for,
Philbin's resistance. Part of "Millionaire" 's appeal, he speculated to me, is
its host's out-of-placeness. "Regis manages to both distance himself from it
and be the star of it at the same time," he said.

At WABC, Philbin occupies a large, windowless room that he uses both as
an office and as a kind of warehouse. On the walls are old photographs,
long-forgotten awards, and aging posters, including a blowup of the cover
of Philbin's one and only LP, "It's Time for Regis!," which was released in
1968. Books and pictures and souvenirs, many of which have never been
unwrapped, cover every other available surface, including parts of the floor.
If there is a theme to all this, it is not show business but Notre Dame
football; there are Fighting Irish mugs and a Fighting Irish clock and an
old beat-up leather helmet and a large photograph of the football stadium,
and, in the place of honor, an elaborately framed letter signed by Knute
Rockne.

Philbin prepares for "Live" each day amidst this clutter, with his CD
player and his TV going at once. On the first, he plays and replays Dean
Martin; on the second, he follows his investments on CNBC, mainly, it
seems, in order to complain about them. "I only hear how much money
he's lost in the market," Tom Battista told me. "He doesn't talk about the
wins."

Philbin has obviously been more than comfortable for quite a while now.
Five years ago, when he and Joy moved to the West Side, they bought two
adjoining condominiums and broke down the walls between them. The
resulting apartment has a white grand piano, wraparound views of
Manhattan, and several large marble bathrooms. Before that, they lived
on Park Avenue.

On morning television, Philbin never really bothered to adapt the logic
of his routine to this success. Kathie Lee was the one entranced by

becoming a big star; Regis was the one always waiting for the show to be cancelled. "He's still the same insecure kid from the Bronx" was how Gifford liked to put it. By now, though, Philbin's shtick has stretched a little thin. At the farewell concert, for instance, he launched into a familiar lament about his daughter's extravagant European travels. "You can afford it, Reege," one fan yelled out, to much appreciative laughter. Nothing about "Millionaire," it seems safe to say, is underappreciated.

Not long ago, I went to talk to Philbin in his office for what I promised him would be the last interview. When I got there, Dino was singing about "*amore*" and tech stocks were tanking. As always, Philbin was in a tremendous hurry. He had just finished "Live," with Dolly Parton as that morning's co-host—ratings for the show, which has had a succession of guest co-hosts, have gone way up since Gifford left—and he was about to head down to Chelsea Piers to do a publicity photo shoot for ABC.

Philbin greeted me with an exaggerated, "here we go again" kind of look. He sat down at his desk, underneath a half-inflated Notre Dame football balloon, and I sat on a chair facing him, next to a doll wearing a Yankees uniform. We talked a little bit about his summer vacation—he had been in California and out in the Hamptons—and about the upcoming television season. Eventually, I asked him whether "Millionaire" fulfilled the dream he had had all those years ago, when he first started out in Los Angeles. I almost hoped he would make me pay for posing such a sentimental question, but, as I should perhaps have anticipated, he tried, instead, to help me out.

"Now that I think about it, you know, I had a sixth sense about television," he told me. "It was available for more or less the common man to be a part of. You didn't have to be a great singer, or a great dancer, or a great actor. You could make it on television without those talents, if you were able to reveal your humanness. And that's the way it happened. I watch myself on TV, and, I must tell you the truth, I say to myself, 'Why me? What's the big deal?' Thank God I'm on the morning show live, so I never see it. But once in a while, if I'm on tape, on a holiday or something, and I see it, I say, 'Oh my God.' I really mean that. I don't get it. I don't even like talking about it, because I'm afraid someone's going to say, 'Yeah! Why him?'"

The Prisoner

July 2001

A T APPROXIMATELY 3:45 P.M. on October 20, 1981, a Brink's truck pulled into the parking lot of the Nanuet Mall, in Rockland County, New York, to make its last pickup of the day. As one of the guards wheeled out a handcart carrying three sacks of cash, a red Chevy van drew up alongside. Gunmen in the Chevy killed the guard standing watch, and, in a matter of seconds, shot out the armored truck's windshield, wounded the guard with the handcart, and made off with $1.6 million. They then drove to the rear loading area of a nearby Korvettes, where a U-Haul truck picked them up.

A teen-age girl spotted the gunmen as they were climbing into the back of the U-Haul. She tipped off the police, who rushed to a nearby entrance to the New York State Thruway, in Nyack. The first U-Haul that they stopped was driven by a white man in his thirties, accompanied by a woman, also white, who was wearing a cotton dress. Since witnesses had identified the gunmen as black, the police weren't sure that they had the right vehicle. They were trying, unsuccessfully, to pull open the back of the truck when the door swung up on its own. The gunmen inside again opened fire, leaving two policemen dead.

By any standards, the Brink's robbery was ugly and cold-blooded; by those of suburban Rockland County, it was violent practically beyond comprehension. One of the officers who stopped the U-Haul had spent much of that day dealing with an obscene phone caller, and what normally passed for a big crime in Nyack was a hot-wired car. In the chaos that followed the shooting, several of the gunmen escaped in other getaway vehicles or by commandeering the cars of passersby. Among those arrested at the scene was the woman in the cotton dress. She identified herself as Barbara Edson, though she was, in reality, Kathy Boudin.

Boudin had last used her own name nearly twelve years earlier, when a homemade bomb accidentally exploded in a Greenwich Village town house. Three members of the Weather Underground had been killed in the blast, two blown up so completely that they were not identified for several days. Just after the explosion, two young women, one half-dressed, the other naked, had wandered out of the rubble, dazed and bleary-eyed, only to then disappear. The naked one was Boudin.

The daughter of a prominent civil-liberties lawyer, Boudin had grown up in Manhattan, graduated magna cum laude from Bryn Mawr, and then, in the fashion of the sixties, become a revolutionary. One of her last acts before going underground had been to co-write a how-to book on dealing with an arrest; its frontispiece showed Liberty, supine, being gang-raped by the police. News accounts immediately after the Brink's robbery played up Boudin's sensational past, as well as the threat of further violence. The gunmen, it was revealed, were linked to the Black Liberation Army, a well-armed spinoff of the Black Panthers. One of the getaway cars was traced to an apartment in East Orange, New Jersey, where police found bomb-making manuals and materials, diagrams of six Manhattan police-precinct houses, and a hit list of multinational corporations. The cost of the security around the Brink's trial was so high that Rockland County eventually had to impose a sales tax to pay for it.

Under New York State law, a participant in a felony can be held responsible for any deaths that result. For her role in the robbery, Boudin, who was unarmed, pleaded guilty to one count of felony murder and was sentenced to twenty years to life. She has not spoken publicly since her sentencing, in 1984, or ever explained what purpose she thought the robbery would serve. Nor has she offered an account of what she believed she was accomplishing by remaining underground six years after the end of the Vietnam War and a year into Ronald Reagan's Presidency. On the morning of the robbery, Boudin had dropped off her fourteen-month-old son at the babysitter's, as usual, packing a little knapsack for him with a bottle of milk, a few diapers, and some pocket-size picture books in which he had recently shown an interest. On her way out, she had run into a friend, who was leaving her young son with the same sitter, and the two mothers had talked briefly about taking the boys to the park that afternoon.

To get into Bedford Hills Correctional Facility, New York State's only maximum-security prison for women, you first have to enter a bunkerlike building with a watchtower attached. Next to the door is a window with a counter where you can drop off food and clothes for prisoners. "No thong, fishnet, g-string or bikini panties," a handwritten sign posted nearby reads. "No lace or sheer bras."

Nearly eight hundred women are incarcerated at Bedford, which is in northern Westchester County, and behind the razor wire life very much goes on. Inmates have conjugal visits, and they produce babies, who are allowed to stay in the prison's nursery until they are up to eighteen months old. Prisoners work and take classes and play softball, and, if they are fortunate, they receive visits from the children they have left on the outside. AIDS has hit the prison population hard—it is estimated that nearly one in five female inmates in New York is H.I.V.-positive—and so, increasingly, women also get sick, die, and are mourned at Bedford.

I interviewed Boudin four times at the prison, in a small room equipped with a few chairs and a round table. Now fifty-eight, Boudin has dark-blue eyes and wavy black hair that is streaked with gray. At each of our meetings, she had on the prison's standard-issue green pants, but on top wore something of her own: a purple velour pullover one time, a white blouse another. We also spoke a few dozen times by telephone. (Although prisoners cannot receive calls, they can make them, collect.) Talking on the phone, I was sometimes able to forget where she was, though not for long. Usually, Boudin would call at around ten o'clock at night, and at ten-twenty-five or so she would start to get nervous. At ten-thirty, she would have to run to her cell for a "count." At eleven o'clock, the line would go dead.

In the last seventeen years, Boudin has been outside Bedford only once, for a medical test. Owing to the nature of her crime, she is what is known as a "tracker"; every time she moves from one building to another, an officer calls ahead to her destination. She remains a tracker despite the fact that she has an exemplary disciplinary record, and, indeed, now lives in an honor unit.

While in prison, Boudin has earned a master's degree in adult education and literacy. She has co-written a handbook for inmates who have children in foster care. In the late nineteen-eighties, she helped design an AIDS support program that is now used as a model at prisons across the country, and, more recently, she created a program for mothers and their adolescent children, which is also expected to be copied nationally. She has published articles in the *Harvard Educational Review* and the *Journal of Correctional Education*, and she won a 1999 PEN award for her poetry. Her cell, which I never saw, but which she described to me, measures eight by ten feet, and contains a bed, a toilet, a sink that provides cold water, two metal lockers, and a plastic chair. With permission from the authorities, she has rigged up a desk by arranging a board on top of the lockers, but, because the lockers are too high, she has to sit on a pillow in order to work at it. Among the many ironies of Boudin's imprisonment at Bedford is that it has been the most productive period of her life.

Bedford has also provided Boudin with a version of the egalitarian society—albeit a state-enforced one—that, as a revolutionary, she was working toward. For the most part, she has embraced this. "Kathy has helped many people who have never had a helping hand in their lives," said Thea Jackson, a former state official, who for many years volunteered at Bedford. Prison rules made it impossible for me to talk to other current inmates, but I spoke to nearly a dozen former prisoners—black, white, and Hispanic—who had served time with Boudin, and they all talked about how much she had done for them. "The one person that was there for me all the time was Kathy," a woman who served twelve years on drug charges told me. "She speaks for women who are too afraid to speak themselves." Another former prisoner, who had spent fifteen years with Boudin and worked with her on the AIDS program, observed, "Coming from a different background and being Caucasian sometimes can cause conflicts for people, but for her it did not. There is probably not one person there who would say something bad about Kathy." The only inmate I heard Boudin herself speak at all disparagingly about was Jean Harris, who murdered Herman Tarnower, the Scarsdale-diet doctor, and was for several years Bedford's most celebrated inmate. Boudin described Harris as "independent," by which she clearly meant that she was a snob, or worse.

Boudin will come up for parole for the first time in August. Her many accomplishments at Bedford, her model behavior, and her efforts on behalf of her fellow-inmates are all strong arguments for parole, to the extent, that is, that any argument could make a difference. Her decision to speak to me was clearly made with this in mind. At the same time, whatever flexibility and small freedoms Boudin now enjoys are granted at the discretion of the authorities, who are not necessarily eager to see Bedford described as a place where former terrorists are permitted to be leaders. Once, when I asked one of the prison officials if I could watch a parenting class that Boudin was "running," the official immediately corrected me. Boudin, she said, was not "running" but merely "facilitating" it. (Permission to sit in on the class was denied.) On another occasion, I asked Boudin about something I thought she had "organized." "I am so afraid of the word 'organize,'" she said. "I feel like it's going to get me in trouble, because you're not allowed to organize. I'd rather say 'create projects.' Have I done that? Constantly."

Boudin was born on May 19, 1943, and grew up in a brownstone on St. Luke's Place, opposite a playground, in Greenwich Village. She was an avid athlete, and her early ambition was to become the first bat girl in the major leagues. In those days, the Village was still bohemian, at least in the eyes of the F.B.I., and one afternoon, when Boudin was seven or eight, an agent came to the door. "My mother was very small—she was four feet eleven—and this guy was very big, and he was handsome," she recalled. "I could not understand what was happening in front of me. He said, 'I just wanted to ask a few questions about your neighbors,' and my mother said, 'I'm sorry, you'll have to leave.' I thought she was being rude to him, and I was really upset about it. I ran down the street, and I said to him, 'What would you like to know?' And he said, 'Well, I just want to know their names.' I told him. And he patted me on the head and said, 'You're going to be a very good American.'"

The Boudins could be described as a classically ambitious, talented, and liberal New York Jewish family, were it not that they were almost too ambitious, talented, and liberal. Boudin attended the Little Red School

House, then Elisabeth Irwin High School, both progressive private schools where many of the teachers had been blacklisted. A typical field trip was a weeklong outing to a steel-making town. Boudin's mother, Jean, was a poet, and her uncle was the journalist I. F. Stone. Judith Viorst, the writer, who babysat for Kathy, remembers her as "from the earliest days on very idealistic."

Boudin's father, Leonard, founded his own law firm in 1947, intending to pursue labor law, but rose to prominence during the McCarthy hearings. At one point, he held the record for the most clients represented before the House Un-American Activities Committee. When he was accused of being a Communist himself, he flatly denied it. "I have a basic cynicism for any political line," he later said. "I'm not a radical, because I don't know where the truth is."

Some of Leonard Boudin's clients, including Paul Robeson, Jessica Mitford, and Dr. Benjamin Spock, became family friends. Ellen Sklar, a schoolmate of Kathy's, describes the atmosphere in the Boudin's living room as being "like a salon—a little intimidating." Leonard and Jean encouraged Kathy and her older brother, Michael, to participate in the free-ranging discussions, and in general expected a great deal from them. "There was an understanding that, whatever they were going to do, they were going to contribute in a big way," Sklar told me. Michael, in fact, went on to graduate magna cum laude from Harvard and then to become president of the law review at Harvard Law School. He specialized in antitrust litigation until he was appointed to the federal bench by President George Bush, in 1990.

When Kathy was nine years old, she came home from school one day to find the apartment smelling of gas and her mother lying unconscious on the floor of the kitchen. Jean spent the next three years in psychiatric hospitals. During this time, Kathy developed a variety of phobias: she wouldn't ride the subway, and refused to stay in the apartment alone. She also resolved to go to medical school. "My fantasy of myself was all about being a doctor, and I think that came out of wanting to heal, to help my mother," she said. Her favorite movie, "Never Take No for an Answer," was about an orphaned Italian boy who takes his sick donkey to the tomb of St. Francis to pray for a cure.

When Jean came home, she tried to pick up with her children where she had left off, but found that her daughter wasn't interested. "I basically said, 'I did fine without you, so why do I need you now?' " Boudin recalled. "She wanted to take me to the dentist. I said, 'I don't need to go to the dentist with you. I've been going alone.' She would say, 'Well, let me buy you some comic books and then we'll go.' And I would know that she was bribing me and trying to get me, out of her own vulnerability, to let her do something, and I would get the comic books."

At school, Boudin was energetic, disciplined, and self-doubting. "I worked hard, but I always felt there were other people that were more talented," she said. "In any area that I could get an A, there was always somebody that maybe got a B or C, but they were really better." She worked one summer at a hospital, the next at a camp for handicapped children, and the summer after that at a blood bank. In 1964, following her junior year at Bryn Mawr, Boudin went west to spend the summer in Cleveland. There she lived in a communal house on the impoverished Near West Side and worked as a community organizer for what was called the Economic Research and Action Project, or ERAP. Her mother, in a piece for *Ms* magazine that was published some ten years later, recalled her dismay. "I still shudder over a visit to their rooms in a Cleveland slum," Jean Boudin wrote. "It wasn't the roaches that bothered me, it was the rats. They lived with the poor, as the poor."

Even before her summer with ERAP, Boudin had begun to have second thoughts about a career in medicine. Although she had taken the requisite premed courses at Bryn Mawr, and had got good grades in them, she had come to believe that she wasn't talented enough—not realizing, as she now puts it, "that you don't have to be a great scientist to be a doctor." For Boudin, this fairly typical college experience was traumatic. She suffered from insomnia and went to see a therapist. In Cleveland, she found a new sense of purpose. "It was thrilling," she told me. "I felt like I was learning about the realities of class, of poverty. It was the discovery that there was a whole other world that I was living next to, part of, and didn't really know about."

ERAP was run by Students for a Democratic Society, the campus group that came to epitomize "the New Left." S.D.S. had set up similar projects in cities like Baltimore, Chicago, Newark, and Boston, all founded on two not necessarily compatible objectives. On one hand, student volunteers were supposed to help out on a practical level—for example, organizing neighborhoods to lobby for improved garbage collection. On the other, they were supposed to be building what they called, with a kind of grandiose innocence, an "interracial movement of the poor." Boudin recalls long debates with her fellow-ERAPers over virtually everything, including the politics of pocket change.

After graduating from Bryn Mawr, in 1965, she returned to the Cleveland project, this time focussing her efforts on welfare mothers. It was, she says, rewarding work, and she was basically happy at it, though the longer she was involved the harder it was for her to reach any decision about her future. "Here were people who could have been a housekeeper or a maid in the house that I grew up in," she told me. "I was living on the other side of that, and it made me feel guilty. I felt increasingly ambivalent about whether I could see myself moving toward a professional life. It seemed like it would perpetuate, in my own life, more privilege." As a senior in college, Boudin had applied to Yale Law School—and only Yale Law School—and been rejected. While in Cleveland, she applied to a variety of other law schools, only to defer her enrollment once she had been accepted. Eventually, she put in a desultory half term at Case Western Reserve, which she chose, she said, in part because of its low standards.

The Cleveland project that Boudin was working on collapsed in 1968, one of the many casualties of that extraordinary year. It was hard for any form of activism to measure up to the events of the time—the assassinations, the riots, the escalation of the Vietnam War. For S.D.S., the increasing pressure to act boldly resulted in dissension and, ultimately, factionalization. For Boudin, it caused more confusion. "When Cleveland dissolved, it definitely left me feeling very anxious," she told me. "What am I going to do and who am I?"

Now jobless, Boudin travelled to Chicago, that August, for the Democratic National Convention. She was in Lincoln Park for the first violent clashes, where demonstrators threw rocks and were clubbed and teargassed by the police. She maintains that she was not involved in the violence but, rather, intimidated by it. "It was scary to me," she said. Still, a few days later, she managed to get arrested in an episode that is, as she describes it, both absurd and ominous.

"The next day, after the Lincoln Park situation, a couple of friends of mine and I were asked whether we would like to do some work that meant that we couldn't go in the demonstrations," she told me. "The word that was used was 'secret,' or something like that. I welcomed it. I thought because it was secret it had a sense of status to it, a higher level of commitment. The first thing we did was spray-paint the door of a C.I.A. office that nobody knew was really the C.I.A. The second thing we were asked to do was to take some liquid that smelled like rotten eggs and put it on the rugs of the delegates' cocktail lounges. We were in the Palmer House hotel, and I remember sitting in the lounge. The two women I was with were at different tables, and they got picked up by hotel security. I watched them be taken, and I remember sitting there and thinking, I could just leave, you know, and in a way I felt like that's what I should do. The other part of me felt like, well, if I leave, they'll be heroes, and nobody will know that I'm doing this work. And it was that anxiety: how am I going to prove that I'm a committed person? I was sitting there, and all of that went through my mind—it wasn't even through my mind, it went through my feelings—and I jumped up and followed them. I think I actually asked someone, 'Where's hotel security?' And I went in there and basically threw myself into the arms of the security. It took me a long time to tell that story because it's embarrassing. I felt embarrassed about the idea that, instead of being a hero, I was somebody who was looking for a way to be a hero."

"You Don't Need a Weatherman to Know Which Way the Wind Blows" ran in the June 18, 1969, issue of *New Left Notes*. The sixteen-thousand-word manifesto, which took its title from Bob Dylan's "Subterranean Homesick Blues" and was written by eleven S.D.S.ers, called for an end to class privilege, bourgeois capitalism, and American imperialism. More immediately, it was a *cri de guerre* in the increasingly sectarian battle for control of the organization.

It is nearly impossible at this remove to write a sympathetic, or even entirely coherent, account of what Weatherman—or the Weathermen, or

Weatherfolks, or, finally, the Weather Underground—was up to. Its founding document is almost too full of grand, synthetic claims about its place in history:

> The strategy . . . for developing an active mass base, tying the city-wide fights to community and city-wide anti-pig movement, and for building a party eventually out of this motion, fits with the world strategy for winning the revolution, builds a movement oriented toward power, and will become one division of the International Liberation Army, while its battlefields are added to the many Vietnams which will dismember and dispose of U.S. imperialism.

At the same time, the group was clearly making up its ideology as it went along, mixing Marx and Mao and Che with whatever else was at hand. According to Weather doctrine—at least some of the time—blacks formed a "colony" within the United States which made them part of "the international revolutionary vanguard." The American government was fated, in its efforts to maintain imperialist power, to overextend itself and fall, and it was the role of enlightened whites to hasten this process along. "The best thing that we can be doing for ourselves, as well as for the Panthers and the revolutionary black liberation struggle, is to build a fucking white revolutionary movement," proclaimed Bernardine Dohrn, a University of Chicago law-school graduate who later became the group's spokeswoman.

Much more than ideology, however, it was sex and violence and, more specifically, the sexiness of violence that the group contributed to the revolutionary cause. The Weatherman leadership swaggered around in sunglasses and leather, looking petulant and cool. Dohrn, before making the F.B.I.'s Ten Most Wanted list, posed for Richard Avedon in a miniskirt. (J. Edgar Hoover reportedly called her "La Pasionaria of the Lunatic Left.") At first, the group's posturing was cartoonish and, it is hard not to believe, self-consciously so. At Weatherman's National War Council, held in late 1969 in Flint, Michigan, a huge cardboard machine gun swung from the ceiling. The Manson murders were treated as an inspired political act. "Dig it," Dohrn declared. "First, they killed those pigs, then they ate dinner in the same room with them. Then they even shoved a fork into a victim's stomach. Wild!" Delegates to the council took to greeting each other with spread fingers signifying the fork.

Boudin made an unlikely Weatherman. During her years in Cleveland, she had never taken much interest in S.D.S.'s internal ideological battles, or made any effort to play a leadership role in the organization, and her persistent self-doubt clashed with the group's sense of style. Yet, by the fall of 1969, she had become an active participant. Boudin attributes her involvement to Weatherman's not quite Marxist position that blacks, rather than workers, made up the revolutionary class. "With black people there was just an understanding that there was something fundamentally wrong with the whole system," she told me.

One of Boudin's first responsibilities was to help plan the Days of Rage, which was intended to "bring the war home" by replaying the Chicago protests of 1968. To build support for the event, Weathermen staged "jailbreaks," storming into classrooms in high schools and community colleges across the country, tying up the teachers and delivering lectures on sexism, racism, and imperialism. They also disrupted other groups' meetings and harangued the crowds for their lack of militancy. In one fairly typical incident, they took hostages at the American Friends Service Committee in Pittsburgh while they used the organization's office to run off leaflets.

For all their efforts, only about two or three hundred helmeted combatants showed up in Chicago that October, producing a protest that looked a lot like petty vandalism—kids trashing cars and stores on the city's Gold Coast. More than a hundred were arrested, among them Boudin, who was picked up while carrying a Vietcong flag through Lincoln Park. Two months later, in Flint, she played a minor role in the antics onstage, and came home to New York with mono and a case of V.D.

As far as bringing down the American government was concerned, Weatherman had no discernible effect. But, for the student movement, it was lethal. The faction took control of S.D.S. at a time when the organization had some three hundred chapters, with between thirty thousand and a hundred thousand members. It had no use for this national infrastructure and set about, quite deliberately, dismantling it. "I hate

S.D.S.—I hate this weird liberal mass of nothingness," one Weatherman founder declared. "You don't need a rectal thermometer to know who the assholes are," came the bitter reply of a Wisconsin S.D.S. chapter.

How, exactly, Weatherman's cartoon violence turned into something more serious—the stockpiling of explosives and the building of bombs—is uncertain. It could be that the group felt trapped by its rhetoric, or that its leaders genuinely began to believe in it. What is clear is that Weatherman began to rationalize its failures, in classic cult fashion, by raising the stakes. According to its self-punitive and self-justifying logic, those truly committed to the cause ought to be willing to sacrifice everything for it; therefore, whoever made the biggest sacrifice was the most committed—a false syllogism, at best. As Bill Ayers, one of the members of the Weatherbureau, the group's high command, put it, victory would come only to those willing to throw it all away: "It's not a comfortable life, it's not just a dollar more, it's standing up in the face of the enemy, and risking your life and risking everything for that struggle."

One weekend last month, I went to visit Dohrn and Ayers, who were married in 1982. (Dohrn was in jail at the time, and received a furlough for the occasion.) The two now live in a turn-of-the-century row house in the Hyde Park neighborhood of Chicago, along with Dohrn's mother, Dorothy, who suffers from Alzheimer's. They have raised three boys: two of their own, Zayd and Malik, and Boudin's son, Chesa, who has lived with them since he was fifteen months old.

Dohrn teaches law at Northwestern University and is, at fifty-nine, still notably glamorous. Ayers, who is fifty-six, teaches education at the University of Illinois at Chicago; his business card reads "Distinguished Professor, University Scholar, Educator, Activist, Peacemaker, Flash-of-Lightning." The night I got to Chicago, the couple was giving a party, timed to coincide with the booksellers' convention, which was being held downtown; as I was arriving, Studs Terkel was just leaving. Ayers's memoir, titled "Fugitive Days," is coming out this fall, and he was handing his guests promotional stick-on tattoos of the Weatherman symbol—a three-colored rainbow crossed by a lightning bolt. He showed me a larger version of the symbol tattooed on his upper back.

The fate of Weatherman's members since the group's breakup, in 1976, bears, it seems, an almost inverse relationship to their original roles in the organization. Though far and away the most famous of the group, Dohrn served only one jail stint of any significance—seven months for refusing to coöperate with a federal grand jury investigating the Brink's case. Ayers has served practically no time, despite cheerfully admitting in his memoir to, among other illegal acts, conspiring to bomb the Pentagon. His best friend and fellow Weatherbureau member Jeff Jones, who is now an environmental lobbyist in Albany, was charged with illegal possession of explosives; he received probation and community service. "We are hugely lucky," Ayers told me when I asked about the way things have played out. Meanwhile, other members of the group, including Boudin's ex-partner— and Chesa's father—David Gilbert, who drove the U-Haul during the Brink's robbery, are serving sentences of seventy-five years to life.

At the time of the Brink's holdup, Dohrn and Ayers were living in Manhattan and had been above ground for nearly a year. They recalled going to visit Leonard and Jean Boudin shortly after the robbery and finding Jean, at that point nearly seventy years old, on the floor with Chesa, trying to figure out how to put on a Pampers. A few weeks later, Chesa went to live with Dohrn and Ayers. Virtually all of the grandparents, in one way or another, opposed the arrangement. Ayers remembers that his father, a former chairman of Commonwealth Edison, thought Chesa might be happier if he were adopted anonymously and allowed to forget his past. Leonard Boudin, for his part, used to have Dr. Spock visit Dohrn and Ayers's fifth-floor Harlem walkup to keep tabs on the boy's development. "He was in anguish about the fact that we were raising his grandson," Ayers said. "And also that we weren't cultivated enough and New York enough," Dohrn added. (Leonard died in 1989, Jean in 1994.)

Chesa was not an easy child—he threw tantrums, refused to wear a coat, even in the middle of the winter, cursed out his teachers, and needed special tutoring. He is now twenty, and a history major at Yale. In her conversations with me, Boudin referred to Chesa constantly, Dohrn and Ayers only rarely. Chesa remains quite close to Boudin, but he calls her "Kathy" and refers to Dohrn as "Mom."

"It couldn't be more complicated," Dohrn told me. "It's totally loaded in every way. And everything that we do that's wonderful should be her doing it, and every risk that we took should be us paying a heavy price for it. And in that sense Kathy's been unbelievably generous and transcendent, and we've all struggled over those obvious tensions and resentments and inevitable conflicts, both in every phone conversation and in the broader, global sense."

Dohrn and Ayers's luck runs, in a perverse form, all the way back to the town-house bombing, in March, 1970. Before the explosion, Weatherman was preparing to commit more serious acts of violence, though to what purpose remained unresolved. Some argued that the violence should be essentially symbolic, a form of guerrilla theatre; others were intent on turning Weatherman into a band of actual fighters. The bomb that was being prepared in the town house was meant for a nearby Army base, and its design—roofing nails wrapped around dynamite—signalled an intention to inflict casualties. When it went off, it killed Terry Robbins, one of the more militant Weathermen, as well as Ted Gold and Ayers's girlfriend at the time, Diana Oughton. In his memoir, Ayers fantasizes that it was Oughton who set off the bomb, and that she did so deliberately, to prevent still more tragic consequences. "The town house knocked us back and forced us to reassess ourselves, pulling us back from that particular abyss," he told me.

For Boudin, the blast had the reverse effect. Up to that point, she had been a secondary figure in Weatherman, and, as its leaders had begun, one after another, to go underground, she had, she says, felt left out. "Occasionally I would see people that I knew and the next day they weren't there, and I was still there," she told me. "And I felt bad, because I felt that something was happening and I didn't know what it was."

Boudin was taking a shower at the time of the explosion. She maintains that she had had no idea what was going on in the town house's basement and that she had initially thought the blast was an earthquake. (She was never charged in connection with the bombing, although the other survivor, Cathy Wilkerson, whose father owned the building, eventually served nearly a year in prison for it.) When Boudin emerged naked from the wreckage, Susan Blanchard Wager, one of Henry Fonda's ex-wives, who lived a few houses down, took her in and gave her some old clothes;

Wager went back outside for a moment, and Boudin slipped away. No one who had seen her come out of the house knew who she was; she was identified a few days later, when a dentist's appointment card with her name on it was found in the debris. Despite the intense publicity, Boudin, who was staying with her parents, kept the appointment. She recalls that she felt traumatized but, at the same time, oddly relieved. "My name appeared in the newspaper," she told me, "and I said, 'Oh, good, now I can go underground.'"

"Foreign Influence—Weather Underground Organization," a now de-classified F.B.I. report, was written by the bureau's Chicago office in 1976. It attempts to detail every significant trip abroad made by every member of the group, going back nearly ten years. The file runs to several hundred pages, and, even so, represents only a tiny fraction of the F.B.I.'s efforts. The bureau planted a mole inside Weatherman, conducted what are now known to have been extensive illegal surveillance operations, and dis-tributed photos of twenty Weatherman members, including a stunned-looking Boudin, on "Wanted" posters around the country. Either the F.B.I. had its own reasons for wanting to fail or it was phenomenally incompetent. Weatherman was made up of middle-class kids with no prior training in covert activities, yet with a few exceptions they managed to elude capture.

Boudin describes life underground as uneventful to the point of being dull. In the early years, operating under a variety of aliases, she went to Mexico to practice her Spanish, picked grapes with migrant workers in California, and worked at a Massachusetts hospital, drawing blood. At one point, the Weatherbureau sent her around to campuses and community groups to try to build support for the antiwar movement, but without the benefit of normal communication tools, like an address or a telephone. "Much of our time was spent continuing to try to play a leadership role above ground, and yet we were underground," Boudin told me. "It didn't make sense, but it's a lot of what we did."

Meanwhile, bombs were going off. All told, Weatherman took credit for some two dozen blasts, including one in the offices of the National Guard in Washington, D.C., and another at police headquarters in Manhattan.

Partly through good planning and partly through good fortune, the group avoided killing anyone, and mostly just damaged buildings. In September, 1970, it teamed up with an organization that called itself the Brotherhood of Eternal Love to spring Timothy Leary from prison in California and spirit him to a Panther compound in Algeria. The following March, Weatherman bombed the Capitol. "We have attacked the Capitol because it is, along with the White House and the Pentagon, the worldwide symbol of the government which is now attacking Indochina," Weather Underground Communiqué No. 8 declared. A month later, according to F.B.I. documents, Boudin's fingerprints were found in an apartment that had been used as a "bomb factory" in San Francisco.

Boudin says that she herself never made or planted a bomb, although as a member of Weatherman she implicitly supported such activities. In 1970, she was one of twelve members of the group indicted on federal conspiracy charges. (These indictments, like most of the other charges against the Weathermen, were later dropped, because of the illegality of the methods used to obtain them.) "There were thousands of acts of violent protest happening all around," Boudin told me. "Every day, you would hear about acts of violence, so it didn't feel unusual in a certain way." Together with several other members of the group, in 1974 Boudin wrote a book, "Prairie Fire," which presents American history as a series of imperialist adventures, and in 1975 she appeared—behind a scrim—in "Underground," a documentary by Emile de Antonio. Although the film seems to have been intended to explain, if not justify, the group's agenda, Weatherman's fundamental incoherence made this difficult. Halfway through it, Boudin talks about what it feels like to be inside an explosion. "It's that kind of time that can't be counted on a clock," she says. "It's that kind of time that seems to go on forever, and you have a chance to see your whole life in that moment, and also the lives of your friends."

As desultory as these activities may have been, they were, in relation to what followed, comparatively purposeful. With the end of the Vietnam War, in 1975, Weatherman lost whatever focus it had left, and disintegrated. The old leadership—Dohrn and Ayers included—was charged with betraying the movement's causes. Accused of representing "agents of the bourgeoisie within the revolution," they were eventually purged in a coup engineered by Clayton Van Lydegraf, a sixty-one-year-old Maoist. Boudin considered giving herself up, but decided against it. She took a series of menial jobs, less because of the difficulties of working under an alias than out of a kind of politicized asceticism. For a while, she lived with friends in Ohio and cleaned houses, a job she says she wasn't particularly good at. By her own account, she would have found it easier to come back above ground if her life underground hadn't been so ineffectual.

"The very status of being underground was an identity for me," she told me during an interview at Bedford. "It was a moral statement. Three years, five years, eight years, ten years, eleven years—that was who I was, and it didn't really matter if I was doing anything. If I had been doing any of the kinds of things that I do here," she went on, "or any of the kinds of things I imagine doing when I go home, I wouldn't have felt the way I felt. In the world we live in, you make a difference in a small way, but it feels like you are doing something. But I was making a difference in no way, so then I elevated to great importance the fact that I was underground."

Several weeks ago, I went to a meeting in the Valley Cottage Public Library, a mile from the site of the Brink's robbery. Sitting around the table were about a dozen family members of the murdered men, as well as a local police chief, a district state assemblyman, and representatives from several law-enforcement agencies. The purpose of the gathering was to come up with a strategy to prevent Boudin from getting parole.

Initially, there had been some resistance to my attending. Just last January, Susan Rosenberg, who was indicted in connection with the Brink's case and later convicted on a federal weapons charge, was freed from prison, a beneficiary of the final frenzied round of Clinton pardons. In Nyack, many felt betrayed by the commutation of Rosenberg's sentence, and by what they saw as the media's sympathetic coverage of it. At the start of the meeting, Diane O'Grady, the widow of Sergeant Edward O'Grady, one of the slain policemen, came over to show me a photo of her family taken shortly before her husband was killed. As it happens, I have three sons who are now much the same age as the three O'Grady children were then, and when she handed me the picture I nearly started to cry. This seemed to reassure her.

All told, the robbery left nine children fatherless, and three of them were at the library that evening. Michael Paige and Peter Paige, Jr., the two sons of the slain Brink's guard, had driven up from New Jersey with their mother, Josephine. Gregory Brown, the son of Police Officer Waverly Brown, was there alone. His presence—Brown is black—pointed to one of the crime's crueller ironies.

Talk around the table alternated between halfhearted efforts at objectivity and expressions of visceral hatred. "We have the right to be bitter," Jim Kralik, Rockland County's sheriff, said. "We have the right to be frustrated. We have a great deal of right, especially you, the families, to have the pain. But the attitude we should take is that we want appropriate justice."

"That Susan Rosenberg was released for clemency is an absolute friggin' disgrace," John Dillon, a retired police captain, said. "I cannot say that loud enough and long enough. This is a network. They came into Rockland County, they killed us, they stopped us one day, but guess what? Rockland County reached out, and every friggin' one of them was caught. Some of them almost got out because of the system. She's not going to get out. She should stay in prison for the rest of her friggin' life and rot. People died, for what? So that these scum could continue their cause against the American dream?"

Among the claims I heard over the course of the evening was that Boudin was still a revolutionary; that her work at the prison was intended only to impress the parole board; that she was utterly unrepentant; and that she was violent and remained a danger to society. Someone even asserted that she had lied about her birthday, choosing May 19th only because it was the birth date of Ho Chi Minh and of Malcolm X. Pointing out that these claims were unfounded would have been not only inappropriate but also irrelevant. The friends and families of the victims are not interested in what Boudin is really like, nor, understandably, are they interested in becoming interested. They want the empathy to run the other way, to force her to experience something of the losses they've endured. "She raised her son while in prison." Diane O'Grady said at one point. "So this child was held and loved, and yet what about our kids? The only sentence that is justified to any of us is life."

*   *   *

Among the poems that Boudin has written while at Bedford is a series that deals directly with her crime. In one fragment, narrated from the perspective of a woman riding in the cab of a truck, Boudin imagines—or describes—what it feels like to be stopped at gunpoint:

> I look into the eyes of guns
> and wonder
> will they shoot me
> My hair is taut
> my skin is stretched
> my eyes are popping
> my breath comes out in short puffs
> Clang metal and metal.

The central event in her life, the Brink's robbery is also the one Boudin had the most trouble talking to me about. There are many quite practical reasons I could imagine for this, some bearing on parole and some on her relations with others, particularly David Gilbert, the father of her child. But her difficulty, I came to feel, also had to do with the same needs that had brought her to Nyack in the first place.

Boudin is, in her recounting of the crime, a strangely passive figure. She is an even more strangely uninformed one. She didn't know, she maintains, exactly who was committing the robbery, how the perpetrators planned to go about it, or what they hoped ultimately to do with the money. She now characterizes this ignorance as "sick," but says that at the time it made sense to her. She had read widely about the Underground Railroad during her years as a housecleaner and, she told me, had come to identify with the white women who were involved in it, sometimes at great personal cost. She also used religious analogies to try to convey something of her mindset: "Had I been Roman Catholic, perhaps I would have been a nun" was a thought she voiced to me more than once.

"I developed a politics: the way for me to enact this issue of empowerment was to put myself at the service of a Third World group," she explained. "My way of supporting the struggle is to say that I don't have the right to know anything, that I don't have the right to engage in political discussion, because it is not my struggle. I certainly don't have a right to criticize anything. The less I would know and the more I would give up total self, the better—the more committed and the more moral I was."

The "Third World group" Boudin chose to submit herself to was the remnants of the Black Liberation Army. Organized in the early nineteen-seventies, the group had taken as one of its missions the murder of police officers, in the name of liberating African-American communities. By the mid-seventies, most of its original leaders were dead or behind bars, and others had hooked up with a gang of armed robbers, known among themselves as "the family," who specialized in sticking up armored trucks. Their code name for the Brink's job was "the Big Dance," and had it been successful it's likely that some of the proceeds would have gone to an acupuncture center in Harlem and some to buying cocaine for "family" members. When I pressed Boudin on her choice, asking how, of all possible groups, she could have chosen this one, I was met with a long and pained silence.

At the time that Boudin began her association with the B.L.A., she was, she says, taking steps toward establishing a normal life. She had recently moved back to New York, where she had renewed contact with her parents, visiting them for the first time in years. She had set about repairing her relationship with Gilbert, with whom she had long been involved. And she had had Chesa. Though her efforts were halting and tentative, she had begun looking for an occupation, first getting certified as a paralegal, then hanging out at Sarah Lawrence to see if she could imagine herself back at graduate school. She had also begun taking Valium for panic attacks that she attributes to the strain of trying to begin again.

She was approached about the Brink's robbery, she claims, just twenty-four hours beforehand, and received her instructions while sitting in a Manhattan restaurant. She was supposed to ride in the U-Haul to Nanuet, and then wait with Gilbert, several blocks away, while the actual holdup took place. The idea was that the white couple in the cab would act as a cover, throwing off the police, who would be looking for a band of black gunmen.

About the robbery itself, Boudin has little to say. When the first gun battle took place, she was, she says, too far away to know what was going on. She claims that she was still unaware that anyone had been shot when the U-Haul was stopped by the police near the Thruway, and that she missed the second shoot-out as well. She recalls being pulled over, getting out of the truck with her hands up, and then, in response to loud noises from the back, running in fear. She was not, she insists, trying to escape. She made it as far as the edge of the Thruway, where she was picked up by an off-duty corrections officer who happened to be driving by.

Several of Boudin's co-defendants, including Gilbert, refused to attend their trials, arguing that they weren't criminals but political prisoners and should be tried in The Hague. Boudin left her defense to her father. The lawyers he picked for the case managed to win an unprecedented two changes of venue, and ultimately negotiated the deal under which Boudin, who had been charged with three counts of felony murder, pleaded guilty to just one, and to one count of first-degree robbery. (The agreement rested on the argument—devised by Boudin's lawyers—that she could not be held accountable for the deaths of the police officers, because she had, in effect, surrendered before they were shot.) The victims' families have always resented the plea bargain, viewing it as another example of Boudin's privileged treatment.

In the eleven years leading up to the robbery, Boudin had more or less made a profession out of misrepresenting herself, deceiving probably hundreds of people, some to quite serious effect. Remarkably, at the time of the holdup, she was sharing an apartment with a reporter, who, thanks to her relationship with Boudin, subsequently lost her job at the Stamford, Connecticut, *Advocate*. Some key details of Boudin's account of her role in the crime have been challenged by witnesses. One of the officers at the scene testified that before the shoot-out began Boudin had asked the police to put away their guns, although he did not make this claim until more than a year after the robbery. The corrections officer who picked Boudin up on the side of the road reported hearing her shout, "He shot him, I didn't shoot him"—something she denies having said.

But, even if one accepts Boudin's version of events, her interpretation of them is problematic. In spite of everything that has happened, she still wants to see herself as a fundamentally good person. Inevitably, this leads her—against her will, even—to something that can sound dangerously close to evasion. "I was responsible for not being responsible," she told me at one point, a formula she clearly intended to acknowledge her culpability, but which also had the effect of denying it.

In her poetry, Boudin's conflict is settled through inversion. The narrator who sits in the cab of a truck in a print skirt is not a participant in a deadly crime but the victim of terrifying violence:

> The truck slowly
> slowly
> Came to a stop
> Along with throbbing of my pulse.
> I stared through the rays of the sun
> into a barrel of a shot gun
> aimed at my head
> through the glass.

The last time I went to speak with Boudin, she was looking forward to a visit from Chesa the next day. He has been coming to see his mother—and also his father, who is now in Attica—since he was a toddler. Typically, they meet in a large cafeteria-like room with vending machines along one wall, though they occasionally also have overnights, known as "trailer visits," for the mobile homes on the prison grounds in which they take place.

Chesa is, by the standards of late adolescence, forgiving toward his parents—both sets of them. He has had to answer questions about his mother throughout his life. "When I was five, six, seven, I would basically tell people that it was like Robin Hood, or it was supposed to be like that, which of course is a vast oversimplification," he told me over lunch one day in New Haven. "But how else are you going to explain something like that?" Recently, he has begun speaking around the country about his experiences and about the problems facing children of inmates.

Chesa's arguments for his mother's release are those one would expect—that she's been punished enough, that it does the victims no good to keep her inside, that a year at Bedford costs more than a year's tuition at Yale—

though he is realistic enough to know that these are not the grounds on which parole decisions are made. "I don't expect the 'life' at the end of her sentence to become a reality," he said. "But I know that it's a possibility. I try not to have any illusions about what's going to happen."

In nearly thirty hours of conversation, I came to feel many things about Boudin, some of them contradictory. Often, I felt sorry for her and, on several occasions, I offered her the opportunity to feel sorry for herself. She didn't take me up on it. I never heard her complain about prison or suggest that her punishment was unfair. On the contrary, she said that in many ways she felt lucky in the community she had found at Bedford, and in the richness of her life there. She told me that when she was first arrested, and held in solitary confinement, she had found herself too distracted and despairing even to read, and that when she finally did pick up books again she could handle only one kind of story—"books about people who have had terrible accidents and have overcome them, in the sense that they've figured out how to build a life, even if it's not the life that they wanted."

Only three times during our often difficult conversations did Boudin weep. Once was while she was showing me a scrapbook. Among the poems and quotations that she had copied into it was a passage about El Salvador and the dreams and hazards of revolution. She started to read it to me but got only as far as a description: "mistakes so terrible that forgiveness may be impossible, and self-criticism hollow."

The second time occurred when we were discussing the days immediately following the robbery. Her mother had come to visit her in jail and had told her that although she had done a terrible thing, she had an obligation to go on, for the sake of her son. Boudin said that she now realized how horrifying it must have been for Jean, who had tried to destroy herself, to see her daughter repeat the pattern.

The third time Boudin broke down, she was talking about an exercise she had completed for a writing workshop led by the playwright Eve Ensler. The assignment had been to describe what it would be like finally to leave Bedford. "When I walk out of the prison gate I will gently touch the air that surrounds me like a shawl," Boudin wrote. "It is autumn and the leaves are floating in circles of reds, browns, and oranges. I am with my child in freedom, a reunion with my family and friends who have lived these decades with me."

Along with the work of several other prisoners, Boudin's piece was read almost two years ago at a Lincoln Center benefit. In it, she goes on to imagine, in terms borrowed from Virgil and Dante, a river crossing to a place where "the flames burn, with spirits." As in the old myths, there can be no going forward without first going back: "My journey cannot be taken without facing your eyes, and those of your loved ones who went on with their lives without you. If only there were a place where the living and the dead could meet, to tell their tales, to weep. I would reach for you— not so that you could forgive me, but so that you could know that I have no pride for what I have done, only the wisdom and regret that came too late."

Postscript: Denied parole the first time she came up for it, in August 2001, Kathy Boudin was released from prison two years later.

The Unfashionable Mr. Lam

September 2001

T HE HEADQUARTERS OF the Chinese Staff and Workers' Association is situated a few blocks east of New York's City Hall. To get to it, you enter through 15 Catherine Street, a grim tenement sandwiched between a fish stall and a Chinese bakery. You then climb a narrow metal staircase, leave the building through a back door above the second floor, and cross an open bridge made of steel plates. This bridge leads down to a second building, which was orginally designed for storage and is completely cut off from the street. The arrangement has certain obvious disadvantages, but a few years ago, when someone hoping to intimidate Chinese Staff tried to set fire to the place from above, it fortuitously turned out that the ceiling was made of concrete and wouldn't burn.

The headquarters is one large room that has been divided into several smaller ones by a series of wooden partitions. Wing Lam, the association's executive director, has his own office—a tiny, closet-like affair almost entirely taken up by legal files—but he rarely occupies it. Instead, he can usually be found in the main room, where two battered metal desks have been pushed together to form an approximation of a conference table. One day this spring, I found him sitting at the desks, clutching a manila envelope.

Lam, who is fifty-two, has a broad face, longish hair that is constantly flopping down over his eyes, and prominent front teeth. He speaks idiosyncratic English, weeps easily, and, in his own quiet way, can talk almost uninterruptedly for hours at a stretch. As soon as I sat down, Lam opened the manila envelope and pulled out a glossy picture of a man named Jian Wen Liang.

Liang had operated a pair of garment factories in Brooklyn that manufactured women's sportswear. He had paid his workers by the piece, had often demanded that they put in one-hundred-hour weeks without overtime, and had systematically skimmed five per cent from their wages. The picture showed Liang being led off to jail on March 5, apparently in handcuffs. Whenever someone new would come into the office, Lam would slide the photo out of the envelope to show it off. "My trophy," he said, chuckling.

Lam could be called a labor organizer, and Chinese Staff a labor organization, although neither term would be entirely adequate. Chinese Staff serves as an intermediary between immigrant workers and labor enforcement agencies, acting as a goad to both sides. Without its encouragement, many workers would be too scared to file complaints against their employers, and without its constant pestering, many prosecutors wouldn't follow up on them.

In New York's Chinese-language newspapers, the Liang case was big news. The last time anyone could remember a similar prosecution was a decade ago, when another sweatshop owner, Stanley Chang, had become the first garment-factory owner in state history imprisoned for nonpayment of wages. Liang's punishment even made English-language papers like the New York *Daily News*, which published the story under the headline "Buttonholed at Last."

In general, Liang's sentence—ninety days and a ten-thousand-dollar fine—was taken as a sign of the peculiar viciousness of his conduct. He had, the *News* asserted, operated "some of the worst garment sweatshops in the city." It would probably be closer to the truth, however, to describe his tactics as fairly typical. Liang ended up in jail because he was peculiarly stubborn, and quite possibly also stupid, but mostly because he was unlucky, this last quality having mainly to do with the fact that he had run up against Wing Lam.

One afternoon when I arrived at Chinese Staff's office, Lam was sitting at the desks with a group of half a dozen women. A collection of clothes labels was spread out before them. The women were grim-faced and Lam looked tense. They were speaking to one another in Chinese, and it seemed clear from everyone's body language that Lam was reading the women the riot act.

After the visitors had packed up their labels and left, Lam explained that the group had come to him earlier complaining about a factory owner who owed them nearly one hundred thousand dollars in back wages. Then he hadn't heard from them for several months. Lam had been trying to impress on the women that they weren't going to get their money without fighting for it. Once Chinese Staff determines that a complaint is justified, its chief concern in deciding to pursue a case—either by filing a lawsuit or by bringing it to the attention of prosecutors—is whether the workers will stick through what can be years of court dates and hearings. "We want them to understand: We are not like government," Lam told me. "They got to be involved."

A lot of workers bring the stories of their hardships to Lam, thinking that he will be moved by their suffering and will try to solve their problems for them. This is only partly correct. Lam is interested in solving their problems but not, as they might like, quietly, through back channels. Lam used to give his business card to nearly everyone he met, but a few years ago, he discovered that workers were simply flashing his card as a way to win better treatment. Now, he rarely hands out cards. "The main thing: We ask workers' commitment to help other workers," he says. "That's the only way we have strength."

Much of Lam's work is anachronistic; the labor conditions he is fighting have been illegal for more than half a century. But having a law on the books and having it enforced are, in this case, two entirely different things. At any given moment, there are more than three thousand garment factories operating in New York City, and it is estimated that two-thirds of them violate such basic labor standards as paying the minimum wage or compensating workers for overtime. In Los Angeles, there are some five thousand garment shops, and there, too, the majority are believed to be sweatshops. Similarly, in the restaurant trade—the other main occupation of recent Chinese immigrants—it is routine for workers to get less than the minimum wage, to put in seven-day weeks, and to be forced to give up part of their tips to their bosses. Restaurant workers come to Chinese Staff for help from as far away as Florida.

Lam has no legal training, and Chinese Staff has no lawyers; nevertheless, the group is constantly generating lawsuits against employers—as many as a hundred a year—most of which are handled by attorneys from the Asian American Legal Defense and Education Fund, and from big firms that donate time pro bono. "Wing thinks that if you fight hard enough and long enough you can change the system," says Ken Kimerling, the fund's legal director. "He's given people an opportunity to fight back who otherwise would have just gone on being victims."

Over the years, Chinese Staff has had many legal victories, in cases involving everything from nonpayment of wages to extortion. Probably its biggest win was a $1.1 million judgment against one of Chinatown's most prominent restaurants, Jing Fong, in 1997; after much legwork by Chinese Staff, the state attorney general successfully sued the restaurant for cheating nearly five dozen workers out of tips and wages. It is these occasional triumphs that keep Lam going, Kimerling speculates, in a trade where long-term improvements in working conditions remain elusive. Especially in the garment industry, he observes, "it's hard to see major changes, except the other way."

Lam is, in addition to lawsuits, an enthusiast of protests, boycotts, and pickets. One picket line he helped organize, in front of the Silver Palace restaurant in lower Manhattan, has been in place for so long now that the placards are in tatters and the cardboard coffin, which is supposed to symbolize the death of "slave labor," has developed a permanent sag. In its complexity and its sheer duration, the Silver Palace picket is an exemplary Lam crusade. (Once, when I asked him how he could possibly remember the intricacies of his many campaigns, Lam waved his hands in front of his face, a gesture that conveyed the recognition that he was, in this respect, not entirely normal.)

The battle began back in August 1993, when a group of Silver Palace workers challenged the restaurant's practice of confiscating part of each day's tips. It continued through a seven-month lockout, an unrelated legal dispute that revealed that the owners were keeping two sets of books, and a lawsuit by the state attorney general on behalf of the workers. In 1995 and 1996, a state court and the National Labor Relations Board awarded the workers a combined $1.1 million; at that point, the restaurant declared bankruptcy and was reorganized, ostensibly under new management. Five years later, not a dollar of the award has been paid.

Lam recounted the saga of the Silver Palace to me one bitter cold evening when I was preparing to go out with the picketers. Chinese Staff has only five full-time employees (whose salaries are paid by membership dues and foundation grants), but every time I visited, the office was filled with volunteers—old men, young women with babies, and college students, many, but not all of them, Chinese. On this particular evening, there was a great deal of bustle as several of the restaurant's "dim sum ladies," together with a collection of volunteers, assembled their gear. I asked Lam whether he found the story of the Silver Palace disheartening. "I'm pretty stubborn," he said.

Lam discovered labor organizing in an accidental sort of way. In 1978, he was working as a shipping clerk in a Long Island City garment factory when, together with another clerk, he learned that the workers were getting paid fifty cents an hour less than their contract required. The factory was a union shop, so the two men took their finding to the union's leaders, who vowed to get to the bottom of the matter. A union representative came to visit the factory and the next day, Lam says, "all the big mouths get the pink slip."

Lam is reluctant to reveal a great deal about his life outside work. When I first approached him late last year, he kept suggesting to me that I write about someone else in the labor movement instead. Eventually, I learned that Lam had been born in Tianjin, had lived in Hong Kong and, later, Brazil. His mother had been a seamstress and his father had worked a variety of odd jobs including, at one point, selling ice cream. Lam arrived in the United States at age seventeen, speaking virtually no English, but managed to get a degree in electrical engineering, a subject he says he found "boring."

After losing his job in Long Island City, he went to work for the same union—the International Ladies' Garment Workers' Union (ILGWU)—that he believed had betrayed him. (The union is now called UNITE.) According to Lam, the only reason he got the job was the union's belief that "the best treatment for the troublemaker is to take them in," and the only reason he took it was that he needed the money. The job involved hiring himself out as a garment worker in order to organize a shop from the inside. Lam found he was quite good at garment work, particularly pressing, but not good at getting along with his bosses. In his three years with the union, he managed to get himself fired twice.

While Lam was still with the ILGWU, a group of workers formed Chinese Staff to push for more effective representation from the white-run trade unions, and Lam acted as an adviser. "Union just for show" is a favored phrase of Lam's, and it is true that while many of the garment factories in Chinatown are unionized, this has not prevented widespread labor-law violations.

For its part, UNITE is equally critical of Lam, saying that he ought to be working with the union, not against it. Steven Weingarten, UNITE's industrial director, says the union is about to launch a campaign to put pressure on retailers and manufacturers who subcontract with sweatshops. "We've got an enormous problem, and the question is, How do we build a strategy that shifts power back to the workers?" he says. Weingarten acknowledges that many garment shops do not fully comply with their union contracts, but maintains that if UNITE pushed harder, the shops would simply shut down. This argument—that the union cannot enforce its own contracts because it would drive work away—is precisely what infuriates Lam.

Official New York views Chinese Staff's efforts with decidedly mixed emotions. The group's work is essential to many labor-law prosecutions, like the Liang case, which according to one of the prosecutors involved would never have gone to court had Lam not convinced the workers to testify. By the same token, Lam is never satisfied; frequently he attacks the very government agencies he is assisting. "He's always demanding a little more of you," the prosecutor says. "He'll say, 'Why didn't you do that one as a felony?' He calls once a week with a new case or a possibility."

"There are people who attack him left and right, but he sticks by it," says Louis Vanegas, the district director of the U.S. Labor Department's wage and hour division for New York. "He's persistent." Vanegas says he has seen many immigrant workers' groups form, only to get discouraged and give up within a few years. Lam and Chinese Staff, he notes, have stayed the course for two decades. "People get burned out in that kind of work very fast," Vanegas says. "But Wing has maintained the stamina."

In segments of Chinatown, Lam is quite openly despised. In early 1995, Chinese Staff organized a picket line in front of Jing Fong, after a waiter who had challenged the restaurant's practice of docking tips was fired. Later, a group of students staged a hunger strike in front of the restaurant, which can seat about a thousand people. A few months into the battle, an ad appeared in several Chinatown newspapers featuring a picture of Lam; the caption called him "the devil that is destroying the Chinatown economy." Around the same time, signs went up in front of the restaurant rendering Lam's Chinese name, Lam Shung, as "Lam Jung," which means "near death." It was at that point that Lam started parking his car in a garage, rather than on the street.

During the battle over Jing Fong, flyers were circulated that accused Lam of extorting tens of thousands of dollars from various restaurant owners. Though no evidence was ever produced to corroborate this accusation, in Chinatown the flyers succeeded in sowing doubt about Lam's motives. In 1996, Lam sued the management of Jing Fong for libel. When the case finally came to trial last winter, one of the owners testified that life in Chinatown would be better if Lam were, in fact, dead. The jury found that Lam had been libeled but was due no damages.

One winter evening when I stopped by Chinese Staff's office, Lam was talking to a young woman with a sad face and a tiny scar at the corner of her mouth. He told me that the young woman had an "interesting story," which I took to mean that she was miserable, and with him translating, she agreed to recount it for me, minus certain details, such as her name, that could be of use to the INS.

The young woman was in her twenties—she declined to be more specific—and had been brought into the country five years ago by a smuggler who had arranged for her passage by way of Mexico. She had grown up near Fuzhou, a port city in southeastern China, where her mother worked in a factory and her father worked for the government. Although her family was not affluent, they were not poor. She explained her decision to come to the United States by saying, through Lam, "Everybody says

America very good." In fact, she had found life here very hard. When I asked if she would have come had she known what she knows now, she said, "I don't know."

The young woman had wanted a job in New York, but hadn't been able to find one and had ended up in a Chinese restaurant in New Jersey. She was making about a hundred dollars a day, eighteen dollars of which she had to give back to her boss. Meanwhile, she owed her smugglers thirty thousand dollars. Eventually she left that job, and now she was working in a restaurant in Pennsylvania. There she was earning even less than she had in New Jersey.

Fifteen or twenty years ago, most of New York's Chinatown was Cantonese; today, new immigrants are increasingly Fuzhounese, and East Broadway south of Canal is commonly referred to as "Fuzhou Street." Like the young woman, a lot of these new immigrants come with huge debts to notoriously unsympathetic creditors. More established Chinese immigrants tend to blame these newcomers—the *wu sun fin*, or "people without status"—for driving down wages for everyone. Lam, too, says that wages have been falling in Chinatown and that the influx of new immigrants is partly responsible; lacking legal protection, they often feel they have no choice but to accept illegal working conditions. In Chinese, he points out, smugglers of illegal immigrants are known as "snakeheads" and their charges as "snakes."

"Where you can find a snake?" he asks. "Under something. Very dark, very wet. That's where the snake goes. No-law land."

But for Lam, the Fuzhounese are, in their desperation, no different really from every other low-wage earner. "People think work is better than no work," he told me. "Unfortunately, the real truth is, even if you work fourteen hours, someone is willing to work sixteen hours." It is this same logic, in essence, that underlies American labor law: The minimum wage and the forty-hour week are supposed to make it impossible for factory hands and seamstresses to undersell one another. One of the results, of course, is that millions of jobs have moved overseas, where no such obstacles exist.

This dilemma is well understood in Chinatown. Often workers are the only good source of information about what is going on in a garment factory or a restaurant kitchen, and typically they refuse to talk. Indeed, sometimes they will go so far as to rally in support of the bosses accused of exploiting them: One of the stranger twists in the Liang case came when the Labor Department impounded some of the illegally manufactured clothes. Dozens of workers marched on the department's offices, demanding that the clothing be released.

Lam's response to this frustrating reality has been to expand his ambitions. Along with the seamstress earning three dollars an hour, he maintains that office workers and freelancers who work without benefits are also sweatshop workers, as is anyone who accepts inadequate wages or ridiculously long hours in order to keep a job. Among his many goals is to transform mothering into a paid profession, compensated somehow by the government.

"People only want to settle for what is possible," he says.

Situated just a few miles east of Chinatown, Sunset Park is an unremarkable Brooklyn neighborhood of attached two-story houses bisected by a busy commercial strip. At one point, the area was populated by Scandinavians, and it is still possible to find a few traces of this era, like the Norwegian flag on the sign for the Sporting Club Gjøa. Overwhelmingly, though, the neighborhood is now Chinese, and the businesses along the strip bear names that translate along the lines of "Million Gold Barber Center" and "Chungyuan Herb Corp." For the last five years, Chinese Staff has operated a satellite office in Sunset Park in what was once a pizzeria— there are still "his" and "hers" bathrooms and a mirrored wall left over from the previous tenant—and a few months ago I arranged to meet Lam there.

Most of the garment factories are found at the southern edge of Sunset Park in a commercial zone given over to old warehouses and auto dealerships. When I asked Lam to tell me what I should look for if I wanted to find a sweatshop, he laughed and said, "Look anywhere." In front of one building, we saw two women carrying a heavy load in a brown sack. Lam identified the load as clothes that had been sewn in someone's home, or homework, which is illegal. In front of another building, a truck was parked and men were unloading boxes of plastic hangers.

Liang's sentence had just been handed down a few days earlier and I wanted to see some of his factories, a project that turned out to be more complicated than I had anticipated. At one point, to try to help me understand the whole tangle, Lam pulled out a piece of scrap paper—a flyer announcing a picket of a new Donna Karan store. (The flyer accused Donna Karan of using sweatshop labor in New York to manufacture six-thousand-dollar dresses, an allegation DKNY denies.) On the back of the flyer, Lam drew a map of the area with dates and names and arrows pointing in various directions. One of Liang's factories had changed its name at least twice, and another had three different addresses in a matter of just a few years, all within five blocks of one another.

To avoid giving Liang any ammunition against him, Lam refused to go into any of the factories Liang had operated or that he suspected him of operating still. But he did agree to show me where they were. In one case I got as far as the building's entryway, which was being used to store bags of shirred fabric in pink-and-purple plaid. In a corner, there was a shrine with a statue of Confucius and an offering of oranges. A heavy curtain covered the entrance to the factory floor. Almost as soon as I lifted it, an elderly man came toward me uttering what I took to be imprecations in Chinese.

Walking down the street, I tried, more or less at random, the doors of nearly a dozen buildings. I began to recognize the sweatshops by their windows—or, more precisely, by the lack of them. Some of the doors were locked; the rest opened into rooms filled with piles of precut fabric, and rows and rows of women hunched over sewing machines. I realized that I had probably walked by dozens of similar shops before without noticing them, which is, of course, exactly what Lam is talking about.

The Calculator

November 2002

A LITTLE MORE THAN a year after September 11th, Kenneth Feinberg, who holds the title of special master of the Victim Compensation Fund, met with a group of firefighters in his midtown office. Feinberg, who is fifty-seven, has a long face, a prominent forehead, and an abrupt manner. Standing, he appears to be straining forward, and even when he is sitting down he leans in, as if about to get up again. That morning, Feinberg had taken off his jacket, and he greeted the firefighters in his shirtsleeves. His gold cufflinks—a gift to himself—were embossed with the scales of justice.

The first of the men to speak was a burly firefighter with a ruddy complexion. He had spent four weeks at the World Trade Center site, initially trying to rescue victims and then to recover remains. He told Feinberg that whatever he had breathed in during that time—pulverized glass, concrete, lead, traces of asbestos; "I call it a bunch of crap," he said— had reduced his lung capacity by more than fifty per cent. He coughed throughout the session.

"Sleeping's tough," he said. "When I'm getting depressed, my wife calls it 'the mood.' She takes the kids out." The fireman told Feinberg that he had recently had to quit the F.D.N.Y. and had taken a job monitoring security cameras at a school. "I can't play street hockey, can't play ball— my son, he can't understand why Daddy can't do nothing.

"This is what I take every day," he announced, holding up a freezer bag filled with medications. "There's a bunch of pills, there's nasal sprays, there's steroids, there's inhalers." He extracted some more medicines from a fanny pack. "This is what I keep on me all the time: albuterol, epinephrine—it's a self-stick. If it gets really bad, I've got to hit this and go to the hospital."

Eventually, a second firefighter—a slight man who sat slumped in his chair—spoke up. He explained that he had spent the afternoon of the attack sifting through the ruins of the World Trade Center concourse. "We were trying to dig this person out of the dirt and the debris and the dust and the smoke. You saw the astronauts on the moon, that dust surface? That was what was coming into your face. Three weeks later, I was coughing up blood, dirt, debris. Since then, I've been in the hospital three times. It's affecting my liver, my pancreas, my stomach, and nobody can really give me a definite answer why. My eleven-year-old son, he asks his mother, 'Is Daddy going to die now?' "

The Victim Compensation Fund, or V.C.F., as it is known, expires a year from next month. Between now and then, it is expected to issue checks to some three thousand families. The fund is the first of its kind, and, to the extent that it has a logic, Feinberg, as special master, has imposed it. It is Feinberg who drafted the rules for disbursing the fund, Feinberg who is determining how the rules are administered, and Feinberg who will hear appeals from people unhappy with the way the rules have been applied. In the case of victims like the firefighters, whose ailments did not manifest themselves until days, or even weeks, after the disaster, Feinberg has the authority to decide not just how much compensation they will receive but whether they will get any at all. By most estimates, the bill for the fund will eventually run to five billion dollars, though it is possible that it could be a good deal higher. How much higher is, once again, entirely up to Feinberg, who has been granted what amounts to a blank check on the federal Treasury.

Anyone in Feinberg's position would have found himself at odds with some of the victims' families; Feinberg has managed to infuriate just about all of them. "I've heard you say that you couldn't put yourselves in our shoes," a widow told him publicly a few months ago. "I think if you could feel our pain for one hour your tone and your mannerisms would be so drastically different than what they are." At the same meeting, a man who had lost his wife and niece said, "You have an arrogance about you that is so painful, you can't possibly believe." Feinberg, who is a lawyer by training, has spent most of his adult life immersed in disaster, and during that time has priced almost every imaginable form of human suffering, from birth defects and infertility to asbestosis and death. If the anger upsets him, he doesn't show it. "Everybody rants and raves," he told me.

The day Feinberg met with the firefighters, he listened, apparently unmoved. While they related their symptoms and fears, he jiggled his knee. He consumed two Halloween-size packages of Necco wafers, then stuffed the wrappers into a plastic cup. When the men were done, they asked him if he had any questions. He shook his head and showed them to the door.

Congress created the Victim Compensation Fund just ten days after September 11th. During the hurried negotiations, several candidates to manage it had been mentioned, including John Danforth, the former senator from Missouri, and George Mitchell, the former senator from Maine. Feinberg took a look at the legislation and decided, as he put it to me, "I've been trained for the last twenty years to do this." He rang up Senator Chuck Hagel, of Nebraska, an old friend of his. "The minute I called, he said, 'I know why you're calling,'" Feinberg told me. "'You're the man.' And he took it from there."

Feinberg grew up in Brockton, Massachusetts, where his father sold tires, and he still speaks—usually emphatically—in an unreconstructed Boston accent. As a kid, he performed in amateur theatricals, and even considered becoming an actor, but after attending the University of Massachusetts he decided, on the advice of his father, to go to N.Y.U. Law School instead. Feinberg clerked for the then chief judge of New York, Stanley Fuld, and later served as Edward Kennedy's chief of staff. He now lives in Bethesda, Maryland—he and his wife, Diane, have three grown children—in a house with a specially designed sound room where he keeps six thousand classical-music CDs. Before September 11th, he routinely got up at 5 A.M.; these days, he is often awake at three. He is in the office by six.

Oddly enough, Feinberg arrived at his current specialty in large part thanks to a talent for burlesque. In the early nineteen-seventies, at a birthday party for Fuld, Feinberg delivered a roast that impressed

Judge Jack Weinstein, of the federal district court in Brooklyn. Weinstein and Feinberg became friendly, and a decade later, when Weinstein took over the Agent Orange case, he asked Feinberg if he would try to persuade the two sides to settle, so that the case wouldn't have to go to trial.

At the point that Weinstein brought Feinberg into it, the Agent Orange case was in its eighth year. It pitted hundreds of thousands of Vietnam veterans who had been exposed to the defoliant, and who had contracted diseases ranging from skin ailments to abdominal cancer, against the federal government and the herbicide's manufactures, including Dow and Monsanto. Virtually no one on either side believed that an agreement could be reached. Nevertheless, Feinberg threw himself into the project, producing an eighty-page proposal in a few weeks. Both sides rejected it. They remained separated by a host of issues, most significantly money—the veterans were demanding a billion dollars, while the chemical companies refused to pay more than a few hundred thousand—and it appeared that a trial could not be avoided. At 3 A.M. on the day that jury selection was set to begin, they finally settled.

"Ken revealed himself as a superb negotiator," Judge Weinstein, who is eighty-one and still serving on the bench, told me. "He was very tough. He understood the case completely, better than either side's lawyers." The night the settlement was reached—the sum ultimately agreed upon was a hundred and eighty million dollars—Weinstein had taken a hotel room in Manhattan, and, just before dawn, he informed Feinberg that he could announce the deal. Weinstein recalls him bouncing on the bed: "He was very excited."

The Agent Orange case was precedent setting. It greatly expanded the possibilities of class-action lawsuits—some would argue disastrously so—and it was followed by a string of other so-called mass-tort cases. Rare was the large, high-profile settlement that Feinberg was not involved in. He was the special master in the DES case, which had a thousand plaintiffs, and he played a similar role in the case of the Dalkon Shield I.U.D., which had two hundred and fifty thousand. Feinberg served as the negotiator for Dow Corning when it was sued by four hundred and fifty thousand women over breast implants, and successfully negotiated the resolution to hundreds of asbestos cases. In the process, he earned a reputation of being highly effective and unusually abrasive.

"He had a style which conveyed a great sense of displeasure at your stubbornness or lack of understanding," Judith Vladeck, an attorney who represented Long Island Lighting Company ratepayers in another case that Feinberg mediated, told me. "It wasn't 'I don't agree with you.' It was 'What's wrong with you, how dumb can you be?' There was a firmness which I can appreciate now, but which I didn't enjoy being a victim of." In 1993, Feinberg left the law firm of Kaye, Scholer, Fierman, Hays & Handler, where he had been a partner, and formed his own firm, the Feinberg Group, with offices in New York and Washington.

Over the years, Feinberg has worked out a method for dealing with sprawling, complex cases, the key element of which he describes as stripping away the complexities. Under this method, individual circumstances are reduced to numbers, so that the whole settlement can be expressed in a set of tables. "The way you divvy up the money is to come up, to the extent you can, with an objective allocation formula," Feinberg told me. He offered the Dalkon Shield case as an example: "We had a matrix—here's what you get. A hysterectomy's worth this, pelvic inflammation's worth this, cervical cancer's worth this, migraine headaches are worth this. Demonstrate medically you've had any of this, and we'll pay you."

Numerically speaking, September 11th is much less daunting than most of the other cases Feinberg has been called upon to settle. "I mean, thirty-three hundred dead and injured is almost quantitatively not a mass tort," he observed. But the rawness of the emotion is something that Feinberg acknowledges he has never before experienced. "I made a very wise decision when I took this job," he told me. "I'm doing this for nothing. I love it when senators or congressmen come up to me and go, 'Ken, what a sacrifice that you're doing this for nothing, in the public interest, that's fabulous,' when of course the real reason I did it in the public interest—It *is* fabulous, if I do say so, it *is* a sacrifice. But, as a Machiavellian matter, can you imagine if these families knew I was getting paid for this, on the blood and bodies of the dead? 'You're only giving me three million, what did you make?' As a Machiavellian matter, I just completely undercut that whole line of criticism by telling people, 'I'm not getting paid for this, you know.'"

During the past year, Feinberg has held several dozen question-and-answer sessions with victims' families, mostly in the New York area but also in Boston, Washington, and Los Angeles. At these sessions, Feinberg explains the workings of the fund and listens to families' concerns, a process that often involves taking a good deal of abuse. On a recent sleety night, I drove out with him and his oldest son, Michael, to a session he was holding on Staten Island. Feinberg had already been out to Staten Island twice; the first time, a man had made what Feinberg, who is Jewish, considered to be an anti-Semitic remark. Michael, an N.Y.U. law student, was accompanying him to the third session to lend moral support.

"Staten Island, that's a Third World country," Feinberg told me, more than once, on the drive out. The meeting, at the Staten Island Hilton, was set for seven o'clock, and Feinberg hadn't had dinner, so before heading into the session he stopped at the hotel gift shop to buy a package of Chuckles for himself and a Snickers bar for Michael. In the lobby, he ran into several people he knew—there are some family members who follow him around from session to session—and he greeted them with wry heartiness. I sat down next to two men, both of whom had lost sons who were firefighters.

"You'll hear it said many times here that people don't care about the money, and it's true, we don't," one of them told me. "But somehow the higher the amount, the more value then put on your loved one's life, the more meaning it has. So I would like them to say we all get a trillion dollars, just so I know my son was worth a trillion dollars, not that I would ever want it."

"That's right," the other man said. "You can't put a value on your son's life, but then they come out with these astronomical figures, and—well, you're not going to get that because of this, that, and the other reason. They kind of promise you something, but they don't deliver." A lot of families, the man added, "feel that this program is just a coverup to bail out the airlines, to bail out the Port Authority; to bail out New York City. It's for them, it's not really for us."

The Victim Compensation Fund was in fact created not for the victims' sake but for the airlines', and, more specifically, for protecting the airlines *from* the victims. In the days after September 11th, the country's major carriers were facing not just billions of dollars in immediate losses but tens of billions of dollars in potential legal claims, and lawmakers were worried that the nation's entire transportation system could collapse. They responded with the Air Transportation Safety and System Stabilization Act, which granted the carriers five billion dollars in cash and ten billion in loan guarantees. The act also limited the airlines' liability for the disaster to the amount of insurance that had been carried by the four hijacked flights. (This is generally believed to be a total of six billion dollars.) It was in a subsection of the bill that Congress created the V.C.F. Families who accept the payments from the fund relinquish the right to sue the airlines, the Port Authority, which owned the World Trade Center, and any other domestic entity; in return, they are supposed to receive from the government compensation for their pain and suffering and for their economic losses.

At the Staten Island meeting, the first few questions put to Feinberg were technical ones. Under the law, payments from the V.C.F. are supposed to be reduced by the amount of compensation that families have received from other sources, and one woman wanted to know whether a certain type of death benefit would count as an offset. (Feinberg has defined offsets to include life insurance and Social Security, but not the sums—in many cases, considerable—that families received from charity.) A man asked who should file a claim with the fund in the case of a family whose members were feuding.

Soon, however, the tenor of the questions shifted. A woman stood up at the microphone, holding a large photograph. "I'm the parent of a single firefighter," she said. "This is my son. Before he became a probationary firefighter, he served his country for five years in the United States Marine Corps, making sub-poverty-level wages. He then joined the Fire Department as a probationary firefighter and he graduated to making poverty-level wages. I would like to know why someone in his category is really being discriminated against regarding what you and the Victim Compensation Fund consider his life was worth?"

A few minutes later, a second woman, who had lost her sister, declared, "I just want to say that it's really a disgrace that a year and some months after the tragedy happened we're still all fighting." Addressing herself to Feinberg, she went on, "We've suffered enough. Why are you making our lives even more complicated? Make something easy, make everyone happy. I know you're all about the numbers, and the statute, and the regulations, and this computation, and this deduction, and 'This doesn't count,' and 'Please come to me and make your plea to me.' We don't need to make a plea. We're not begging for money. We want our people back."

Feinberg told the woman he could not bring people back, and he could not make them happy.

"Yes, you can," she insisted.

"No, I can't," he repeated. "I can't make them happy."

"But your children are alive and breathing, right?" someone called out.

"Thank God," Feinberg said, casting a glance in Michael's direction.

"Explanation of Process for Computing Presumed Economic Loss" is one of a series of papers that Feinberg has posted on the V.C.F. Web site. In it, he provides the formula that he will be using for compensating families, as well as an explanation of the assumptions underlying it. Much of the document is abstruse—at points, it seems, even deliberately so. At the end, however, Feinberg, in keeping with his usual practice, resolves these complexities into a set of tables. Using them, anyone can plug in a few basic facts about a victim—his or her age, income, and number of children—and derive an estimate of what the fund can be expected to offer the family.

At first glance, the tables defy most notions of equity; the more needs a family is likely to have, the less well it fares. For example, the tables show that the widow of a twenty-five-year-old who had no children and was earning a hundred and twenty-five thousand dollars a year can anticipate a payment, before any offsets, of nearly four and a half million dollars. The widow of a man who was earning the same salary and was similarly childless but was forty can expect half that amount, while the widow of a forty-year-old who was making fifty thousand dollars and had one child can expect a quarter of it. Finally, the widow of a forty-year-old with two dependent children who was making twenty thousand dollars does worst of all. She can expect about a fifth, or slightly more than nine hundred thousand dollars.

When Feinberg is questioned about these sorts of inequities, he responds, invariably, that his hands are tied. "What you're really asking is: All lives are equal, why isn't everybody getting the same amount of money?" he told the mother with the photograph on Staten Island. "A very fair question, ladies and gentlemen. The answer is: Congress told me that is not the way to compute these awards. Congress said you must take into account the economic loss suffered by the victim's death." This claim is a useful one for Feinberg, and, up to a point, also accurate.

Aside from the inequities, what is most striking about Feinberg's tables is that a lot of numbers are missing. In those rows where the economic losses would be the greatest—low age crossed with high salary—instead of posting numbers Feinberg has put rows of "X"s. Moreover, he has declined to publish any figures at all for victims who earned more than two hundred and twenty-five thousand dollars a year.

It is unclear exactly how many victims Feinberg has left off his tables, but because the World Trade Center housed several large financial firms, where relatively young men and women routinely earned hundreds of thousands of dollars a year, the number is almost certainly a high one. Following a strict economic-loss calculation, some of these victims' families would be entitled to payments of ten, twenty, and, in a few cases, even thirty million dollars from the government. This, apparently, is what lawmakers mandated when they created the V.C.F., but it is not, it seems clear, what they—or just about anybody else—actually want to see happen now. Feinberg noted to me that both Senator Kennedy, a Democrat, and Senator Hagel, a Republican, had offered him the same advice on this point, which he summed up as "Don't let twenty per cent of the people get eighty per cent of the money." Exactly how Feinberg intends to treat what he calls the "high-end" families is not known—he keeps putting off resolving this issue—but he has indicated that, except in extremely rare cases, he is not going to give out awards of more than six million dollars.

Not surprisingly, Feinberg's position has infuriated the families of the most highly paid victims, who accuse him of acting arbitrarily, unfairly, and, finally, illegally. One day, I was sitting in Feinberg's office when a man whose wife had earned nearly four hundred thousand dollars a year came in to appeal his award. After several million dollars in offsets because of a life-insurance policy, the man was set to receive two million dollars. He felt he deserved at least another million. Feinberg asked the man whether he thought payments ought to be made solely on the basis of income, even if this meant that some already affluent families would receive ten million dollars in taxpayer money.

"Yes, absolutely," the man responded. "The idea is to compensate me so my life style doesn't change, and my life style is different from a guy washing dishes. I don't live in a two-hundred-and-fifty-dollar-a-month apartment. I live in a place that costs me five thousand dollars a month in mortgage payments."

Cantor Fitzgerald, the bond-trading firm that lost six hundred and fifty-eight people in the attack, has issued an eighty-page critique of Feinberg's handling of the fund, which notes that Congress instructed him "to determine economic loss—not to make value judgments about different groups of income earners." Stephen Merkel, the firm's general counsel, told me that Feinberg had sought "the power to make awards on whatever basis he feels like" and that his actions demonstrated "a complete disregard for the law itself." When confronted with criticism of this sort, Feinberg offers precisely the opposite defense from the one he gave the mother on Staten Island.

"The law gives me unbelievable discretion," he says. "It gives me discretion to do whatever I want. So I will."

Perhaps because of this discretion, a number of conspiracy theories swirl around Feinberg: that he has cut a nefarious deal with the Bush Administration, that he is secretly taking orders from Attorney General John Ashcroft, that—and this is really a subset of the first two—he is using the Victim Compensation Fund to advance the cause of tort reform. Although Feinberg is an outspoken, Teddy Kennedy-style Democrat, he was appointed special master by Ashcroft, a conservative Republican, who also— theoretically, at least—has the power to un-appoint him. At every opportunity, Feinberg praises Ashcroft, calling him his "No. 1 ally."

When I asked him how he and the Attorney General had managed to bridge their not inconsiderable political differences, he smiled and said, "It's either a tribute to bipartisanship or very Machiavellian, or a little bit of both."

Feinberg uses the word "Machiavellian" to refer to his own actions surprisingly often. The first time I heard him do so, I was puzzled; by the third or fourth time, I realized that he didn't mean it as self-criticism. During the weeks that I followed Feinberg around, I attended half a dozen meetings at his conference table, at which a total of about thirty cases were discussed. Feinberg was by turns gentle and hostile, confiding and with-holding, depending on what seemed most efficacious. With awards below the average—currently about $1.5 million—he was almost always willing to add a few hundred thousand; on one occasion, I heard him promise to give a widow an additional half million dollars for no other reason than that she had come in with her two small children and asked for it. As far as I could make it out, Feinberg's reasoning in these cases amounted to: Let's do what seems to work, and worry about how to justify it afterward. With awards in the very upper reaches, by contrast, he was staunchly, even theatrically, recalcitrant. One lawyer told Feinberg that he had calculated the proper payment for his client to be between sixteen and seventeen million dollars.

"You've lost your fucking mind!" Feinberg exclaimed. "This guy should file a suit."

"He might—you're giving him every reason to," the lawyer replied, calmly.

"I want him to!" Feinberg said. "And do me a favor—hold a press conference. Say I wouldn't give the guy sixteen million dollars—tax free!"

So far, only about eight hundred families, or a quarter of those eligible, have submitted claims to the fund, a proportion that is lower than Feinberg would like, but one that he maintains he is not, at this point, particularly concerned about. Feinberg's stated goal is to have ninety per cent of the families accept payment from the fund, and so relinquish the right to sue the airlines, the Port Authority, or the City of New York. Accepting the payment doesn't necessarily mean being happy with it, or even feeling that it is fair; it just means recognizing that it is better than the alternative, which is years of litigation and a high risk of getting nothing. "Who's going to fight?" Feinberg told me. "No one's going to fight."

One evening after a series of meetings with victims' families, I stayed behind to talk to Feinberg. We sat in the empty conference room, which offered a view of several lanes of rush-hour traffic and a sliver of the East River. I asked him for his own views on the fund and whether it was structured fairly. Was it right for some families to receive huge payments while others, who needed help much more, received comparatively little? This was, he said, an "interesting and debatable" question, but by no means the most difficult one, which, in his opinion, was whether the fund should exist at all.

"I'll show you e-mails from people that'll break your heart," he told me. " 'Dear Mr. Feinberg, my son died in Oklahoma City. Why not me?' 'Dear Mr. Feinberg, my son died in the first World Trade Center bombing, in '93, why not me?' Anthrax—why not me? African Embassy bombing— why not me? U.S.S. Cole—why not me? And then you get even beyond terrorism. 'My husband died last year saving three little girls in a Mississippi flood—why not him?' " If there was an essential distinction between September 11th and these other tragedies, Feinberg didn't offer it. "Where do you stop?" he asked. We talked for a while longer, and then Feinberg told me, politely but firmly, that he had to leave. He was meeting Michael, and they were going to the opera.

Tumult in the Newsroom

June 2003

NOT LONG AFTER I graduated from college, I went to work at the *Times* as a copyboy, or, in more enlightened terms, copy person. The job title was left over from the days of typewriters, when stories were filed on sheaves of carbon paper known as ten-part books, but by the time I got to the newsroom, in the mid-nineteen-eighties, the process had been computerized, and copy persons mostly just answered the phones and sorted the mail. Whenever we could, we shirked these responsibilities to write our own stories, which were usually printed, without a byline, deep inside the Sunday paper. Working at the *Times* in this way was a heady experience—yes, that was my piece on the Hmong folkfest that ran next to the numismatics column—and also a humiliating one. As a group, we copy persons excelled at cataloguing our grievances, collecting gossip, and daydreaming. One colleague—now a television news producer—developed a particularly vivid fantasy of revenge, which he was constantly adjusting to reflect the latest slights, real or imagined. As I recall, it began with his leaping up from his desk, shoving aside various senior editors, pushing his way across the newsroom, and hurdling over the "bullpen." It always ended the same way: with a Bruce Lee kick delivered to the head of the executive editor, Abe Rosenthal.

I hadn't had much reason to think about this fantasy in recent years; then events at the *Times* brought it back in all its cartoonish violence. The paper's travails are, by now, well known, having been chronicled perhaps most extensively by the *Times* itself. In late April, the *Times* discovered that one of its young reporters, Jayson Blair, had, journalistically speaking, gone off the deep end. In a fourteen-thousand-word article that ran as the paper's off-lead, it documented his multifarious sins, which ranged from poor nutrition and fraudulent expense statements to plagiarized quotes, fabricated scenes, and imaginary sources. Not long after that story appeared, the paper reportedly suspended one of its most celebrated writers, Rick Bragg, after a caller raised questions about his work as well; Bragg, the *Times* revealed in an editors' note, had relied almost entirely on the reporting of a freelance journalist to compose a feature about oyster fishermen in Apalachicola, Florida. (Bragg has since resigned from the paper.) Finally, the newspaper's executive editor, Howell Raines, and its managing editor, Gerald M. Boyd, stepped down, and Raines's prede-cessor, Joseph Lelyveld, was summoned out of retirement to run the paper. The *Times* also played this story as an off-lead, under the headline "TIMES'S 2 TOP EDITORS RESIGN AFTER FUROR ON WRITER'S FRAUD." In the accompanying photograph, the paper's media reporter, Jacques Steinberg, could be seen standing behind the publisher, Arthur O. Sulzberger, Jr., intently taking notes. His description of the editors' departure was a classic of *Times* understatement: "Mr. Raines grabbed a straw hat from the office he had just vacated and walked out of the building. Mr. Boyd followed a minute later. (Neither man responded to requests for interviews.)"

Even at the *Times'* lowest moment, which may be right about now, it is almost impossible to exaggerate the paper's significance. Not only is it bigger and better than its rivals; it enjoys a whole different ontological status. An event it doesn't cover might, in a manner of speaking, just as well not have happened. At the same time, the *Times* is a place where people show up to work, which is to say also to whine, conspire, feud, and slack off. (When I left the paper, after fourteen years, I found that, no longer consumed by *Times* gossip, I had added an extra hour to my day.) The mechanics of the paper's production and its eminence as an institution have always been in tension, and part of what made the *Times* the *Times* was its ability to repress this. In this sense, Blair's bogus stories were almost less damaging than the accurate ones that followed: here was all the *Times'* institutional stature and gravity of tone being brought to bear on its own screw-ups. And, once the *Times* picked up the story, it had to see it to the end. Woe to the editor whose newsroom becomes the news.

*   *   *

One of the best accounts of life inside the *Times* comes from a historian of the French Revolution, Robert Darnton. (Darnton, now a professor at Princeton University, is a member of a *Times* family: his father, Byron, was killed in the Second World War while on assignment for the paper; his younger brother, John, who won a Pulitzer Prize for his reporting out of Poland, is now an associate editor at the *Times*; and Darnton himself briefly worked in the newsroom in the mid-nineteen-sixties.) Darnton's article "Writing News and Telling Stories" appeared twenty-eight years ago in *Daedalus*, ostensibly in response to an academic study of the media. Whatever its contribution may have been to the field of communications theory, it was so astute about *Times* affairs that it was passed around among reporters as a kind of in-house Masters and Johnson. Somebody gave me a smudgy Xerox when I started out at the paper, and for years I kept it in my desk, under a pile of notebooks.

The *Times* that Darnton describes is a rigidly hierarchical, almost neurotically status-conscious place. The star reporters, like Homer Bigart and Peter Kihss, occupy the front of the newsroom. The young reporters— the "greenhorns"—are banished to the back. In between sit the rewrite men and the middle-aged veterans, who include, among others, "foreign correspondents who have been sent home to pasture" and "bitter, ambitious men who have failed to get editorships." Darnton relates how reporters would be summoned over the newsroom's public-address system to the city desk for assignments, and the terror this could induce. To avoid an editor's "hungry eye," grown men were known to resort to hiding in the bathroom or behind the water fountains.

At one point, Darnton imagines a reporter named Jones approaching the desk: "Jones can feel his colleagues thinking as he walks past them, 'I hope he gets a lousy assignment or that he gets a good one and blows it.'" At another point, Jones is dispatched to cover a meeting in Brooklyn. When his story on the event, a mere two hundred words long, gets poor play, he is depressed, especially as Smith, who sits next to him, "made the second front with a colorful story about garbage dumping." To those who read it, the *Times* may be a record of wars, famines, and Broadway openings; to those who write it, Darnton observes, it is just another reminder of who is getting ahead and who isn't.

This kind of anxiety is institutionally useful, which is one of the reasons it persists. " 'Did you see how Smith handled that garbage story?' the city editor will say to Jones. 'That's the kind of work we need from the man who is going to fill the next opening in the Chicago bureau.' " But, if it is tempting for editors to manipulate reporters in this way, it is not without risk. The newsroom's very competitiveness can, paradoxically, inspire a subversive sort of solidarity:

> Chronic insecurity breeds resentment. While scrambling over one another for the approval of the editors, the reporters develop great hostility to the men at the other end of the room. . . . The reporters feel united by a sentiment of "them" against "us," which they express in horseplay and house jokes. (I remember a clandestine meeting in the men's room, where one reporter gave a parody of urinating techniques among "them.")

By my day, Bigart and Kihss were gone, the seating plan had mostly broken down, and the public-address system had been replaced by multi-line telephones. But, aside from these details, life at the *Times* was basically the same. My colleagues and I worried endlessly over our positions in the hierarchy and had worked out to several decimal places which assignments were to be coveted, based not on their intrinsic merits but on their status. (City Hall was better than Police Headquarters, Police Headquarters was better than the Brooklyn courthouse, the Brooklyn courthouse was better than Trenton, and anything was better than Long Island.) We rushed to get the early edition of the paper as soon as it appeared on Manhattan newsstands, which in those days was around 11 P.M. The pleasure of a really great story was usually mixed with envy, while the pleasure of a really awful one was pure and uncomplicated.

At the same time, we were a community, bound in no small part by the countless stories that would never—could never—make it into the paper. (A favorite concerned an Arabic phrase that the *Times*, relying on a clerk who happened to be Muslim, had rendered "There is no god but Allah" but which actually meant "National Bank of Kuwait.") Gathering at a restaurant—now defunct—called the Hawaii Kai, first as copy persons and later as reporters, we inevitably came to the conclusion that, in our sleep, we could run the paper better than our bosses. A game I remember with particular fondness was called Most Fucked Over: the winner was the one who, as the name suggests, could recount the day's best example of editorial imbecility—the lead mangled beyond recognition, the story assigned at nine hundred words, then cut to a news brief. After one Metro editor we especially disliked was pushed out, someone pencilled in his name on a list of history's greatest disasters that was posted by the rewrite desk. It remained there until the newsroom was renovated, a decade later.

Just after the revelation of Jayson Blair's transgressions, Sulzberger, Raines, and Boyd held what the *Times* referred to as a "town-hall-style" meeting with their staff. To accommodate everyone who wanted to attend, the session was held in a rented movie theatre on West Forty-fourth Street, and it was also piped in, via telephone, to the paper's many, far-flung bureaus. The *Times* closed the meeting to news coverage—a throng of reporters stood in front of the threatre's entrance—and, in a somewhat convoluted effort at high-mindedness, barred its own media reporter as well, forcing him, in effect, to rely on leaks from his colleagues.

One after another, reporters rose to dress down their bosses. "I do not feel a sense of trust and reassurance that judgments are properly made," Joseph Sexton, a deputy editor on the Metro desk, announced in front of several hundred *Times* employees. Shaila K. Dewan, a Metro reporter, demanded, "What will you do to restore our faith that there is a modicum of fairness in the advancement process?" Alex Berenson, a reporter for the Business desk, asked Raines point-blank if he had considered resigning.

During the years I worked at the *Times*, there were three different executive editors. Abe Rosenthal retired shortly after I got to the paper, and was replaced by Max Frankel, who served until 1994, when he was succeeded by Lelyveld. In that time, I'm sure there were some editors and reporters who felt that they were being well treated and their talents properly recognized; however, they were careful not to admit it. The level of disaffection in the newsroom may even, at moments, have approached that of the past few months, but the resentment never had much in the way of coherence. In narrative terms, it lacked a theme, or, to use *Times* shorthand, a "nut graf."

Though neither Frankel nor Lelyveld could be described as easygoing, both men tended, as executive editor, to underplay the part. They would often act, and perhaps genuinely were, unaware of the extent of their power. I don't recall either of them ever articulating an overarching goal for the paper. The implication was that their own sensibility didn't matter; they were there to run the *Times*. This neutral posture was, of course, the posture of the paper itself.

Raines, who became the executive editor on September 5, 2001, showed no interest in this sort of studied self-effacement. He often invoked Bear Bryant as a model leader; in an interview for this magazine last year he told Ken Auletta, "When Coach Bryant walked onto a football field, everybody in that stadium knew that football would be played here today." He was, without a doubt, the only *Times* man to show up at work in a white Panama hat.

Throughout his tenure, Raines sent out *Times*-wide e-mails addressed "Dear Friends and Colleagues." Typically, they included expressions of praise—often extravagant—for the work of the previous weeks. "You have managed to make every page of the newspaper a richer, deeper read and a more gratifying visual treat day after day," one from last year went. "The intellectual depth and professional quality of the journalism in our paper, on the Web and in our expanding television and book operations has no peer anywhere in the world." The terms of Raines's praise were, as a rule, both triumphalist and agonistic: Sports "spotted the ice judging story early and dominated it all week"; the Business staff and the Washington bureau "continued to dominate the Enron story as they have all winter." When, in April, 2002, the *Times* won an unprecedented seven Pulitzer Prizes, mostly for its coverage of the World Trade Center attacks, Raines declared that the paper's reporting on 9/11 would "be studied and taught as long as journalism is studied and practiced."

Raines had a very public goal for the *Times*, which was, as he repeatedly put it, to raise the paper's "competitive metabolism." What the practical import of this metaphor was depends on whom you ask. During Raines's tenure, several high-level editors who had been moving steadily up the ranks found themselves sidelined. Similarly, several veteran reporters who had expected to be able to negotiate their next assignments were told, rather summarily, that this would not be happening. (A number of them left the paper.) Meanwhile, a new élite of writers and editors emerged. Some were people who had distinguished themselves in the aftermath of September 11th; some were known as stylish, or at least flashy, writers; some were aggressive risk-takers; and some, it appeared, were just people Raines could push around. The net effect was to centralize authority, which one has to assume was deliberate on Raines's part, and to create widespread resentment, which one has to assume was not. Reporters in the Washington bureau took to calling the masthead editors the Taliban and Raines Mullah Omar.

Most of the newsroom's grievances never got much beyond the *Times*. Usually, they centered on some example of editorial heavy-handedness—an article ordered up to fit a preconception, a lead dictated from on high. In one case, Raines, or one of his deputies, interfered so insistently—and wrongheadedly—with a piece on the State of the Union address that the front page had to be reset at the very last minute to repair the damage. (The incident left a top editor at the paper in tears.) During the controversy last fall over the Augusta National Golf Club's refusal to admit women, Raines killed two columns on the subject, one by Dave Anderson and one by Harvey Araton. Both columns appeared to question the significance of the controversy, which the *Times* had devoted thirty-three stories to. It is almost unheard of at the *Times* for a column—even one that runs in the news pages—to be spiked, and eventually Raines reversed himself, but not before news of his decision had leaked out and became a minor scandal. Raines defended his actions, saying that they had been based not on ideology but solely on the quality of the columns, a claim that almost no one took seriously. In what turned out to be a preview of things to come, the *Times* felt compelled to report on the whole embarrassing incident in its own pages, in an article headlined "2 REJECTED SPORTS COLUMNS TO BE PRINTED BY THE TIMES."

Raines was clearly aware of the growing discontent in the newsroom. "I know that inaccurate reports have stirred anxieties among some of you about how people will be treated as we pursue this energetic vision," he noted in a "Dear Friends and Colleagues" e-mail dated February 15, 2002. But even his efforts at mollification could be read as an admonition. This same e-mail stated, "As we move forward, we will be doing so as a team, and we are determined to leave no one behind who wants to participate in the *Times's* kind of journalism."

In "The Kingdom and the Power," Gay Talese, himself a former *Times* man, recounts what was, at least until Blair, the paper's classic story of youthful indiscretion. The tale's hero, as it were, is Clyde Haberman, who now writes a column for the Metro section. In June, 1966, Haberman was the City College stringer, and had the unenviable task of transcribing for the *Times* the names of the winners of the hundreds of awards that the college was bestowing at commencement. Apparently out of boredom, he added a prize of his own, the Brett Award, "to the student who has worked hardest under a great handicap—Jake Barnes." When Abe Rosenthal found out about the joke—an allusion to the tragically disadvantaged narrator of "The Sun Also Rises"—he called Haberman, who had been a favorite of his, into his office. "Sit down," he is reported to have said. "You will never be able to write for this newspaper again." (It took more than a decade for Rosenthal to relent.)

Somehow, in my early years in the newsroom, I missed this story, or, more likely, I heard it but failed to take it to heart. In 1986, I got my first big assignment as a probationary reporter—to follow Bishop Desmond Tutu on a cross-country tour. By the fourth or fifth newsless day, I decided to amuse myself with an obvious—and therefore, I thought, harmless— parody. As I recall, it was datelined Hartford, Connecticut, and began with something witty like "Today Bishop Desmond Tutu and his wife had breakfast in their hotel room here." Shortly after I filed it, I received a call from the Metro desk's weekend editor, informing me that he was doing his best to get the story killed out of the *Times'* computer system. He suggested that if I was attached to my job I had better hope that he succeeded. The tone of his voice—anger mixed with panic—was instructive, and I was never tempted to try anything like that again.

Blair was hired by the *Times* in the summer of 1999, right after finishing, or, as it turns out, not quite finishing, college. In his first two years at the paper, he racked up some fifty corrections. "An article on Saturday about a Long Island man who killed his wife, Elsa Rolan, misstated the way she died," a correction dated January 25, 2000, read. "She was strangled, not shot." He was admonished—in an evaluation in January, 2002, the Metro editor, Jonathan Landman, warned Blair that his correction rate was "extraordinarily high by the standards of the paper"— but he never seems to have really got the message. Nor, apparently, did the *Times*.

A few months after Landman submitted his negative evaluation, he sent a note to newsroom administrators saying, "We have to stop Jayson from writing for the *Times*. Right now." Instead of being terminated, though, Blair was placed in a sort of journalistic rehab program designed specially for him, and then, in October, sent off to Washington as part of the team covering the sniper shootings. Soon after arriving there, he produced a front-page exclusive, relying entirely on unnamed sources. Raines sent Blair a note congratulating him on his work, which he called "great shoe-leather reporting." A few weeks later, Blair produced another front-page story on the sniper case, once again relying on anonymous sources.

Over the next several months, Blair was supposedly in constant motion, filing stories from twenty cities in six different states. At one point, he was sent to Hunt Valley, Maryland, to interview a couple awaiting news of their son, a marine stationed in Iraq. He updated his editors on the progress of the interview via e-mail. "I am giving them a breather for about 30 minutes," he wrote in a message to the national editor, Jim Roberts. "It's amazing timing. Lots of wrenching ups and downs with all the reports of casualties." Blair, the paper later discovered, never met the couple. Indeed, the entire time that he was claiming to be on the road, it seems, he was sitting in Brooklyn, doing his reporting, such as it was, from his apartment. Not surprisingly, many of the pieces he composed this way contained grievous errors. In perhaps his most celebrated invention—a feature about Private Jessica Lynch's family datelined Palestine, West Virginia—Blair placed the family's home on top of a hill and described Lynch's father, Gregory, choking up "as he stood on his porch here overlooking the tobacco fields and cattle pastures." The Lynch home actually sits in a wooded valley.

When the *Times* finally went looking for evidence of Blair's malfeasance, it found it everywhere, and certainly in retrospect it seems incredible that his deceptions should have continued for so long. Key details of Blair's first front-page piece on the sniper shootings had been challenged by senior law-enforcement officials; after the second, a prosecutor involved in the case held a news conference to denounce the story. Yet no one at the *Times* ever seems to have asked Blair to identify his sources. In five months of near-constant travel, he never filed a single receipt for a hotel room, or a rental car, or an airplane ticket, yet no one seems ever to have taken note of this.

Still, to read Blair's story as a failure of supervision is to misunderstand the nature of the problem. The *Times* doesn't check up on its reporters—it is taken for granted that they will get things right. Daily journalism, for many practical reasons, depends on this sort of trust; that's why the Brett Award cost a favored young reporter his job. The problem in Blair's case is that the *Times* bent its rules to keep him on—an indulgence that by its own logic was bound to end badly, though just how badly no one could have predicted.

After the *Times* confronted Blair, he dropped out of view, and there was some fear that he might harm himself. Instead, he produced a book proposal. "I really screwed up" was its opening line. In the proposal, which was quickly faxed around to half the journalists in New York, Blair, who is African-American, cast himself on the one hand as a black urban professional Everyman and on the other as a sort of latter-day Nat Turner. "I want to offer my experience as a lesson, for the precipice from which I plunged is one on which many young, ambitious, well-educated and accomplished African Americans and other 'minorities' teeter," he wrote. His story, he continued, would be "about a young black man who was told he could not succeed by everyone from his white second-grade teacher to his editor at the *Times*, who rose from the fields and got a place in the master's house, and then burned it down the only way he knew how."

In the great rehashing of Blair's story, many commentators quite reasonably focussed on race. Howard Kurtz, the Washington *Post's* media critic, for example, speculated on CNN that the *Times* tolerated an error rate like Blair's only because he was a young, promising African-American: "I wonder if a middle-aged hack would have gotten away with fifty mistakes and still be at that job." As many noted, Raines was especially concerned about diversity: he had written a book about the civil-rights movement, had won a Pulitzer Prize for an essay on his debt to his black nanny, and, in choosing Gerald Boyd as his second-in-command, had appointed the *Times'* first African-American managing editor. Initially, Raines denied that Blair's race had mattered. Responding to Kurtz, he told the *Observer*, "If someone wants to have some unbecoming speculation on their television show, that's their prerogative. We have a diverse staff, and we manage them in a very evenhanded way." Later, speaking to his own staff, he took a different position: "You have a right to ask if I, as a white man from Alabama, with those convictions, gave him one chance too many by not stopping his appointment to the sniper team. When I look into my heart for the truth of that, the answer is yes."

If Blair had been an isolated problem, Raines's suggestion that he had been misled by his own best impulses might have won him a sympathetic hearing. Conversely, had there been no Blair it's possible that *Times* staff members ultimately would have adjusted to Raines's overbearing style. But the two came together, and, in the end, it was the coincidence that seemed to lend the matter its moral clarity.

By pushing the newsroom to be faster and more aggressive, by demanding that stories be "dominated" instead of just reported, Raines had defined himself—or, what amounts to much the same thing, had allowed himself to be defined—against the traditions of the institution. Even his favorite formula—raising the "competitive metabolism"—could be read as a version of the old critique of the *Times* as slow and fustian. In this way, the everyday grievances of the newsroom acquired the force of principle. What Raines was doing wasn't just making a lot of people miserable; it was undermining the *Times'* highest values. Blair, with his fraudulent exclusives and his spurious hustle, was spectacular confirmation of Raines's mistake. Or, at least, he was close enough.

The People's Preacher

February 2002

THE REVEREND AL Sharpton knows that you do not take him seriously. Racism is like that. A man can win eighty per cent of the black vote, and still white people will question whether he really represents anyone. This is an outrage, and also a matter of no small personal satisfaction.

Nearly two decades have passed since Sharpton first made his appearance on the New York political scene and was dubbed by Ed Koch "Al Charlatan." In that time, there is hardly a form of contempt that he hasn't elicited; he has been variously condemned as a hustler, a demagogue, a symbol of all that is wrong with race relations in America, and a stupid joke. To the extent that the criticism has been damaging, it has not been to Sharpton—a pattern whose implications his critics, even today, seem unable fully to grasp. Just this past fall, a series of cartoons ran in the *Post* showing Sharpton in an assortment of poses with then Bronx Borough President Fernando Ferrer. One of the cartoons pictured Ferrer, who was hoping, with Sharpton's support, to become the Democratic mayoral nominee, perched, Charlie McCarthy-like, on Sharpton's knee; another depicted the two at the altar, Ferrer in a wedding dress, Sharpton bursting out of a tuxedo. Ultimately, one of the cartoons found its way onto a campaign flyer for Ferrer's Democratic rival, Mark Green; it showed Sharpton presenting a blimp-sized rear end to Ferrer's puckered lips amid clouds of what can only be assumed to be flatulence. Chaos ensued. Democratic leaders lined up to mollify Sharpton, among them Bill Clinton, who spent the night before the general election driving around midtown Manhattan in a vain attempt at mediation. The whole mess probably cost Green the mayoralty, but, more important, as far as Sharpton was concerned, it provided new material.

"Blacks and Latinos made a statement this year that plantation politics is over," he announced to much applause in Harlem a few days after the election. "We may have a bad date with Michael Bloomberg, but I'm not going to be the battered wife for the Democratic Party. That's what battering husbands do: beat their wives, talk about 'Nobody wants you but me,' slap them around, say 'Who else is going to buy you a dress?' Well, I'd rather walk naked than wear your wretched dress."

Sharpton, who is forty-seven, has been successful enough at what he does that his staff now numbers twenty. This includes a scheduler, a field director, and a full-time driver, who ferries him around the city in a black, Eddie Bauer-edition Ford Expedition. His organization, the National Action Network, has twenty-three chapters in fifteen states. Though it is still dangerous for white politicians to deal with him, it can be equally dangerous for them not to. Over the years, Sharpton and the New York press corps have worked out a symbiosis much like that of the crocodile and the Egyptian plover, though whose teeth are being cleaned by whom isn't always obvious.

If Sharpton were interested in conventional political power, he clearly could have acquired it by now; there are at least half a dozen congressional districts that would gladly elect him. Instead, the races he has taken on—two for the United States Senate and one for the mayoralty—have all been manifestly unwinnable. When, for instance, in 1994 he mounted a primary campaign against Senator Daniel Patrick Moynihan, Sharpton received eighty per cent of the black vote and twenty-five per cent of the total—a stunning result, and yet still several hundred thousand votes shy of victory.

Sharpton's latest plan is to run for President of the United States. He is assembling an exploratory committee, which is headed by the Harvard professors Cornel West and Charles Ogletree. In the next few weeks, he plans to make his first visit to New Hampshire. Once again, it's easy to see where all this is headed. Sharpton will lose, and before that he will be reviled—mocked and derided for even putting himself forward. Running is, for him, an absurd decision, and, given the scope of his ambition, an irresistible one.

*   *   *

The House of Justice occupies the second floor of a weary, low-slung brick building on Madison Avenue, just south of 125th Street. Above it is the Israelite Church of God and Jesus Christ, and down in the basement is a used-record store, open only sporadically, which specializes in "oldies but goodies." Next door is a West Indian restaurant, Flavored with One Love, and next to that a fish place with spiritual aspirations. "Servants of God" reads the awning, right above "A Taste of Seafood."

For the last five years, the House of Justice has been Sharpton's base of operations, home to his office, and also to the auditorium where each Saturday he holds forth to his secular congregation. The rallies are broadcast on WLIB and WWRL, two black-owned radio stations, and several weeks ago I went to hear one live. Sharpton's lawyer, Michael Hardy, made the introduction: "Let me bring to you now the soul-reacher, the liberation-seeker, the people's preacher, the president of the National Action Network." Then Sharpton led off with his trademark call and response:

"No justice!" he shouted.

"No peace!" the crowd shouted back.

"No justice!"

"No peace!"

"No justice!"

"No peace!"

"What do we want?"

"Justice!"

"What do we want?"

"Justice!"

"When do we want it?"

"Now!"

"When do we want it?"

"Now!"

"Hug the person next to you and tell them you love them."

Sharpton speaks entirely without notes about whatever happens to be on his mind. His method is to pick topics apparently at random—these range from Bible stories to current events—and then, in a final bravura rush, tie them all together. He is, as a speaker, both rambling and brilliant. "The guy's one of the finest preachers you will ever meet," the Reverend Floyd Flake, the former congressman from Queens, told me. (Almost every year, Flake invites Sharpton to speak to his congregation at Allen A.M.E. Church, one of the largest in the city.) On this particular Saturday, more than a month after Bloomberg's victory, Sharpton was still dwelling on the election. His other topics included Attorney General John Ashcroft, the fighting in the Middle East, a turbulent flight he had been on earlier that week to Chicago, and God's mercy.

The House of Justice auditorium is decorated with an assortment of posters and paintings of civil-rights leaders, among them Frederick Douglass, Marcus Garvey, Jesse Jackson, and—mostly—Sharpton. (One huge photograph shows him dressed in prison garb.) In one corner, partly hidden by a column of stacking chairs, stands an enormous wooden fist. About a hundred and fifty people were in the room that Saturday, including a woman in the front row who was holding aloft a handwritten sign advertising a booklet with the names of "70 more copkilled black males since October, 2000, in the NY tristate area alone." There were frequent cries of "Teach!" and "Tell it, Rev!" and also much laughter.

At one point, Sharpton described a recent breakfast he had had at an upscale restaurant with a young aide. The aide had ordered a poached egg and apricots—Sharpton recounted this part of the story in a fake British accent—while he himself ordered grits. "You go around town trying to act like you're eating fried roaches as a delicacy," he said. "You say, 'Oooh, this is *interesting*.' What does this do for you? Well, it'll kill you if you eat it. You can make anything look right. You take some mess, put some chocolate on it, sprinkle sugar, and the wanna-be Negro will stand in line to buy it."

Usually pictured as angry, Sharpton is, in fact, a satirist who specializes in bathos. He is forever poking fun at the "wanna-be Negro," or his close cousin the cocktail-sipping Negro. According to Sharpton's typology, this figure, who surprisingly often seems to have attended Harvard, is consumed by a self-hatred he pathetically mistakes for ambition. At the same rally, Sharpton also told a story about an executive wanna-be. Hoping to curry favor with his boss, the executive had assured him that he could ignore Sharpton. Then, when promotion time came, the boss denied him the promotion. "And the only one who could have fought the issue was me," Sharpton announced. "It wasn't nothing for me, but I could make it something for you, if you wasn't so dumb."

Although he is not a separatist or a black nationalist—he labels these views "escapist"—Sharpton is nonetheless a fatalist. Whites, he argues, haven't changed the way they feel about blacks, and perhaps they never will. "The bus driver didn't change his mind, Rosa Parks changed hers," he likes to say. Above all else, the wanna-be is a stand-in for those who don't understand this truth, or refuse to accept it, a group that includes Sharpton's moderate political rivals, as well as those members of his audience wavering in their commitment. "This is real," he declared at one point. "This ain't no part-time, do-it-when-you-like-it, I'm black today, having a black attack, then I'm going back to normal tomorrow. Many of you at home get black attacks. Well, cop stopped the car, so we're mad. So you go to two rallies. Let me tell you something. What we can't convince you of by preaching, the forces are going to force you into."

Toward the end of his address, Sharpton told the parable of the prodigal son. In his race-inflected version of the story, the son leaves home because he feels his family isn't good enough: "I ain't with this no more; you all ain't sophisticated enough for me." He squanders his portion amid high-living strangers, only to be scorned by them. Eventually, the son comes to a realization: "I ain't got to live like this, you all disrespecting me, you all acting like I'm nothing, like I'm lower than the hogs." And so he returns to the place that, in his self-loathing, he had originally rejected.

" 'Well, what are you saying, Sharpton?' " Sharpton asked himself. "I'm telling you it's time for us to come home. We wandered out there. We tried to be what we're not. You boogied around the White House for eight years because Clinton didn't mind letting Negroes in the big house. But you didn't take care of the people. You were too busy posing for Christmas pictures, rubbing your nose in champagne jars. But now you're lower than the swine—Ashcroft rubbing your face in the mud. None of your Christmas cards in the White House mean nothing now. You're eating the husk that the swine eat.

" 'Well, well, Rev, what are you talking about?' " he went on, his voice rising as he prepared to gather up the morning's many loose threads.

" 'Mark Green lost!' Yeah, but we didn't. Because to have coöperated we would have lost our dignity. To coöperate with being marginalized and demonized we would have lost our self-respect. When we didn't have no money in Birmingham, when we didn't have master degrees from Ivy League colleges in Selma, when we didn't have the ability to write memos on computers in Mississippi, we always had our self-respect. We always had our dignity. And when I think about them little nameless, faceless black women that marched in Birmingham, them babies that laid in front of water hoses, they had some self-esteem and self-respect. Columbia can't give that to you. Harvard can't give that to you. You've got to go home and find out who you are. And something will rise up in you never to fall again. And you can climb through the turbulence. You can survive through the storm. God will make a way. Hold on just a little while longer. We don't have a minute, but hold on anyhow. Because if you hold on, if you hold out, He'll make your enemies leave you alone."

Then Sharpton started to sing, as he always does at the end of a rally. "Everybody sing 'Amen,'" he began, and the audience took it up. "Everybody sing 'Amen.' Everybody sing 'A-men, amen, amen.'"

After the rally, Sharpton ducked into his office with Michael Hardy and closed the door. Soon the two were joined by Sharpton's wife, Kathy Jordan. A strikingly attractive woman who wears her hair in a mountain of reddish curls, Jordan used to sing backup for James Brown and now sings in the choir for the Saturday-morning rallies. As she swept by, several people told her how much they admired her outfit—a white leather top paired with a black leather skirt. Married for twenty-one years, Sharpton and Jordan renewed their wedding vows at a ceremony last summer attended by many of the city's most prominent politicians, including two former mayors, Koch and David Dinkins. Sharpton and Jordan live in Flatbush and have two teen-age daughters, Dominique and Ashley.

After Jordan and Hardy left, Sharpton called me into the room. Most of the office is taken up by a large L-shaped desk that holds several stacks of papers and a computer. The computer was in its screen-saver mode, and the phrase "No Justice, No Peace" kept scrolling across the monitor. Sharpton retreated briefly to the bathroom to change; when he emerged, in a fresh white shirt, I asked him about the point of the Saturday rallies. He answered in the most pragmatic terms possible, saying that the rallies were useful to him. "I have my own communication network set up," he told me.

I then asked about some of the stories he had recounted, like the one about ordering grits. "I try to make people not feel like they have to apologize for their authenticity," he explained. And the one about the executive who didn't get the promotion? "The most stable secret support group I have is people that played by the rules," he told me.

Sharpton went on to cite the example of the defamation suit that arose from the Tawana Brawley case. The case remains, in many ways, the defining event of his career, and a continuing source of conflict. In the fall of 1987, Brawley, a fifteen-year-old high-school student, was found lying in a garbage bag covered with feces, and said that she had been raped by a gang of white men. Her tale was later shown to be a hoax, but only after Sharpton and Brawley's other "advisers" had named Steven Pagones, then an assistant district attorney, as one of her assailants.

Pagones subsequently sued for defamation and infliction of emotional harm. The suit dragged on for a decade, until, in the summer of 1998, a Poughkeepsie jury found in his favor. An award of a hundred and eighty-five thousand dollars was levied against Brawley, who didn't show up at the trial, and to this day remains in hiding. Sharpton was ordered to pay Pagones sixty-five thousand dollars, but he never took the trouble to settle up, instead ducking subpoenas and insisting he had no assets. (Sharpton has still not expressed remorse over any aspect of his role in the debacle.) When he was finally deposed, last winter, and his unorthodox financial arrangements came to light—Sharpton claimed under oath, for example, not actually to own his suits but simply to "have access" to them—several of the country's most prominent black businessmen, including Earl Graves, the chairman of the magazine *Black Enterprise*, and Percy Sutton, the chairman emeritus of Inner City Broadcasting, stepped in to bail him out.

Shaming as the whole episode might have been to some, Sharpton invoked it that morning as another illustration of the high standing that whites can't, or simply won't, credit him with. "No one ever stopped to say, 'Well, why would these guys do that?'" he said, referring to his wealthy patrons. "They had nothing to do with the Brawley case. It's because in their own minds and their own hearts they feel I'm saying and doing things they know are right and can't do themselves. And I have any number of corporate executives and political insiders who say, 'You do what I wish I could do, and I'm going to help you to keep doing it.' Percy Sutton used to have an expression, 'If we didn't have an Al Sharpton, we'd have to invent one.' All right, fine, I have enough charisma, or fire, to draw a crowd. But why are business leaders—you're talking about multi-millionaires—they're not mesmerized by me. Let's be serious. What people have never stopped and thought about is that no one can survive as long as I have unless somebody needed them."

Sharpton was born in Brooklyn on October 3, 1954, the same year that the Supreme Court handed down Brown v. Board of Education. As a child during the great civil-rights struggles of the nineteen-fifties and sixties, he had little direct experience of segregation. Of the many stories about growing up that he told me, only one—about a trip down South to visit relatives—involved overt bigotry. "I remember one night we were driving, I don't remember if it was to Alabama or Florida, but we stopped somewhere in North Carolina, and my father and I went in to get some hamburgers and the guy refused to sell them," he said. "It was obviously a segregated place, but I didn't know anything about segregation. My father said to him, 'You don't understand—we're not going to eat here, we just want to take them out,' and the guy humiliated him. 'We don't serve niggers here.' It was the first time I saw someone defy my father."

Sharpton's father, Alfred, Sr., was a contractor who invested in real estate on the side. He was successful enough at both vocations that Sharpton led a sheltered, even privileged (by the standards of black New York) childhood. When he was still small, his father moved the family to Hollis, Queens, a racially mixed neighborhood, where they lived in a ten-room house and kept his-and-hers Cadillacs in the driveway.

Almost as soon as Sharpton could talk, he began preaching. He would line up his sister's dolls, put on his mother's bathrobe, and use a candle as a microphone. "I'm not talking about once or twice," he told me. "I would do this every week." Not a religious man himself, Alfred, Sr., didn't much care for his son's sermons; still, by the time Sharpton was four he had begun preaching regularly at the Pentecostal church favored by his mother, Ada—the Washington Temple Church of God in Christ—before a congregation that often numbered more than a thousand. At ten, he was ordained by the church's pastor, Bishop Frederick Douglass Washington, and during the 1964 New York World's Fair the "wonder-boy preacher," as he became known, held forth at a gospel-night celebration featuring Mahalia Jackson. She was sufficiently impressed to subsequently take him on tour with her.

During the school week, Sharpton attended P.S. 134, where he remembers being uninterested in sports or games or, for that matter, anyone else's opinion. "I would always put on my school papers 'the Reverend Alfred Sharpton,'" he recalled. "And the teacher kept telling me, 'You can't put that there!' And I said, 'But that's who I am.' And it would drive her nuts. I was in third or fourth grade, and I remember that my conclusion was I didn't care what they said, that's what I was going to do. And I kept doing it. I don't even remember if they agreed, so much as they said there's no use trying."

One day in the spring of 1964, Sharpton came home from school to be told by his mother that his father was moving out of the house. Ada had a son, Tommy, and a daughter, Ernestine, by a previous marriage, and they had been living with the Sharpton family in Hollis. Ernestine, who was in her late teens, had, it turned out, been having an affair with Alfred, Sr., and was now pregnant by him. "My mother got very sick, and basically my father abandoned her," Sharpton told me. "We couldn't pay the bills. For many months, we had no lights, no gas; we had to try to wash up any way we could, at a neighbor's house, because we had no hot water, and no phone. And you got to remember now, we're in this middle-class neighborhood, and eventually everybody in the neighborhood knows this."

Ada finally moved what was left of her family back to Brooklyn and went on welfare. Bishop Washington became something of a surrogate father to Sharpton, the first of many. Sharpton remembers Washington buying him, among other things, a new suit for Easter. Because the Bishop was an avid reader, Sharpton became one, too. "I used to sit in Bishop Washington's office all the time after Sunday service, and he'd sit and underline parts of books," Sharpton recalled. "I remember even before I could understand what I was reading, I used to sit and underline books. I mean, I'm walking around, twelve years old, with ten books, underlining. People say, 'Either this kid's a genius or a fraud, or both.' "

Practically every Sunday morning, Sharpton still preaches, usually at a black church in New York, or, if he happens to be on the road, in Chicago or Atlanta or Los Angeles. In December, I went to hear him at Dunton Presbyterian Church, in South Ozone Park, Queens. A neighborhood of tightly packed one-family homes, South Ozone Park suggests from a distance middle-class stolidity; viewed close up, it suggests something nearer to poverty. It was the Sunday before Christmas, and the pews of the small brick church were full.

Sharpton's Sunday-morning sermons function more or less as the inverse of his Saturday-morning speeches—current events subordinated to faith. At Dunton, he spoke about the meaning of Jesus' birth, the legacy of Martin Luther King, Jr., and the importance of self-sacrifice. "I'll tell you, the hardest job of a black preacher is to preach the funeral of an insignificant Negro," he told the congregation. "Most folks shouldn't even have a funeral. Most folks should go straight from the morgue to the cemetery. Because most folks ain't done nothing we can talk about. Bought you a nice house. Who cares? We'll sell your house as soon as you die. The only thing that will matter two minutes after you're gone is if you did something for somebody other than yourself."

After he was finished, he changed his shirt, and made a brief stop at a luncheon that was taking place in the basement. "It's Reverend Sharpton! I can't believe it!" a teen-age girl exclaimed. The crowd broke into a chorus of "For He's a Jolly Good Fellow" as he posed for pictures. The church's choirmaster, a tall, gray-haired man wearing a Christmas tie, came up to Sharpton and said, "There's only two people I know that have lasted like you—you and Cassius Clay. You never compromised." People kept urging Sharpton to stay for lunch, but he said he had to go; he was on his way to a meeting with executives at PepsiCo about advertising in the black media.

Sharpton might well have become a conventional preacher with a conventional congregation—it was Bishop Washington's hope that Sharpton would one day marry his daughter and take over the Temple—had he not discovered something even more attractive. Poking around a bookstore one day when he was in elementary school, Sharpton came across a ninety-nine-cent biography of Adam Clayton Powell, Jr. He bought the book, and as he read it he became, in his words, "absolutely mesmerized."

At that time, in the mid-nineteen-sixties, Powell was the pastor of the Abyssinian Baptist Church, in Harlem, the congressman from New York's eighteenth district, and the chairman of the House Education and Labor Commitee. Sharpton decided that he wanted to meet Powell, and began pestering his mother to let him go to Harlem. Finally, she relented, and one Sunday he took the subway uptown with his sister, Cheryl.

"To this day, I have never got the rush and the excitement that I got when I first saw Adam Clayton Powell," Sharpton told me. "I told friends of mine that I thought I had seen God. He was very tall, very erect, almost majestic. He didn't walk to the pulpit, he, like, strutted. He preached a sermon about love. My sister was absolutely unimpressed, and I'm ready to leave the world. After church is over, hundreds of people are filing out, and I go with my presumptuous self and ask, 'Where's the pastor's office?' They show me where it is. And I walk over, down this long hall, and, I'll never forget, in those days they would have doors where you could open the top and the bottom was still shut. So you could barely see me over the bottom. And I'm knocking on the door. Finally, the lady comes and looks over, and I say, 'I'd like to see Reverend Congressman Powell.' She says, 'What?' I said, 'I'd like to see Reverend Congressman Powell.' She kind of smiles, and says, 'Who would I tell the pastor is calling?' I said, 'Reverend Alfred Sharpton.' She's, like, this is the biggest joke in the world, and I'm, like, what's wrong with you? She goes about her business, totally ignores me. So I knock again. And she again ignores me. The third time, she gets a little irritated, and she goes somewhere. And she comes back and—I remember it like it was yesterday—with this look of disbelief on her face. And she says, 'Follow me.' And she brings me in this inner room and Adam Clayton Powell is standing there, and there's two or three old women around, he has his arm around them, and he looks down—now, mind you, Adam was about six-three, six-four—and he says, 'Alfred Sharpton, boy preacher from F. D. Washington's church in Brooklyn.' And I say, 'You know me?' 'Sure, Washington's an old friend of mine.' Now I know he's God. Adam Clayton Powell knows me!" That very afternoon, Powell took Sharpton with him to one of his favorite haunts, the Red Rooster, a bar on Seventh Avenue, and Sharpton watched as the Congressman held court in the back. "It was the most amazing scene I'd ever seen," he said.

Sharpton came out of a denomination—Pentecostalism—that explicitly discouraged secular pleasure. Powell was nothing if not worldly. He liked to drink, to date beautiful women—he went through three wives—and to live well. "Keep the Faith, Baby" was the title he picked for a volume of his collected sermons, printed to pay off a libel judgment. Sharpton nonetheless attached himself to Powell, becoming, at the age of thirteen, an unofficial member of the Congressman's entourage. He was called "the kid," and in this capacity was introduced to everybody who was anybody in Harlem politics, or was hoping to be.

"I met Percy Sutton, Charlie Rangel, David Dinkins, all of them, when I was 'the kid' in Adam Clayton Powell's operation," he told me. "So it might have something to do with how I see them. They were just guys with dreams, hanging around. And I was one of the court jesters to the King of Harlem."

Sutton, who became Manhattan Borough President in 1966, remembers Sharpton as an almost preternaturally facile student. "He was an assembler of information and knowledge," Sutton told me. "He ingested material, and—how shall I say it?—regurgitated it much enhanced. Many people sort of adopted him, because they wanted to share with him."

It was on Powell's behalf that Sharpton staged his first protests. In 1967, Powell, who had been accused of misusing travel funds, was barred from taking his House seat pending an investigation. The following year, although he was reëlected, he was still prevented from voting. Not long afterward, Sharpton met Jesse Jackson, then the director of the Southern Christian Leadership Conference's Operation Breadbasket. Sharpton, who had dangled a pencil from his lips in a schoolboy's imitation of Powell's cigar, approached Jackson in much the same spirit. "I had my own little crew of ten guys," he told me. "I had security. I'm little Jesse Jackson in school, because whatever Jesse was doing, that's what I was doing." As Sharpton recalls it, Jackson's first advice to him was "Choose your targets, do your research, and then kick ass." I asked Sharpton what targets he had found in high school.

"Everything," he said. I asked for an example. "One day, we were eating lunch, and I said, 'This food is inferior.'" He laughed. "'Boycott it!' We called a boycott. I'm serious. Everything."

On an icy evening last month, Sharpton invited me to accompany him to the swearing-in ceremony of Charles Barron, an old friend of his who had just been elected to the City Council. When I arrived at Sharpton's office, he was watching a homemade video, one of a library of tapes he has compiled of Jesse Jackson's television appearances. Sharpton has continued to study Jackson—"It's like going over the text before you take the test," he told me—even as their relationship has changed. During the Clinton Administration, Jackson became quite close to the President—in the midst of the Monica Lewinsky scandal, he came to the White House to pray with Bill, Hillary, and Chelsea—and later he campaigned hard for Al Gore. According to Sharpton's general outlook on race relations, Jackson's efforts can mean only one thing—that he has given up the struggle. Sharpton is clearly attracted by the idea of displacing Jackson—his Presidential bid is both an homage and a challenge—and he has taken to hinting publicly that it is time for Jackson to retire. "If you want to be comfortable, you should do what Muhammad Ali did," Sharpton has said of his old mentor. "You should get a ringside seat and watch the fight."

After a while, we set off in Sharpton's Expedition for City Hall. We arrived late, but not as late as Barron. Council members are free to choreograph their own ceremonies, and Barron, who represents East New York, had chosen an Afrocentric theme. The ceremony began with the pouring of libations. This was followed by African drumming, an African dance, and, finally, a rendition of "Total Praise" by a gospel choir. Everyone joined in for "Lift Every Voice and Sing"—the black national anthem. The council chamber, which holds more than five hundred people, was packed, and, aside from a handful of council members there to advance their own political careers, I was, as far as I could tell, the only white in the room. (This was a common experience during the months I followed Sharpton.) Eventually, the oath of office was administered, by the Reverend Herbert Daughtry. Daughtry, who is seventy-one, heads a group called the National Black United Front. He cautioned the audience that there was a chance he might misstate the oath and instead of asking the new councilman to uphold the laws of New York ask something else: "Do you, Charles Barron, commit yourself to the ongoing revolution of the people?"

Barron, a former Black Panther, was wearing a blue tunic with gold trim and a matching peaked cap. He began by announcing that it was time for the council chamber, an ornate room hung with portraits of various early American heroes, all of them white, to be redecorated. "We are the new majority," he said to a roar of approval from the audience. "And we should have the majority of pictures on the walls!" Barron went on to advocate freedom for America's "political prisoners" and to vow to fight for reparations for slavery. "We built the bridges," he said. "We built Wall Street. Our ancestors cleared Brooklyn. In return, we were raped, we were murdered. And you have the nerve to say we should forget that? Not in your lifetime!"

When it was Sharpton's turn to speak, he recalled that it was exactly sixty years ago that the first black had been elected to the City Council. "His name was Adam Clayton Powell," he said. Sharpton reminisced about time that he and Barron had spent together in the Brooklyn House of Detention as a result of a protest, and he praised Barron as a man who "personifies politics at its best." In closing, he spoke about his own political ambitions, and the detractors who would, inevitably, mock them. "They ask me, 'Why are you going to run for President?' " he said, emphasizing the "why." "If I wanted to be a ballplayer, it would be all right. If I wanted to sing and dance and switch my hips, it would be all right. But I want to think and use my mind and my heritage to run the United States."

Sharpton left the ceremony as soon as he had finished speaking. Heading to his car, he checked the messages on his cell phone. We had been at City Hall for an hour and a half and in that time he had received fourteen messages. Two concerned the race for City Council speaker, five were about the fight between Harvard's Afro-American studies department and its president, Lawrence Summers, which was then making front-page news, and the remaining seven were about Vieques. Over the summer, Sharpton had joined the protest against Navy bombing on the island, and as a result had spent ninety days in federal jail. It took him approximately five seconds to realize that the latest development in the battle—a judge had dismissed an anti-bombing lawsuit—was newsworthy, and not a whole lot longer to figure out how to become part of the story. On the way uptown, he got on his cell phone and called a press conference, to be held at the House of Justice at eight-forty-five. It was eight-fifteen.

Sharpton became "Al," as opposed to the stodgier "Alfred," one night during the early nineteen-eighties in a hotel room in Miami. He was sitting around with James Brown, when, as he recalls it, the Godfather of Soul turned to him. "You need to cut that," Brown said. "It's got to be quick, something people can grab onto." He recommended "Al Sharp."

Sharpton regards Brown as the last and most devoted of his surrogate fathers. The two met not long after Brown's son Teddy was killed in a car accident, and they quickly became close. As part of his apprenticeship, Sharpton helped arrange for Brown to perform at the Rumble in the Jungle between Ali and George Foreman, in 1974. This led to a friendship with Don King, which, in turn, led Sharpton to serve briefly, under circumstances that remain murky, as an F.B.I.informant—a career twist that he has alternately denied outright and tried to explain away. (Among those he is reported to have provided information on is Danny Pagano, an organized-crime figure later convicted of racketeering.) In 1981, Brown and Sharpton cut an album together, "God Has Smiled on Me," with Brown singing and Sharpton preaching, and when Brown's manager had a heart attack Sharpton filled in for him, which is how he met his wife. Sharpton also got his curious hair from Brown, a style he adopted, he told me, "somewhere between admiration and duress."

As an impresario of protest, Sharpton draws heavily on the skills he learned from Brown, not the least of them being the art of self-promotion. In recent weeks, he has, among other things, proposed himself as a mediator between India and Pakistan in the conflict over Kashmir, requested permission to lead an ecumenical council to Guantánamo

Bay, and held a town meeting with Enron employees in Houston. Rare is the Sharpton production in which he himself does not play a central role. In this regard, Vieques was fairly typical. During Sharpton's incarceration, his supporters camped in tents outside Brooklyn's Metropolitan Detention Center while he conducted a hunger strike to protest his imprisonment. Later, Sharpton had a wooden platform built next to the jail so that when he emerged, some thirty pounds lighter, he could immediately hold a rally. The event—covered as a homecoming and a weight-loss story rolled into one—made the front page of both the *Times* and the *News*. Whatever the seriocomic spectacle accomplished in Vieques, in New York it established Sharpton as a hero in the Latino community.

"You know, New York is theatre, street theatre," Ed Koch, who has softened considerably toward his old enemy, told me. "You have to respond. Sharpton in large part is street theatre. It's a shtick, and it's effective." After the police shooting of Amadou Diallo, an unarmed Guinean immigrant, in 1999, Sharpton arranged what was probably his most ambitious protest: two weeks of civil disobedience that resulted in the arrest of hundreds, including the state comptroller, Carl McCall, and the actress Susan Sarandon. Koch remembers approaching Sharpton, in effect, to arrange a booking. "I called him up and I said I wanted to get arrested on Monday, but could I get arrested at ten in the morning?" Koch recalled. "He said, 'I can't do it at ten; I can only do it at eleven.'"

Sharpton gleefully exploits the logic of celebrity culture, by which a protest he is leading will make news because he is leading it. According to his detractors, this game of mirrors is all there is to him. When I told Michael Meyers, the director of the New York Civil Rights Coalition, that I was writing about Sharpton, he blew up at me. "Al Sharpton is a media hound," he said. "He's a racial buffoon, a publicity stunt, and you guys fall in line. I want to know what has he ever done for quote-unquote his people, whoever they are?" Meyers, who is also a columnist for the *Post* and is black, went on to argue that the press's coverage of Sharpton represented, in itself, a form of bias. "The credibility he has has been given by the New York Paternalistic *Times*," he said. "It's racism. It's sheer lunacy, but it's also racism."

On the night of Barron's swearing-in, we arrived back at the House of Justice at roughly the same time that crews from WABC, WNBC, WCBS,

UPN, and NY1 were pulling up. Once they had set up inside the auditorium, Sharpton delivered a brief statement, composed en route, saying that the ruling in the Vieques case should be appealed. Then he vowed, if need be, to go back to jail. Under what circumstances this would be necessary, or whether it was even a serious promise, were matters of minor significance. The crews had what they needed for the eleven-o'clock news and, as soon as they had packed up their equipment, dispersed into the night.

Every Monday evening, Sharpton's most committed supporters get together for what are called organizing meetings, at which they discuss whatever protests, or "actions," are in the works. Often at these volunteer meetings, dinner is provided; on a Monday not long ago, the menu was fish stew, and the agenda included a planned boycott of the *Post*. When I arrived, about fifty people were sitting in the House of Justice auditorium at long tables. In contrast to the Saturday-morning rallies, where the audience had always been welcoming, the evening group was openly hostile. One woman came over and demanded to know who had told me I could come. Another said that she had never heard of a reporter being allowed to attend an organizing meeting and let me know that if it were up to her it wouldn't happen again.

The immediate inspiration for the *Post* boycott was last fall's Ferrer-Sharpton cartoons, and the group had produced flyers that showed six of the offending drawings on one side and the message "No Justice, No Profit" on the other. "We should not support any entity in our community that espouses racism," the flyers said. "The last thing we New Yorkers need is the fostering of ethnic and racial divisions." Most of the discussion, however, centered on a second piece of campaign literature, which, because of some lapse, still wasn't ready.

Sharpton clearly found the conversation tedious. "What I'm saying is, if he couldn't get the literature done, he should have reported that to somebody," he observed, trying to put an end to the finger-pointing.

"That's what we're saying, too," an elderly man insisted, refusing to let the issue drop. "We'd like to know what happened and why we can't get this going."

After still more discussion in this vein, Sharpton retreated to his office. The stew was served, and then people began putting together a mailing for the House of Justice's fifth-anniversary celebration. At one point, an older man, apropos of nothing in particular, began to rail about the role that Jews had played in the slave trade. This matter, he said, had not received the attention that it deserved, even though he had been talking about it for forty years, and he went on to say that his mother had worked as a cleaning woman for Jews, who were very dirty people. A younger woman agreed with this assessment, and added that Jews were not good to work for, because "they try to squeeze every penny." I couldn't quite catch the connection, but another man who had joined the conversation complained that the media were still spreading lies about the Brawley case, and that it was impossible to get the truth out, even on black radio.

Sharpton calls himself a civil-rights activist, but the term, of course, has never accurately described what he does. Many of the issues he's taken up over the years have been, at best, tangentially related to the cause of civil rights, while others have been antithetical to it.

In 1995, for instance, Sharpton joined the campaign against Freddy's, a clothing store on 125th Street whose owner, a Jew, had tried to expand into space leased by a black. Sharpton's Saturday-morning rallies were used as a platform by many of the organizers of the campaign, which had an overtly anti-Semitic thrust, while Sharpton himself referred to the store's owner as a "white interloper." Eventually, a protester set fire to Freddy's, killing eight people, including himself. (Afterward, Sharpton apologized—sort of—for the "interloper" remark by saying he shouldn't have used the word "white.") For his work in the Diallo case, Sharpton received praise from many quarters, and the New York Civil Liberties Union briefly considered giving him an award for it. But even in this case Sharpton quickly exceeded the limits of civil-rights advocacy. Before the grand jury had finished hearing the evidence against the four officers who shot Diallo, he was demanding that they be indicted. As Michael Meyers put it to me, "You cannot regard someone as a civil-rights activist who does not believe in due process of law."

Nor, in the end, is it necessarily accurate to view what Sharpton does even as activism. Most of the critical challenges of the inner city, like improving child care and education and housing, don't lend themselves to protests or marches or civil disobedience. Sharpton isn't interested in causes like these. Just half a block from the House of Justice is an empty lot surrounded by a wooden construction barrier. A sign proclaims it the "Future home of the Harlem Children's Zone," a school and community center. I first noticed the sign about a year and a half ago, and in all that time there has been no hint of progress.

I once asked Sharpton which of his accomplishments he was most proud of. He pointed to his campaign against racial profiling and his performance in the mayoral primary of 1997, when he received a third of the vote. On another occasion, I tried to press him about why he didn't pursue more concrete goals. "I have no desire to be an inside player, and no desire to be in social service," he told me. "Building housing is good. But I'll support Johnny Ray Youngblood"—a Brooklyn minister—"in doing that. I do social change—broad, policy climate-setting. And that's what I always will do."

In his book "Race Matters," Cornel West, the co-chairman of Sharpton's 2004 Presidential exploratory committee, devotes a chapter to what he calls "The Crisis of Black Leadership." There he argues that the failure of black politicians to provide either moral vision or practical role models has left a void to be filled by figures of "even narrower visions, one-note racial analyses, and sensationalist practices." As examples of these "protest leaders," who according to West operate in a "myopic mode . . . often, though not always, reeking of immoral xenophobia," he names Louis Farrakhan and "the early Al Sharpton."

By West's accounting, the year Sharpton matured as a leader was 1991, the same year he was nearly stabbed to death by a white man in Bensonhurst. (Visiting Sharpton in the hospital, Jesse Jackson joked that the only reason he had survived the attack was that he had seven inches of fat and the blade was just six inches long.) Sharpton, too, has cited 1991 as a turning point. "In the past I have been guilty of letting ungodly things around me, of excusing hate and violent intent and imagery in my presence," he wrote in "Go and Tell Pharaoh," his 1996 autobiography. "After the stabbing I saw the gravity of what we were doing and realized that I had to choose sides, to decide who I was and what I stood for. I started taking myself, and my movement, a lot more seriously than I had; I started judging the means as well as the end."

In early 1992, the new, more morally disciplined Sharpton gave a speech at Kean University, in New Jersey. "Why did they make us slaves?" he asked at one point. "We were the masters of the universe, so if you want to build an empire, you get people who know how to do that. That's historical fact. That ain't racism; that's facts. White folks was in the cave when we had built empires. . . . We taught philosophy and astrology and mathematics before Socrates and them Greek homos ever got around to it."

Whether or not Sharpton has genuinely changed, his status has. No longer a widely despised and marginal figure in New York politics, he is a widely despised and central one. On a fairly typical day I spent with Sharpton recently, he began the morning by putting in a call to Senator Charles Schumer. Later, he received a request for a meeting from Alan Hevesi, who is running for state comptroller, and a visit at the House of Justice from state assemblyman Adam Clayton Powell IV. (Powell had two sons, Adam Clayton Powell III and Adam Clayton Powell IV.) Toward evening, Andrew Cuomo, who would like to be New York's next governor, also pitched up.

Politicians are pragmatists, and in courting Sharpton they are simply following the numbers. Every one of Sharpton's campaigns has taken place under absurdly adverse circumstances. In 1992, when he ran for the United States Senate for the first time, he had recently been on trial for fraud, was still under tax indictment, and had virtually no campaign funds. Nevertheless, he received two-thirds of the black vote and, in the four-way Democratic primary, came in third, outpolling the sitting city comptroller, Liz Holtzman. In his mayoral race, in 1997, Sharpton received eighty-five per cent of the black vote, and by so doing nearly forced a runoff for the Democratic nomination. These results reflect support that extends far beyond the crowd at the House of Justice. By Sharpton's account, he has maintained this support not despite all the efforts to discredit him but in part because of them. "If my critics were more even-handed, they probably could keep people more against me," he once told me.

I spoke to many prominent black New Yorkers about Sharpton.

Although they expressed mixed feelings toward him, they generally agreed on the nature of his appeal and also on his immunity from white criticism. "When Sharpton did Tawana Brawley, that was perceived by most of the white press, and most white New Yorkers, as a disaster," Phil Thompson, a former Dinkins-administration official who is now an associate professor of political science at Columbia, observed. "It seemed like 'Why keep fighting this battle when you're losing?' What that misses is there's a black tradition of fighting against long odds. It's called 'speaking truth to power.' Sharpton said, 'I'm going to support and believe in this child,' and there's something profoundly resonant in the black community about that."

Eric Adams is the co-founder of a group called A Hundred Blacks in Law Enforcement, which has worked sometimes with Sharpton and sometimes against him. To explain the breadth of Sharpton's support, Adams recounted a recent conversation he had had on the subway with a black Wall Street trader. "Our conversation started because he was reading the paper, and he mentioned something that Sharpton spoke about," Adams told me. "And he said, 'That's why I like this guy!' He started to talk about his life on the trading floor, and how this glass ceiling is there, and how he wants to just go in and punch his boss in the nose. He said that his boss was so pissed off when Sharpton did a rally down on Wall Street that his boss turned red and had conniptions. And he said, 'I wish that Sharpton would march every week so I could piss my boss off the way he pisses me off all the time.'"

Adams continued, "Many black professionals thought if they burned the midnight oil, if they got those A's, if they went to the prestigious institutions and made it out, they would follow the same professional track as their white counterparts, and reach for that American dream — only to find out it was a nightmare. And Sharpton is the only one that allows them in their cocooned, professional state—they're too tied up, they've got to meet that Mercedes payment, keep that house in the Hamptons, send their kids to private schools—Sharpton is all they have to stand in the face of the people they would love to stand in the face of and give them a bloody nose. And that's why they love him."

*   *   *

Far and away the biggest event of the year at the House of Justice is the annual Martin Luther King Day celebration. Called a "public-policy forum," the event isn't really a forum and doesn't deal much with public policy; rather, it is a series of speeches delivered by a parade of community leaders and public officials. In a different setting, such a holiday gathering could easily devolve into a feel-good celebration of racial harmony; at the House of Justice, there's little risk of this. Two years ago, for instance, one of the speakers at the forum told a rambling but still recognizably anti-Semitic tale about being fired by two Jews and hired by a third. (The last Jew was Jesus.) A few minutes later, Hillary Clinton, then a candidate for the Senate, mounted the stage.

Every year, the list of politicians who come grows longer. Last month's attendees included Senator Schumer; the state attorney general, Eliot Spitzer; the state comptroller, McCall; the city comptroller, Bill Thompson; and the city's public advocate, Betsy Gotbaum. Charles Barron was given the honor of introducing the new City Council speaker, Gifford Miller. Miller noted that just a few days earlier he had received a gift from Barron: "a hammer and some nails so we could put up some new pictures at City Hall."

Many of Sharpton's guests come in a spirit of fear, a condition that fits well with his sense of the holiday. "I've said throughout the years, and I'll say again, 'Ultimately, Dr. King won,'" he told the crowd. "Because today even in Mississippi, where it was once against the law for us to read and write, the libraries are closed for Dr. King's birthday." He went on, "Even in Alabama, where in city halls they wouldn't let us register to vote, they can't go to work today, because it's Martin Luther King's birthday."

During his tenure, Rudy Giuliani refused to deal with Sharpton. He never came to the forum and, as Sharpton likes to point out, also was never invited. This year, though, Mayor Bloomberg accepted an invitation, and, what's more, brought along his police commissioner, Raymond Kelly. Sharpton could have treated the gesture as one of good will, but instead told a joke exposing it for what it was. "There will be some cynics who say, 'Mr. Mayor, did you kiss Reverend Al's ring?'" he announced. "First of all, let me take my ring off." When it was Bloomberg's turn to speak, he promised to keep coming back to the forum "for each of the four years that the voters of the city of New York have given me." The Mayor went on to assert, with his usual blithe optimism, "We shouldn't forget that the world, or at least America and particularly New York, is getting better." The crowd met the remark with silence. (Later, Sharpton told me, "Let's hope that he and I are speaking every year," a prospect that did not seem terribly likely.)

Like Bloomberg, most other whites probably want to believe that post-civil-rights America is a fairer, better place. Sharpton's entire extraordinary career can be seen as a response to this view, an effort to prove it not only false but, more essentially, self-protective. When he is attacked as a race-baiter, which is just about all the time, Sharpton turns the accusation around. "What they're really saying is I should accept we can't walk in Howard Beach," he told me. "And to go out there is not exposing racism but I'm fanning the flames. Like I went out there and taught the people in Howard Beach and Bensonhurst how to use the N-word." (In 1986, a white mob in Howard Beach chased to his death a black man who had stopped in the neighborhood for a slice of pizza; in 1989, a white mob in Bensonhurst killed a black man who had come to look at a used car.) Those who claim that he is exacerbating racial tensions are, he said, "those that want to deny that racism exists, and don't want someone to pull the covers off. I knew that all I had to do is walk down the street in Bensonhurst and they would prove the case. And how did I know it? Because I grew up in New York and I knew where I was. What did I do to exacerbate that? Get off a bus and walk down the block?"

The irony of his position, of course, is that it tends toward its own kind of conservatism. Ambitious and energetic as he is, Sharpton looks at the world and sees a set of limits. These limits are the theme of every rally and protest, and even of his upcoming race for President; by running, he will show not what is possible for a black man in America but, once again, what isn't. Like all good theatre, his campaigns are about mobilizing emotions. Sometimes the process is productive, but often it is just the reverse—a summoning up of passions that only ends up dissipating them.

After the forum was over, Sharpton went into his office. I asked him how he thought the afternoon had gone, and he pronounced himself satisfied: "You couldn't think of anybody we wanted who wasn't here." He turned on the TV, and clicked to NY1, where every few minutes a clip of the forum was airing, sometimes showing Sharpton taking off his ring, sometimes the Mayor promising to come back. Sharpton watched himself appear and reappear on the screen five or six times. Then he packed up his things, spritzed on some cologne, and headed out to a taping downtown at Comedy Central. In the short walk to his car, he ran into an elderly woman. She was leaning on a cane, and when she saw him she smiled. "I am blessed to see you," she said.

Acknowledgments

I DON'T THINK anyone could hope for better editors than I have had for the last five years at *The New Yorker*. I especially want to thank David Remnick, Dorothy Wickenden, and John Bennet. Every story here has benefited from their counsel, their prodding, and, in many cases, their cuts. I am also grateful to Ann Goldstein and the magazine's superb copyediting staff. Too many fact-checkers to name have pored over these pieces, and, in the process, greatly improved them. Any errors that remain are, as they like to say, entirely "on author."

I'd also like to thank my former colleagues at *The New York Times*. Adam Nagourney and Jennifer Steinhauer, even on deadline, were always willing to talk politics. Sam Verhovek, Nick Goldberg, and Todd Purdum, old Albany and Room 9 hands, provided invaluable help and also friendship. Todd remembered details about New York politics that I had forgotten and knew things that I had never known, and many of the insights here are his.

Gillian Blake and Kathy Robbins made this book possible, and to a large degree gave it its shape. I am grateful for their enthusiasm and for their advice.

I owe a different kind of thanks to Marlene and Gerald Kolbert, George and Edith Kleiner, Lorri Sparks, and Elena Lopez. They have been enormously generous to me, and to my darling, if not always obedient, children, Ned, Matthew, and Aaron. Dan Kolbert, Melissa Kantor, and Annemarie Maass were the kind of unsentimental—if disparately inclined—readers that I always tried to keep in mind.

Finally, not one single word here would have been written without my husband, John Kleiner, to whom my debt is so large that (as he points out) it can never, ever be repaid.

A NOTE ON THE AUTHOR

Elizabeth Kolbert was a reporter for *The New York Times* for fourteen years before leaving to becoming a staff writer covering politics for *The New Yorker*. She and her husband, John Kleiner, have three sons. They recently moved from New York to Wililamstown, Massachusetts.

A NOTE ON THE TYPE

Linotype Garamond Three is based on seventeenth-century copies of Claude Garamond's types, cut by Jean Jannon. This version was designed for American Type Founders in 1917, by Morris Fuller Benton and Thomas Maitland Cleland, and adapted for mechanical composition by Linotype in 1936.